passages north
anthology

PASSAGES NORTH ANTHOLOGY

Edited by Elinor Benedict

Preface by Charles Baxter

A Decade of Good Writing

Milkweed Editions

PASSAGES NORTH ANTHOLOGY
© 1990, text by *Passages North*

All rights reserved
Printed in the United States of America
Published in 1990 by *Milkweed Editions*
Post Office Box 3226
Minneapolis, Minnesota 55403
Books may be ordered from the above address

93   92   91   90   4   3   2   1

ISBN: 0-915943-48-4

Passages North Anthology was made possible by support from the National En-
dowment for the Arts, the Arts Foundation of Michigan, Bay de Noc Community College, the Michigan Council for the Arts, and Borders Bookshops.

The paper used in this publication meets the minimum requirements of American National Standard for Information Sciences—Permanence of Paper for
Printed Library Materials, ANSI Z39.48-1984.

∞

Library of Congress Cataloging-in-Publication Data

Passages north anthology / edited by Elinor Benedict ; preface by
  Charles Baxter.
    p. cm.
    ISBN 0-915943-48-4
    1. American literature—20th century. I. Benedict, Elinor, 1931–
  . II. Passages north.
  PS536.2.P36 1990
  810.8'0054—dc20
                                                                90-5457
                                                                CIP

Frontispiece Photo by Brainard Childs, circa 1880.
Used by permission of Jack Deo.

EDITOR'S FOREWORD

After the first ten years of *Passages North* literary magazine's publication, now comes a new decade of writers who will find encouragement from the magazine under Ben Mitchell's editorship at Kalamazoo College. In editing this volume from the magazine's old headquarters at the William Bonifas Fine Arts Center in Escanaba, we have surprised ourselves at how many of the writers we published in their early days have since produced their first or second books, a number of them winning prizes and critical praise. Our emphasis on "emerging writers" proved prophetic. We also find the emerging themes and voices of this collection informative of what the North and Midwest may mean in the literary world. "Telluric," says Charles Baxter in his preface. "Earthy and human," say we who edited the magazine. And we think there may be some prophecy there, too, for the world in the coming decade. Perhaps the nineties will bring a touch less dour isolation, a dash more wit and a breath more air than Baxter saw in *Passages North*'s first decade.

But for the present it's enough to say that once upon a time there were a few people in a certain place called the Upper Peninsula of Michigan who made something happen that, in a microcosmic way, perhaps, made a difference to literature. The editors lived in an isolated spot, but the manuscripts came from many states and foreign countries. The circles are still expanding. The people who tossed the first pebbles include Carol R. Hackenbruch, Larry Leffel, Mary Joy Johnson and Anne Ohman Youngs. A special word of gratitude also goes to Stephen Cole for his assistance in reviewing poems and stories by or about Native Americans. The Upper Midwest is a place where the Native American heritage is strong, even when partly unconscious. The weather, animals, images and spirits remind us who and what was here before we came.

—Elinor Benedict

ACKNOWLEDGMENTS

We gratefully acknowledge permission from all authors to reprint their poems and stories, which originally appeared in *Passages North*. We also acknowledge the following publications in which some of the works appeared subsequently and for which permissions also have been granted:

Robert Boswell, "Little Bear," *Dancing in the Movies* (University of Iowa Press, 1986).

Debra Bruce, "Father, Son, Grandson," *Sudden Hunger* (University of Arkansas, 1987).

Sharon Chmielarz, "My Father and Mother," *Different Arrangements* (New Rivers Press, 1982).

Jim Daniels, "My Father Worked Late," *Places/Everyone* (University of Wisconsin Press, 1985).

Michael Delp, "Checking the Neighbor's Deer," *Over the Graves of Horses* (Wayne State University Press, 1989).

Jack Driscoll, "Early Summer Concert," *Fishing the Backwash* (Ithaca House, 1984; "Winter Fishing,' *Twin Sons of a Different Mirror* (Milkweed Editions, 1989); and "The Love and Fear of Fire," *Building the Cold from Memory* (Ithaca House, 1989).

Randall R. Freisinger, "Door Hanging," *Running Patterns* (Flume Press, 1985).

Diane Glancy, "After the Loss," *The Tonia Poems* (The Writers Voice, 1990).

Linda M. Hasselstrom, "Drying Onions," *Roadkill* (Spoon River Poetry Press, 1987).

Patricia Hooper, "Coming Back," *Other Lives* (Elizabeth Street Press, 1984).

Margo LaGattuta, "Fires She Could Have Died In" and "To the Impressionable Children," *Diversion Road* (State Street Press, 1983).

Philip Legler, "The Survivor," *North Country Images* (Scarlet Ibis Press, 1988).

Robert Hill Long, "Simple Holdings," in *Juggler's World*, 1986.

Orval Lund, "For John, Who Did Not Choose Baseball," *Take Paradise* (Dacotah Territory Press, 1989).

Patricia McConnel, "The Floor," *Sing Soft, Sing Loud* (Atheneum/Macmillian, 1989).

Bill Meissner, "Winter Fishing," *Twin Sons of a Different Mirror* (Milkweed Editions, 1989).

Sheila E. Murphy, "Rosie," *Late Summer* (Piernian Press, n.d.).

Anne Ohman Youngs, "Annie," *Ball State University Forum* (Autumn, 1981) and *Markers* (Andrew Mountain Press, 1989).

Susan Rea, "Watching Fish" and "The Man Who Waves," *Daily Rhythms: Three Women Poets* (Sing Heavenly Muse! 1989).

John Reinhard, "When Fathers Speak for Daughters" and "The Fundamentalist Argues Against Darwin," *Burning the Prairie* (New Rivers Press, 1988).

Eve Shelnutt, "Orchard Winter," *Recital in a Private Home* (Carnegie Mellon University Press, 1989).

Keith Taylor, "First Dance," *Learning to Dance* (Falling Water Books, 1985).

Lee Upton, "Photographs," *The Invention of Kindness* (University of Alabama Press, 1984).

Mark Vinz, "The Trouble with Poems," *Mixed Blessings* (Spoon River Poetry Press, 1989).

Diane Wakosi, "Red in the Morning," *Lady of Light* (Black Sparrow Press, 1990).

Jeanne Murray Walker, "Shirt" and "The Bag of Stones," *Coming into History* (Cleveland State University Press, 1990).

Jan Worth, "World Travelers," *Home During a Dry-Spell* (Ridgeway Press, 1989).

Gloria Whelan, "The Showing," *Playing with Shadows* (University of Illinois, 1988).

* * *

Quotation from Wallace Stevens, ''An Ordinary Evening in New Haven,'' *Collected Poems* by permission of Alfred A. Knopf.

Brainard Childs, *Photograph for Frontispiece*, circa 1880. Permission given by Jack Deo.

PREFACE

Faced with the challenge of saying something at least marginally true about the work of over one hundred poets and a dozen prose writers collected within these pages, I have been staring out through my study window toward a stand of leafless January trees, fiddling with the sentence you are gliding past right now, and thinking about Escanaba, Michigan. The first time I saw it, I noticed its strip of motels (one in particular with a neon "Yah" and "Nope" vacancy sign), its collection of gleamingly American fast-food restaurants, and its one visible industry, paper milling. It seemed, at first glance, more or less indistinguishable from many other slightly remote American towns of its size. Turned toward Lake Michigan, with an eroding municipal beach, it had, on closer acquaintance, certain discreet charms: a number of citizens with almost imperceptible traces of Northern European tongues in their speech (umlauted *o's* and a gentle conversion of hard *t* sounds into *d*), a morning disc jockey who rang a cowbell every ten minutes or so to wake up his listeners, and a bowling alley with a dance floor and a great jukebox. It had an arts center, and houses, to quote a line from Robert Bly, "built right on the ground." Behind Escanaba stretched the isolated vacancies and beauties of Michigan's Upper Peninsula. Along with these other features, for many years Escanaba has harbored a literary magazine, *Passages North*, edited by Elinor Benedict, the results of which, in part, you now hold in your hand.

Although interesting enough in its own way, Escanaba is not exactly what most people would immediately think of as a literary metropolis. Nevertheless, for many years serious writers sent their work there, and it is now apparent, on the evidence of this anthology, that a certain tone was being established in the magazine, whether through the accidents of manuscript submissions, or the tastes of editorial selection, I wouldn't be able to say. It remains for me to describe—perhaps a fool's errand—what that tone might be.

The sections here have been grouped by subject: among them, travel, parents (especially fathers—this anthology is an outpost of fatherhood), sex, birthing, aging, nature, and God or the gods, floating through the debris of the cosmos. The poems are largely narrative; the pure lyric, the freeplay of words loosed from their significations, is not much in evidence here. An East Coast fluency in the mediations of high culture, and a West Coast celebration of popular culture—they, too, are mostly absent. There is laughter here but not much pure comedy. One has the sense repeatedly—and this is the strongest impression the anthology left upon me—of experiences stored up, guarded almost in secret, and then set down without too much elaboration. It is a trait that some writers share with rural people I have known, this tendency to say something only after having thought about it for a long time. The arts of decoration have been kept, here, to something of a minimum. It is as if what is being said is too precious to decorate. What I think I am describing is a kind of art that arises largely out of isolation.

This kind of art—Albert Pinkham Ryder's paintings and Eric Satie's liturgical piano pieces are analogues—is not noted for its vivid color or its easy wit. It inhabits a kind of middle, even plain, style, and it bears within it an aura of belief that what is being said here is, before man and God, the truth. There doesn't seem to be much recourse to fictionalizing or the more extended flights of the imagination. Instead, such art, in a time of complication and elaboration, prizes an effect of simple nudity.

Reading through these poems and stories, and coming upon over forty names of writers I did not recognize, I had an occasional thought that I was reading that writer's only published poem or story, and that the words were, for that reason but others as well, that much more precious. A reader may have the feeling that much is at stake here. In at least a few cases, *this* poem or story may be the one utterance the writer has come out of his or her silence to give you. Many times here, the pronouns "I" or "we" seem to have a kind of burnished quality, as if the pronouns themselves were threatened by some silence behind them.

It may be that the Midwest does that to you: out of these spaces, these forced marches through a solitary life, you are forced into an elemental sincerity. Rhetoric isn't much help when there's no one around to listen to you. You save up what you have to say; you say it; and then you go back to your life. A few weeks ago I was reading an English critic who had described a Midwestern poet's work as "telluric." Well, I looked up the word. It means *earthly*, or *terrestrial*, and it doesn't seem like much to say about a poet. How can anybody's work not be terrestrial? You'd have to be from Mars to escape *that* calling. But no: probably what he meant was that this poet's work was dominated by the earth, and, metaphorically, by gravity. And what we have in this anthology are many poets and prose writers who are similarly dominated by the earth, its grave force as an element. You may notice how often in these pages a speaker is brought back to earth, or down to it. If the four elements have their poets, then this anthology is dominated by those of the earth, and secondarily by those of fire. There are less than a handful of air-poets, of those who get free of something, and stay free. The writers here depend on their truth(s) to be ordinary, luminous, and beautiful; and so they are.

I have resisted singling out individual poets or prose writers because nothing is gained by doing so. Some of the poems and stories here gave me a sense of unarguable and amazing quality, of the kind that makes a reader feel gratefully alert, but for the others I am grateful too. And the fact is that, as I read from page to page, I grew less interested in the individual names and more intrigued by the effect of a collective voice speaking behind these individual authors. This is not to deny any praise to the authors themselves. If you happen to know any of them, by all means praise them. But what I am getting at is the effect good focused anthologies sometimes have: going from author to author, a reader may feel that our individuality and therefore our isolation are not so important as we may think they are, and that something, some set of conditions, or even a presence of sorts, may be behind us and is speaking through us.

Those barren January trees are still out there, beyond this window, and they make me think of Wallace Stevens' meditation on barrenness and the ordinary in "An Ordinary Evening in New Haven." (Many of the writers in this anthology are interested in the odd and surprising resources of the ordinary). Stevens says in that poem that barrenness is actually "a coming on and a coming forth." And then, in the conclusion of the poem's ninth part, he uses a phrase that may summarize better than I can the sense of an anthology such as this, any coming-together of perceptions. Let it stand as an entryway, a door, into these poems and stories first printed in Escanaba:

> *The glass of air has become an element . . .*
>
> *   * * ***
>
> *It is not an empty clearness, a bottomless sight.*
> *It is a visibility of thought,*
> *In which hundreds of eyes, in one mind, see at once.*

—Charles Baxter

PASSAGES NORTH ANTHOLOGY

THE BLOOD REMEMBERING

THE SAME DOOR

THAT FOOLISH FLYING

OMENS OF FIRE AND ICE

LISTEN !

This Is the Time, the Place

Shall we always be hurting for more territory
And the moon tired from watching our last steps?

—John Garmon,
"Hurting for More Territory"

GOING NORTH

Going north means going
into something deeper than silence.
Mist hangs for hours in the woods
and the apparitions singing in dreams
know places we will never see.
You will know you are north
by the edges of the day
and the slight aura surrounding the trees.
Something in your muscles will be trying
to remember ancient directions,
the way into old hunting grounds,
and if you died and someone
threw your bones into the water
they would swim together
and form a long arrow pointing north.

LEAVING HOME

We could have stayed, we say to ourselves when mom sounds
the least bit lonely on the phone or we read in the round-robin
that dad doesn't change the oil anymore; we could have

taken over the store or the farm, or at least come back
after college and lived close by, pursuing our own careers.
There would have been the living to make and tv and the weather:

nostalgic autumns, mild winters with false spring
in January, then the long real spring, and then summer,
its heat broken by those dramatic storms off the plains.

We tell ourselves we could have stayed and raised our kids
and shared our parents' lives, the way it's supposed to be.
But we know we couldn't, and that if we tried no one would be

more horrified than they. Where after all did we learn
this leaving home if not from them, whose genes must look
like passports, with Poland, Russia, Flanders, Germany

stamped on the helixes? When these foreparents weren't ducking
the draft or looking for a quick zloty, they moved anyway,
for scenery's sake: from New York to West Virginia,

Ohio to Kansas. Some moved from Stockton to Sikeston.
Who could tell the two apart? But these people
argued the trees, the taste of water and the width of streets,

and liked the new place better, and stayed awhile.
So it should be no surprise that our parents are packing up,
selling out, moving away. We worry about their trauma;

I think we feel it more. Old Mason jars and dusty books,
plaster hands that prayed in the darkness of the garage
for thirty years—when these are knocked down at auction

for a half dollar, part of us gets knocked down, too.
But to our parents it's all just junk. They're happy
to see the house clean, even if they had to empty it,

they're happy about the new town, the new place,
the plumbing's new and so are the kitchen cabinets.
Come visit anytime. Stay as long as you like,

they say. But they know we've got to be moving on.
We need practice in this rootless, seedlike freedom,
in the almost casual gracefulness of their letting go.

GROUNDSWELL

At six years, I vowed not to move,
but to stay always in this place, looking
at the sky. On my backyard grass I would
turn with the earth and see every sun,
tangible as footsteps. The crabapple
tree would tumble down its leaves: moist
papers, smelling of age. Soon, I would
go into the ground, wait for the cold
to stitch my self evenly there, its
valley and ridges the coils in a bed,
my back chilled. Snow would melt
into me, a welcome sigh. My
cheek turned to the earth as it rang—
an alarm to my drowsiness.
A parent, as far away as India, was
calling. I lay afraid and hoping
I would not be able to move.

THE ROOFTOPS

After forty Decembers the pastures
of upper Michigan continue to fall
into rust along the Detroit River,
where all of winter is descending
as I look south from Superior
past Michigan, Huron, Erie and Ontario
through miles of snow to find
the people who gave me their names,
the fuel whenever I was numb,
a balcony of blankets and sleep
if I was lost, water to pray from.
All the quiet teachers of healing
who dressed me to climb from loss
as from gain, for they are one,
who let me use my fears by opening them,
farmers who could feel the snow ripening.
They are standing together again
around my last belongings
lifting the weather above them,
a few pages, some cloth, a trunk
of maps and three photographs,
all the gifts I stored once
beneath the rooftops of these people —
the rafters still above me.
One night, with another blizzard
at its peak and their village
low on fuel, I want to know the bones
in their hands and arms held outward
above these gifts, warming themselves.

THE POTATO HOUSE

A feed store, a potato house, and our house lined one side of the rutted dirt road. Running counter to this was the railroad track; beyond it the depot, then Sweenland, population almost a thousand.

The potato house hadn't been used for years, except by us kids in winter. When the snow was deep we used the storage part for a hill to slide down. The slant of the roof—all that could be seen of the building above ground—would take us across the long lot to the next road. It was an exhilarating ride, especially at night with the moon up.

Attached to the roof and rising above it was the office, a little faded coop of a place roosting at the top of a short flight of decaying steps.

"Someday you'll break your neck over there," Mother warned. But my father, who examined the place yearly, always said it was safe enough.

The office never intrigued us much. The grimy windows were high and small-paned; and though by standing on tiptoe we could see a rusted stove, a truck scale, a cupboard, and the door to the storage pit, we were far too busy freezing and sliding to be curious.

Then one morning when I was twelve and the roof of the pit had begun to rot and sink, a young couple moved into the delapidated office.

Mother, who did her ironing in front of the dining room window, spotted them first. With one end of the ironing board resting on an open drawer of the sideboard and the other end on the dining room table, it was easy for her to see past my swing and across the garden to the potato house.

It was late September and we were at noon-dinner when she said accusingly, "Someone is living in that old potato office!" Her eyes took in my father, the two hired men—Maxie and Rupert—and myself.

Maxie spoke first. With no teeth and his napkin tucked under his chin, not to mention his loaded knife part way to his mouth, he said, "It's them Haleys."

"What do you mean 'them Haleys'? There's only one boy in that family. The whole tribe left town a year ago and *he* was brainless." My mother looked at my father and repeated, "*Brainless.*" Then she added, "And so is any girl who would marry him. Why, that's just a *child* over there!" She put down her napkin and went quickly into the kitchen.

Between her short pounding trips in and out of the pantry to dish up the banana cream pie, she issued such statements as, "If they're married, who married them, I'd like to know," and other sharp remarks about indolent people who allowed calamitous things to happen to non-thinking halfwits.

Maxie shuffled his feet uneasily, grinned, fiddled with the flatware, and waited for his pie. The other man, Rupert, did much the same, except for informing us that the Haley boy was a long drink of water with a head like a pin.

Slowly my father swung around in his chair, pulled aside one panel of the ecru curtains, and observed that the garden had done well for such a dry season.

"Garden, my foot," Mother said, marching in with a tray full of pie. "I resent having idiots stuck under my nose when I'm raising a daughter." To me she said severely, as though I'd done something wrong, "Nancy, take these dinner plates into the kitchen and don't let your ears grow."

As I left the room, Maxie, like someone forced to confess, remarked awkwardly that the girl at the potato house was a fat little thing knee-high to his elbow and had a dimple in her chin like the blossom end of a pear.

Then not to be outdone, Rupert put in, "I heard some backwoods preacher married them. He claimed they was living in sin, but now they ain't; she's a dwarf, you know, and don't stand no higher than this." His eyes were critical as his hand with the crippled finger lifted, then dropped to hover a few inches above a corner of the table.

Dad sighed, rapped his knife against his dinner plate, looked at Rupert, and said sorrowfully, "What would I ever do without you, Rupert?" And thick-skulled Rupert grinned happily and said, "I dunno, John."

The men always called my father by his first name and Mother by her full title, Mrs. Warren.

Mother said, "Nancy, when you're through with the plates, I want you to look in the rain barrel and see if the water needs straining — I think it does."

Bit by bit, facts and hearsay began to accumulate, causing my mother to desire heavier curtains at the dining room window. My father wouldn't hear of it. I heard him say, "Damnit, Mollie, they're not dogs."

A day or so later Maxie, who was probably angling for a second piece of pie, said, "They got a little three-quarter iron bedstead over there. It's kind of scabby and saggy, but I guess it'll hold 'em."

Mother frowned and said, "Hold your tongue." Whereupon Maxie shrugged and blurted, "They ain't no different from nobody — I guess."

"How a man living in a woodshed can criticize a man living in an office is beyond me," said my father, meaning Maxie, who lived in Mrs. Grumbuski's lean-to.

Once I heard my mother say, "Night and day I suppose those children are over there wallowing around in that office!"

"Well," my father said, "they've got to do something; they can't read or write."

By late fall it was just beginning to snow, and everyone in town knew that the Haleys were on dole and that she was pregnant. As the winter progressed, we grew used to the sight of their lamp at dusk and formed the habit of glancing out the window to see if there was smoke coming from their chimney. It was a poor runt of a chimney, merely a piece of rusted pipe; and though none of us really called on the Haleys, Father sent Maxie over to fix the steps. On that day, and others, Mother sent baked goods and vegetables.

"They'll never need potatoes," Maxie said. "It's the biggest smell they got. My God, John, how long have those things been buried there?"

"Hard to tell. But if he wanted to lift that trap door and throw in a couple of yeast cakes . . ."

Rupert said, "She ain't so pretty anymore, but she's kinda cute being so little and podded out like that."

"Wait till that pod cries," Mother said grimly.

"They giggle, reel around, and hold hands a lot," Maxie told us. "And they watch each other. If he says something, she leans way over and hangs on his every word. And when she speaks, he looks at her like she's God."

"Don't blaspheme," said Mother.

Maxie ignored her and told my father, "These days, he lugs her from the street all the way upstairs to the doctor's. And let me tell you, she must be quite a load for him to carry, thin as he is."

"One frail as a bird, the other full as a tick," mourned Mother.

And after a heavy snow Maxie said, "You won't believe this, but he's haywired a box onto an old hand-sled, and now he takes her to the doctor's in that. I doubt if she could lift them little legs of hers to get through the drifts anymore."

"I hope to heaven he dusts that box," Mother said. "He uses it to steal coal in."

It was well-known that the railroad detectives would never arrest them for stealing coal; in fact, whenever the weather turned bad, somebody usually left a big tub of coal at the door of the office.

"They're turning into pets," Dad said. And I imagined the littlest baby in the world walking and talking by summer.

Maxie worried out loud about rats one night, but my father hushed him. Later I heard Dad banging around in the woodshed with things that rattled and clanked, and I knew that whatever the Haleys needed, and couldn't get for themselves, my father would provide.

Whenever a late wind picked up and howled, and the snow drifted, Dad would look across the garden and say, "I hope to God he's got sense enough to keep that stove going — ."

I knew he would. But I didn't expect him to show up at our house late one night. It was storming, of course, and we were all in bed. The midnight train had just left the station and was blowing on its way out of town when the Haley boy began pounding on the door. It woke us, and I could hear my father cursing between hasty cries of "Hold on, I'm coming."

Mother and I followed Dad to the head of the stairs and watched him descend in long underwear to the hall and open the front door. He yanked the bareheaded Haley boy into the hallway and slammed the door on the storm outside. "What is it?" my father asked, shaking him. "For God's sake, what is it? Tell me."

There was no answer, just a wild working of jaws and long bare hands jerking toward the office. My father nodded and reached for the hall phone, at the same time yelling for Mother, who already was throwing his clothes downstairs.

It was impossible for my father to understand suffering, and it shocked him that after two days of agony, both the girl and the baby should die.

They were buried together from our parlor. "No county funeral," my father said. "By God, I won't have it."

The Ladies' Aid made the shrouds, and flowers came on the morning train from Bay City. I don't know who ordered them, but I think Mother did, for Maxie and Rupert. There were no family mourners except the boy. No Haleys could be located, or none of her kin.

I saw the bodies just once, the morning of the funeral. My father opened the double doors leading to the parlor and beckoned to me. I went inside and he slid the doors shut again and took my hand. The parlor was chill and hushed, the green blinds drawn. Together we crossed the room to the lace curtained windows where the coffin stood.

Being small for my age I had to stand on tiptoe to look at them. They were both strangely beautiful and waxen. Her lashes lay long and dark on her cheek, and one of her arms held the baby like a doll.

Later my father told my mother, "It's all right, she understands."

The services were at the graveside. "I want it outdoors in the air," my father said. It was terrible for the boy; he cried until she was buried, and then his eyes took on a dry, empty look. It was awful to see him stumble around staring, his hands hanging loose and helpless like his mouth.

Day after day my father went over to the office and tried to get him to eat or talk or stand up — *anything*, but he just lay on the bed, his face to the wall.

One day Maxie said, "His Adam's apple is beginning to look like a crop. He's in bad shape, John."

"I know it," my father said. "I know it."

Mrs. Hines, who washed for us, went over and came back shaking her head. I heard her talking to Mother between rinses; and it seems he was lying there in a wilt, and that the rats were stirring. "Getting bold," she called it, "and coming up to see."

But I was sure if the boy would just try and live until summer so he could smell the sweet clover that grew around the office, and hear the strutting pigeons carooing on the roof, he'd be all right. I even thought maybe I could talk to him sometime and make him laugh, but Mother was adamant and said, "Not on your life. Keep away."

He died early that March and the sheriff came at night and carried him off covered with rat bites. About a week later the sheriff told my father to go to the potato house and look things over. "There can't be much," he said, "but there might be something."

Maxie and my father went the next afternoon and I tagged along, expecting any minute to hear my mother call me back. There were no pigeons on the roof that day. The sky was leaden, and it was after four o'clock. A severe wind had sprung up from the east and it whittled against us as we climbed the worn steps to the office.

Once inside, my father opened up his mackinaw, gnawed his lips, looked at the box on the sled, shook his head, and said, "Jesus."

They had used the rusty scales for a combination towel and clothes rack, and her bonnet still hung beside his coat with a couple of hairs clinging to it, catching the light. Across the room Maxie bent over and hauled a chipped chamber pot from under the bed. He said, "Dry as a bone," and threw it outside on a heap of trash.

The scaly iron bed was bowed and skimpy-looking. There were no pillows, just two rough quilts home-made from men's dark worsted suiting. Maxie pressed down on the thin gray mattress. "The jail's got better," he said and threw it on top of the chamber pot.

The office was clammy cold, and the sour, moldy potato smell was strong. When I opened the cupboard there was nothing in it but a tin cup and some rat droppings that struck the bare floor like hail.

After a while my father stopped puttering, looked at me and said, "Come on, Nancy. It's suppertime."

We went back home and I set the table. I took a long time with the cloth and the silver. Nobody talked. Maxie tried, but no one paid any attention. I listened to the clock for five minutes.

Then while Mother was frying potatoes, I slipped out the front door and went back to the office.

It was almost dark now and the steps were icy. Just the same I hurried, and climbed up to one of the little dark windows, rubbed the grime away, and looked inside. But there was nothing to see.

WORLD TRAVELERS

My father stops
to catch his breath. Everything
in his orchard seems to draw up,
saving air in case he needs it.

His arm curls around me and he says:
Apple trees have a life span
like you and me. It is important to notice
when they keel and make knotty fruit, yet
you must treat them kindly and with respect,
remembering the gifts they have
borne you, what applesauce, what cider!

He walks me through the ryegrass
so delicately. I want to be
his Magellan, but I come home
full of stories I never tell.
What matters here are two new trees,
fragile as fawn legs,
he just planted among the Jonathans.
I think I'll live to eat
an apple from this, he says,
tweaking the little Winesap
like a grandson.

And then he stoops to wonder at
the humus, black and pliable,
a foot deep. He says
you can tell what to do
with the soil by tasting it.
Pinches some between his finger tips
like a bit of snuff. Sweet!
He smiles. Savor this! Believe me,
it started out sour and hard as slate.
You can taste your whole history,
the summers of alfalfa and clover,

the snowstorm of '53, even your
lightning and thunder is in there.

He never tires of walking his domain,
rarely asks about mine.
This is why: nothing I have ever done
or no place I have gone equals
the sum of this small continent,
its contours like
the roundness of his palms.

HUSBANDRY

The first time I saw a man sew anything
it was my father patching binder canvas.
He took good care of such things.
On his chair at the kitchen table
he draped the coarse cloth (Ma made him
bang the dust out before bringing it in)
over his knees like a skirt. Beside him
an oily box kept on the Bible shelf—
a shoemaker's kit with awls, needles,
line tough enough to reel in salmon—
held his tools. Ripe, grainy smells
filled the kitchen. Pa sat up
late, bent to his work, stitching on
bright new patches, binding frayed edges,
his head heavy as oats in the dewy field.
We lugged the dark canvas out next morning,
careful not to drag it in the damp grass,
and spread it for an apron back of the sickle bar.
After threshing we rolled the parched cloth,
packed it under the rafters in a dry shed,
keeping in mind to take good care. And now,
now in a strange city or along some lakeshore
I still hear the thrum of canvas, the swish
of oat stems, a bundling clatter of gears—
shocks of harvest in a far, golden field.

FARMER

The farmer lives next door
in a weather-warped house
bleached as a barn,
on the small farm
of a fenced backyard,
with a town widow
who tells the world
they live in sin.

She's remorseless.
On days their welfare comes
she waits out front
to flag the mailman down
before the farmer
gets to him
and trades their foodstamps off
for Chesterfields and gin.

They live on Spam
and the vegetables
he tends from a sagging lawn chair—
hoeing the Burpee Big Boys,
draining a six-pack
while pole beans shinny
rotted drainpipes
and cukes inflate.

Each afternoon nap
is a stroke,
head lolled back
beneath the sun,
mouth agape,
and dirty hands
still working in his lap
as if peeling an onion.

LIVING IN THE GROUND

Sometimes, just off I-94, people live in basements.
That's where they live, and they hear
the traffic between Detroit and Chicago,
gruff as the rain on their tar-paper roof.

I don't claim much for their dreams,
but they rise two storeys, at least,
then mist out into a picture window,
with a lamp that looks like light cancer.
The folks send you off into wedlock
with surreal appliances, hoping
you find your way to heaven.

They've gone through two dogs now,
and they still come up out of the stairway,
he in the Texaco shirt; she with her hair
combed back over her ears. She has never stopped
at the tray of lip gels at Sears.
He is plain, and she is plain, and the kids.

The yard straggles back into thin pine.
There's the snowmobile, under the tarp,
and snow tires, and some other bulks and waiters.
Sometimes the dog pisses and sometimes it doesn't.
The Detroit people face their destiny in Chicago,
and the Chicago people have given up prophecy.

They live in the ground and the TV comes down
the antenna and puts little square pictures
in their eyeglasses, and that's what they see.
Each year the house grows like dust in a drawer.
As they come up to the pickup,
into the first bites of December,
they look back at the home, flat as snow hummocks,
where they dream flock and doilies,
when they may stride into the lipid gel

of TV, which told them over and over
why they live in the ground.

They almost understand
where they have come from, and where
they are going.

MORNING

In the quiet of darkness you rise,
with the silent song of bedsprings,
as you move from the comfort of quilts,
from the bed of your seventy-eight years.

The worn wooden stairs know your feet,
the stiffness and the swellings,
just as the chair by the fridge has memorized
the weight and depth of your body.

In the kitchen, you drink coffee
from the day before, staring at the land
that has become as familiar to you
as your own face, your own mind.

When the time seems right, you move
to the landing. Like a priest in his vestry,
you take each article of clothing
carefully from the place it's been assigned.

The knitted scarf you place around your neck.
The jacket, passed from some dead
brother-in-law or brother, has now taken on
the shape of your own huddled frame—

you slide into it easily enough.
The hunting cap hugs your head;
the gloves, stiff with soil,
bury your knotted hands.

When you finally leave the house,
you walk the gullied path.
The old sheepdogs, the fat rabbits,
dance a slow dance of greeting as you pass.

They are happy to see you, it seems,
even if, by now, their eyes are too old to see.

For this, to them, means morning, salvation
from the night and from the cold,

that once again, they've been given the simple promise
of another day. You understand this, give them food,
touch their hairy heads, as if laying on hands,
and then move on, to the barn, the coop, the fields.

A farm is a big place in the morning; this
is something you've come to know.
And across it, you move in a ritual
even older than yourself, walking down and down
into the pale white light of morning.

BEFORE NIGHTFALL

I walk out

past the fallen stones
fencing nothing,
past the knotted thorn apple
and the one immovable boulder,
dusk huddled at its roots;

I walk into the darkness washing over the hills,
flooding the fields, lapping against the steps
that fall down from the house where my wife
nurtures the one fire that feeds us;

I walk with the snow falling into my eyes
like so many seeds of light; I walk out
like any man whose life belongs to no one,
whose hands bear fruit, whose heart rises
red above the rivers flowing under his skin;

I walk out to the limit of the land I live in.

And I say:
let the winds that lift these fields
along the last row of saplings
at the edge of winter resound
in the empty barn of my throat;

let stars rise from my lips
to shape one constellation of song
to hang in the heavens
blackening, everywhere, above us;

let every living thing sing
just once, together, and for all
as the night comes down; let us shine.

HURTING FOR MORE TERRITORY

Tonight the roads run away from me
with my feet aching to walk them.

I am old enough to remember too much.

Once all my hours were so many minutes.
I had days I threw away on work.

These things I am telling myself are for you.
And the roads running away.

Shall we always be hurting for more territory
And the moon tired from watching our last steps?

NORTHERN LIGHTS

1

The sow in Vermont slumbers
in the barn. Her sucklings
shiver in the straw.
And cow's bell trembles thinly
up the hill.

The vaulted sky seems veiled
by wings. Not swans,
this feathered light,
though surely now in late October
the icy lake has set its face
against them.

Aurora, mother says,
and children murmur after.
The father, too, some distance off
(who waked them in his awe to see)
stands gaping up.

The great eye blinks
so coldly over us.

2

All religion begins
in yelps.
Out of the choir loft
and into the cold baptistry waters
we glided, white.

One after another we sank back
and then were raised again, children,
the minister's right hand
against our wingless shoulder blades.

3

One misty spring the field
grew up in bayonets.
The radio was full of blood
and numbers.
Tell us, uncles, why this winter sky
reminds us hair keeps growing
underground.

Whose sons were they,
planted so thick and deep?
Who were the women by their beds
with flowers? Must there be
women blossoming with rue?

Perhaps our elders everywhere
will walk out tonight
and see the burning edges
of the world
and know what they see
is not lace.

A PLACE ON A SLENDER RIVER

We share the way
this slender river finds
for its journey through low country,
hardwood paddles flat across our knees.

When you whisper
"These are the best times," I nod,
listen to the wind bend the tall gray grass,
look hard below the canoe
for the quiet current that carries us along.

We scrape over deadfall,
pass half a footbridge anchored
in mud. No path leads away.
We guide our turn around deep bends,
kneel through tunnels of tangled bush.

Then, an impulse. We drive our paddles
hard and deep into this passive drift.
We slice along a straight-away;
the edges blur, our world tightens.

We hear the beat of our own quick breath,
ease our slender boat into a lagoon,
rest over a shallow, black bottom.
Among the sprawl of lily pads,
amid the water bugs' skittish searches,
we breathe the ripe smell of swamp,
of beginnings and endings.

When our place on the river comes by again,
we push gently out of the calm,
away from these smooth, gray-fingered elms,
and drift again with the river,
as though, for now, it had no end.

AT THE SLEEPING BEAR DUNES

No skyborne seagull can beguile
A lofted thought from me, or call,
Like cherubs in some canvas oil,
My soul to disembodied joys.
No fishing in the sky for me.

Instead these acres I'll embrace
Of glacial sand that ran, and runs,
One inch a year to drown, someday,
The lake beyond with crystals from
This hibernating age.
I like my progress slow.

Grind eons in my mortar, gods,
Drop anchors in these shifting ribs,
Where western winds whip traceless wisps,
Upon a formless, normal face.
The skin can change, the rest endure.

Just sleep me with the sleeping bear;
Sing eras to my ears.
Tonight I'll hug the earth, and wake,
Gods willing, from an epoch's dreams,
Here, high atop this airy beach,
Where gulls ignore a grounded man.

BEAUTIFYING SONGS

for my wife
  Look at me very beautifully.
  Let us talk very beautifully.
  There is no loneliness—
  So let us talk!
    —translated from Cherokee
    by Jack and Anna Kilpatrick

I

for the Great Sioux Nation
Wounded Knee, 1973

I am clean and dancing.
Today, the first in a lifetime,
I sing a rattlesnake's voice

in the rocks, I shy from no one.

But I still have fangs,
poisonous or not, and an urge
to feel the warm ball of a fieldmouse
dissolving inside me

the vibrations of rain drumming
across dry hills, a stretch of moist
sunlight along my body.

II

When I breathe inside you

we are remade. When we cross
our steps the earth underneath
warms with the heat of the sun
although we are walking darkness.

When we say our dream-names
our dreams leave their pockets
the brush and dance after us.
This is why we are standing together.

This is why today our shadows,
bright as the reflection, water,
chase each other through our eyes,
mouths, nostrils, why our bodies inside

lift like dragonflies from the grass.

III

The river runs diving beetles,
snapping turtles bellying
into the water, alligator branches,
low swarms of gnats, a cottonmouth
twining with the current
along the surface. This morning
fishing we watch our blood flow,
barefooted in marshgrass
tuning our eyes
with the sun through the trees.

IV

I have come to stand in
your heart, to slip my
feet, hands into your hands
and feet, slide my arms and
legs into your arms, legs,
wear your face, talk without
speaking, share shadows,
sing to each other in the
same small voice, sleep
in the same wide dream together.

V

This morning I am cricket
rubbing my fingers together,
bush noise and grass tongue
brushing fog from the lake
calling water and sunlight
into the roots, trees, night

leaning west in the east,
my fingers stop speaking.
Birds awake daylight and I rest.

VI

The wind winters
in birds' nests, grass
hasn't left its place

through the center of hills

winds we haven't touched
or thought about reaching
into the grass, nests
with eggs to return to.

This evening the sun
shuts down, winds
find a river to follow
and spring will always come

we can still grow gardens
carry eggs from the grass

when we meet the wind

like love from someone
waiting with a fire, food
and a warm place to eat.

VII

Tonight, rabbits, birds
crossed the road, snow
piled along ditch banks,
winter wheat, green under white
stars crackling, we touched tongues,
tasted snow and the universe.
Wherever we are we hear
the sun moving closer,
through the roots, winter wheat,

grasses, birds and rabbits
drinking from the places we've been.
My spirit cries out for you.
I cannot stop loving these winds!

VIII

All day long I live
in your voice, today painting,
listen when the wind drops
between trees, untangles,
runs wide through the snow, fields.

The colors I hear
like wind from a willow tree
ripple and swirl, water
with voice, air the color
of thoughts in small dreams.

Filled with every color
I see like the sunrise.

IX

for the Three Fires

The sky rises between
day and darkness,
wet grass, goldenrod
in a field of light fog,
quiet rain, morning
opening in the roots
filled with the blood
of sunrise, a tremolo of crickets.
I send a voice. Rainwater
whistles in the fire, sings.

X

When I listen
the earth crackles where
I walk. Brown leaves,

life at the center of death
glows in each leaf,
trees as colorful
as the birds gone south,
yellows, reds, a blue sky
sitting in this birch
like a prayer. I watch
the sun go down. Blue
fades into the nearest star.

XI

for Lance Hart

Our canoe like a dance
crossed the lake
and the moon crossed
with us, stars
like the eyes of fish
glowing under water,
our muscles moving
in tune with our hearts
pulling us toward the trees.
Pine, spruce,
we camp in a place
above the beach listening
to the fire, warm
and infinite, a small wind
drawing smoke from a tree
into the trees. All night
the fire burns in a circle
and all night the fire
tells stories.

XII

We are like hawks
rising on evening breezes
waiting with the wind
crossing blue grass, pines,
going into the mountains.

Trees sit still, the hills
darken, your voice
quiets the earth
touching your hair
is like touching
a whisper, touching
the colors of sunset
dancing so close,
dancing in one heartbeat.

XIII

I can hear you
breathing the winds
run like rain
through the trees
the ice is thick
in places the snow
seeps wet to the bones
I burn my hands
every winter and tremble
when the stars sit
quiet and bright
in the cold north sky
I sit fading like a
fire in the fog
you make the night
go easy.

XIV

They say a man dies
without magic.
They say the womb
never lies, a woman's
spirit is the warmth
a fire makes in the dark.
I am only one moment
but together we are
alike and alive
when we listen, talk,

make love far into the night
dancing toward sunset
on the soft summer sand.

XV

for Little Hawk

The whistle is hawk
weaving the distance
grown close where I
walk through the woods
hearing bluebird, sparrow,
redwing, crows. Crickets
weave with the grass
down around roots near
the day morning dew
singing like dancers
with bells where
I walk with the trees
woven with wind, leaves,
feathers they say
all fit together in song
pulse in one blood
rippling the creek across
pebbles, stones,
whistle and hawk
where water spiders
glide along silence
with water, air.
Sometimes I think
a basketmaker made
us all, weaving the dawn
with one life breath
until then, today.

THE GROVES, THE HIGH PLACES

Bark piles up no matter how deep
the drought. Bark knows water,
floats on a film molecules thin.

Trees cored for syrup last
longer than most marriages
across tables made of wood.

We kiss under mistletoe
snipped from live oaks,
carve our names in bark

warping like smoke rings.
Nights, we crouch on pine needles
and dream in sleeping bags

near timberline. Trees thrive
in sandstone or white caliche,
in granite, balanced on cliffs

in thin perpendicular air.
Even posts nailed to barbed wire
learn now to live with rust.

A WOMAN'S LIFE THROUGH TREES

A stippled sycamore hovered over
The white house in a small town ruled by trees.
Above her bed, shadows of leaf and light
Patterned the ceiling and her memory
For the names of wood, those both soft and hard—
Her life is described by those pithy names.

My mother has forgotten the first names
Of neighbors, but not the cedar over
The sandbox behind the house they worked hard
To make picture-perfect, with fence and trees.
House with cedar stands in her memory
As the symbol of fresh hopes and new light.

She talks of the fall of late summer light
On the lake. Using her fingers she names
The summers spent there. There is memory
Of hemlocks tall in a pure stand over
On the other side of the water. Trees
That drooped with snow when the winter was hard.

Then in Florida, those cypress knees, hard
And knobby, were turned into lamps whose light
Filled the house. She planted two orange trees
And made her Yankee children learn the names—
Slash pine, coral bean, royal palm over
Boulevards, a tropical memory.

Black and white snapshots aid the memory
For the move back north; the kids had it hard
Making friends again. The cold stars over
The new place stretched to the Muskegon Light.
The yard held ten blue spruce, which she gave names.
She didn't like the house; she liked the trees.

The cemetery grows catalpa trees;
The cool markers retain memory

Of family. On veined stone their names
Greet her. Her husband's letters are still hard,
Not yet worn by wind or faded by light.
Trees will still be here when her life's over.

Once she knew their Latin names, but it's hard
To keep the trees straight in her memory,
Where rings of light and shadow lap over.

MEETING MY FATHER AT THE RIVER

On this evening path from camp
to river's bend, shadows
roll over and lie down in hollows,
then rise from rotting stumps
to drift along the lowland.
They stalk my boots' dull thud, branches
opening, closing overhead.
The cabin's lamp, the glowing stove,
burn behind me now in memory.

At the river, my father
still stands in light.
This will be his last trip to these waters.
His arm lifts, his line wavers,
settles over the pool.
I have often dreamed this motion:
me watching from the bank, him casting,
the whir of reel, the bend and dip of rod and arm.
Now a small trout rises to the fly.

He calls, "I got one!"
It surfaces, flickering in wetness.
He is pleased I am here to witness
and leans with grace in hip boots
for the ritual of netting,
stepping sure as a young man again.
"Good one," I cry, and wave.
He wades slowly out of sight
around the bend, creel bumping at his side.

Simple Holdings

. . . these arms no weapon, these hands no claim.

—John Reinhard,
"When Fathers Speak for Daughters"

FATHER, SON, GRANDSON

Your father tosses your baby toward the sun.
They both laugh. Their faces glisten.
You watch, listen, as if that's what you've come
back to do. The red-faced father you knew
leaned across your math book after supper,
flicked his pencil inches from your face,
hissed your name as he snapped it in two.

Now your father's summer garden blooms
around you. He kneels there
with his grandson, stroking the round,
ripe shapes he names so slowly:
cantaloupe, eggplant. Those hands
that used to twitch toward his belt
until you ran and ran.
Who is this man who takes the time
to touch inside a flower? A shower
of pollen powders his fingertips.
He brushes his lips across his grandson's cheek.

You watch from under a tree,
too far away for your father to see
the first wisp of skin just slipping
loose from your neck, though your back
is straight as a boy's. It tastes
so bitter—this grass you've picked up
to break a blade on your teeth and tongue
and give a whistle so sharp
they both look at you and wave:
first your father, then your son.

WHEN FATHERS SPEAK FOR DAUGHTERS

As I see my daughter, she is soft
with fur. It is always twilight
when the boys call out her name,
boys who would run their fingers through her,
ride her off into the night where
I dream my daughter, her voice
a fine line between mother
and father, one day and another.

*

I wrote a man to tell him I loved his daughter
and wanted to elope with her. Maybe go north
to a small cabin by the big lake. He wrote back
I wd. lock up my daughter — which one? — ere
I gave her hand (or any other part) to you
(or the likes of you), filthy of mind, unclean
of talon.   I'm serious.

*

When a woman exploded almost
in the stars, the reporters gathered
around her father, asked him about
what a father does when his daughter
disintegrates among the clouds.
As though only a mother's grief remains
unspoken, as though only a mother
might travel with a daughter
into places beyond words.

*

But what of the father who takes his daughter
as he would a wife. Maneuvers his body
and blood over hers. Says love is secrecy.
And when she becomes enough woman
to tell him, No, he jabs an awl into her belly,
bleeds her to a young death in the straw,

buries her in a field without trees
— nothing to keep the dust in its place.

*

I will have to tell my daughter that she
is on her own like all of us. Tell her
there is no longer any such thing as
protection. But in the always twilight
I will cradle my awkward arms, holding them
out to her as some slight shelter, father to daughter,
these arms no weapon, these hands no claim.

THE STUDY OF ASTRONOMY

My father in old age is obsessed
with stars,
cosmic mysteries, how light
travels through space from exploded suns,
how constellations
form and solar systems,
galaxy after galaxy,
recurrence of comets,
timeliness of meteors,
possibilities of black holes.

My father reveres the novae
of Tycho Brahe
visible in full daylight,
the envelope of Nova Persei,
the supernovae of 1006
in the constellation Lupus,
the wolf star.

He writes about the runaway stars
flying from their orbits
to race through black fields of space
like white horses,
of the process of infall,
the red shift of quasars.

He says he needs to know
the laws that govern stars. Theories
of creation, dissolution. Because he is getting old
and there is not much time now
to wish on the first star
or the falling star.

MY FATHER WORKED LATE

Some nights we were still awake
my brother and I, our faces smearing the window
watching the headlights bounce up the driveway
like wild pitches of light
thrown by a tired moon.
We breathed in the huge silence
after the engine died
then ran to the door, grabbing his legs
as if we could hold him there
through night, morning, forever.

Some nights when he wasn't too tired
he took off his shirt
and sat in the middle of the floor.
We wrestled, trying to pin
back his arms, sitting on his chest
digging our heads into the yellow stains
under the arms of his t-shirt.
Each time we thought we had him
Do you give, huh, do you give?
he sat up, cradling us both in headlocks
in the closest thing to an embrace
that I remember, and carried us to bed.

Other nights he looked right through us
mechanically eating his late dinner
yelling at anything that moved.
Some mornings we woke to find him
asleep on the couch, his foreman's tie twisted
into words we couldn't spell.
We ate our cereal as carefully as communion
until our mother shook him ready for another day.

My father carries no wallet full of lost years
carries no stubs, no guarantees, no promises.
We could drive toward each other all night
and never cross the distance of those missing years.

Today, home for a visit,
I pull in front of the house.
My father walks down the steps
limping from his stroke
he is coming toward me
both of us pinned to the wind
he is looking at me as if to say
give, give, I give,
as if either of us
had anything left to give.

CLOSING THE CABIN

1

A boarded door swings open in the afternoon.
A woman in a borrowed coat splashes toward
the dirt road. She grabs a downed branch
at its jagged break and drags it to the woodpile
but that's collapsed, washed out from under
and the family totem pole has been toppled
in this same storm. She turns, squinting
at the raw sky, then finds her father's head
pitched by wind into the barberry.

2

The shrub's stiff arms embrace the wooden
head split off from the totem in its fall.
Thorns bite into the painted stripes that
clarify her father's cheek. The woman plunges
her chapped hands into the brush, pulls them
back bitten by the crimson bristles. She
wedges her boot into the brittle nest, edging
his head out, catching it.

3

Kneeling in the mulch, the woman cradles
the wooden head, scraping nodules of mud
from his tempera blue eyes. Her fingers
like caterpillars curve over his weathered
nose. She peers into a nuthatch hole behind
his ear where the small birds have nibbled
away at his brain, below the brim of the
carved fedora, mossy velveteen, dotty
with orange blossoms. Can the hat be salvaged
with the head? She wraps them in the canvas
Mackinaw and they come in out of the rain.

4

His head rests before the fire on newspaper
pillows. She waits for the appearance of
creatures drawn out by the heat or some
radiant illumination of the hollow skull.
Steam, only, curls from his porous skin.
All that's left to do is drag the rowboat
to the shed. She turns the kerosene on high
before she goes, though it's just her and
the head. She stares at this grinning totem
that he has always been. Who better to burn
this crumbling trunk than the oldest limb?

FOR JOHN, WHO DID NOT
CHOOSE BASEBALL

Because I loved the bone-white hardness of the ball
that fit like a perfect toy in my hand,
the way my fingers ratcheted its tight red seams
as if I could wind up joy and let it fly,
the way I swam beneath the spinning ball
popped up in a child-blue sky,
the satisfying thunk into my glove,
and the around-the-horn with other boys,
I wanted so badly to give it to you

a seven-year old lefty behind the house,
whose loose control burned my face red
and led me to zip the ball back into your tears,
but we kept on, a tyrant reigning behind a cardboard plate,
a subject red-handed. And you,
at your first and last game, standing
on the raised mound, the game spinning
about you like a merry-go-round gone mad,
the ball large and sour as a grapefruit in your hand,
missing the plate pitch after pitch,
I gripping the wire fence with white hands,
the white-haired coach shouting angry words
until he took you out, the bases loaded.

Now, at fourteen, out you go,
like a thoroughbred garbed in blue silks,
your baggy old-time hat tilted jauntily,
your lean legs loping across open fields,
I try to keep up but can't, and marvel
at the nervous grace of your long body.
When I see you, the cemetery milestone turned,
running back to me, you smile and wave
your open hands, and I, yes, I
garbed in my drab clothes of guilt and age, yes,
I smile and open my hands to you.

COMING BACK

All evening I've sat in this chair
reading until the snow
whitened the road, and the clock
lengthened its heartbeat. Now
the plow passes our house
and my husband and child, returning
from a late walk to the park,
trudge through the drifts home.

At their voices I shake myself
from a kind of slumber. It seems
I had almost forgotten the place
I remained in, or how long
it has been since they left the room.
Soon they will enter, breathless,
smelling of snow. I will hold
their coats as they take them off,
and breathe for a moment the fresh
place they have come from . . .
                              Perhaps
they too are forgetful, uncertain
what street has unfolded, and stand
looking in at the warm room
they will wake to: and who is this
familiar stranger who sits
in the lamplight, as if returned there
by their minds alone?

BACKRUB

I've just come from a place
where the shadows are inappropriate
for the middle of the day. My stepfather's bedroom
has its shades pulled, air conditioner on
and king-sized bed made except for
his portion, where he has climbed in naked
after undressing in silence,
unseen, laying his barreled chest and massive arms
against the chilled sheets, his slender
legs trailing down almost invisible
like a fold in a curtain. Soon he will begin
to snore, dreaming as a shark dreams,
moving through dark water, swimming to stay
alive. He will sweeten the air around him
with breath that smells of bananas. But before
he falls asleep he will call out one of our names,
today mine, tomorrow my brother's. I go
because he is a shark and there's no escape.

When I reach his room atop the stairs
I enter softly and close the door,
the air cold as a path through snow,
and go around his bulk and lie beside him
hoping he is asleep. Then I ask
"Daddy, where does it hurt?"
and he tells me to rub his back
all around, shoulders and thick neck, lower
where the shrapnel entered
before I knew him and before he knew us,
lodged where the spine curves
like a tail between his legs. I make circles
on his back with my fist, folding the flesh
like a tailor's cloth; he tells me
use both hands and I work harder
till he calls out for punches and chops
and I am pounding away at him

because he doesn't budge or talk and still
he will not snore.

He lies there, like a god
I no longer believe in.
Beyond the shades
a day is wasting. When I try
once more to rise he stirs
and I know it is too soon to leave,
that I must go on running my fist
up and down his spine in a futile effort
to heal him.
        Finally his snores begin, growing louder,
a sign that soon they will break on shore
and he will turn and go deeper, heading out
to the colder waters in his dream;
and I think of a day when I will be released,
though it means he is dying. His snores
catch like cloth torn in mourning
as I speak to be free.

MY FATHER AND MOTHER

They don't fight anymore.
Mornings they listen to the radio
for the weather and the names
of those who died last night.
After breakfast we women wash up.
He goes out to water the garden.

Irises border it
like an afterthought:
things he threw out in the alley, grew.
They remind me of the old days;
they have a little dried blood
on their tongues.

JACOB STAP
1893–1976

Farmer and carpenter
soldier in the Old Country
stubborn old Dutchman alone for thirty years
in the whitewashed house falling in on itself
its walls leaning like a house of cards.

Each winter your dirt cellar was ankle-deep with walnuts.
The well-water tasted like the night air in the woods
and there were bad dreams when your big face
swung like a lantern above me.
I closed my eyes tighter, but it was no good.

Now I fear your absence.
Forty-seven acres of your land is planted
with corn this year. Your land, I thought.
A new shopping center lights up a corner of the country sky.

It's all slipping away.
You never knew why
and I see now that I won't either.
On your deathbed you were climbing a ladder.
My mother was trying to help you down.
Steady girlie, you said,
hold it for me at the bottom.

THE DESCENDANT

My mother sews a quiver
from rough, dull leather
in a room smelling of rotting fish
and ginger root.
Her needle pierces hide
like an arrow through
a boy's sun-browned thigh.
In the instant of light
remaining at dusk,
her face is as warm and brown
as the leather she sews.
From my place on the matted straw floor,
it is as if her face and the quiver
are continuous, and she stitches
her own skin.
She sings a low, chanting melody
she learned as a girl,
of her ancestors who stained their faces
with poisonous berries
and followed buffalo
in ever-tightening circles.
I watch the day die on her face
as she turns to the window,
searching for what died
on another day,
for what was once clear,
but now crouches just beyond
this circle of light.

SOMEHOW WE MANAGED
for Ollie Napesni

In the mornings I awoke to the sound
of my mother's pounding rock
and the tart smell of chokecherries
Somehow we managed to get by
before the checks made it easy
Always there was work to be done
and there was a rhythm to life
In late June the turnips were ready to harvest
and in August when the berries were dark
we'd travel by wagon to the Niabrara River
where the bushes were heavy with fruit
By summer's end the clothes line would droop
with strips of squash and meat drying in the sun
Somehow we managed to get a beef
and then we'd dry that for the long winter
On cold days we'd boil the hooves for hours
this made a rich broth and kept the house warm
The muscle that came loose was a delicacy
and the bones could be made into a toy horse
We Lakota like that dark green squash
to this day I grow some in my yard
and I keep in mind lady friends
who don't have a plot of land
or who are unable to dig at their age
I took one out to the yard one spring night
the moon was out and oh! those yellow blossoms
"Look," I said, "how pretty they are . . .
This summer we'll be drying squash"

THE SINGING BRIDGE
for my mother

In the backwash of a low light,
against the dark wing of velvet maroon,
you smiled into the slope of one slow afternoon.
We are a pair.

You play the yarn, twiddle your divine
fingers, making pyramids, loops, and dives.
I am sitting on the floor, looking toward

your face. I think
I could find the gist of the yarn, in the glide of your hands,
in the maneuver
of your hands

I could find it. You have wound
your legs beneath you,
coiled yourself tight as a seed
and in that chamber

braided yourself into royalty.

The yarn. I remember it. Soft as skin.
And the sway of a bridge, and its singing.
Barksmell of old rope played on
by the wind. Old bridge. Old fear,
humming, the ropes
throbbing like wings, and I think they are
couriers, flapping a sombre message through
acres of dark:
Do not cross. It is death to cross.
But one day, the sky lowering its whiteness
to me, to every possible horizon beyond
like sweet-smelling terror of the woods,
I chance it, fearing the collapse
of everything that holds me.

The yarn is no longer between us,
but my arms are still toward you
as if they were locked in duty, or love,
or supplication. Surely this small
human act, this pleasure of an afternoon's labor: nothing
so difficult.

RAY SHOWS HIS BROTHER THE BARN

Ray hands me my coat, gloves, and says
he wants to show me the barn, the six acres
he ploughs, the ten cord of wood up on the first
tier, all hand-split, his hands, his ax. Out
in below zero, he looks for his wife in the window,
walks with another man's steps, toes
pointing in, like a pigeon's, like our
father's, whose ghost skulks around the house
at night, Ray whispers, especially
in winter, just one light on in the kitchen
where Ray likes to sit and smoke. In
the darker shadows of the barn, he flashes
the light on the bodies of rabbits
hung from the beam, their empty
skins swinging easily in the wind
that knocks slate dust down from the roof.
Blood, he says, pulling out his knife
to hack a leg off, one or two drops forming
on the thigh, the fur stiff, hard as a brush
Ray makes me touch and then says
Dad puts his face upon his face
at night and breathes fearful dreams
into his head. By flashlight beam
I see Ray's eyes are our father's eyes,
his nose, his teeth, even the voice now
becoming that low rumble as he moves deeper
into the barn where he keeps
the cows and one horse, turning around
just once, the light held by his face,
afloat in the dark.

SUNDAY DINNER

Nobody's father,
I am uncle to the whole world.
Dressed in a brown suit
worn at the pockets and cuffs,
pants shining on my thighs where my hands rub,
I come for Sunday Dinner.
My belly bulges against the vest
where the gold button pops free.

Around my knees
the children pull at my watch fob
like little sailors weighing anchor.
For them I have chocolates wrapped
round like coins in gold foil.
From my great parcel
I pull toys: old fashioned
wooden cars, bright, ring-painted tops,
stiff dolls with hair of rag.

From the kitchen, rice and chicken,
hot bread, clatter of plates.
My nephews wrestle behind my chair,
I tell my nieces stories as they play
with my fat fingers, "And then
the little girl was lost in the dark
forest. She was sorry and afraid
and cried for her uncle to come . . . !"

All week I wait in the shadows,
sit in corners with the dust.
I wait for Sunday, when I come
to dinner. Feed me
bread and chicken, Sister's crystal,
the blue-edged china plates.
I am uncle to the whole world;
no one's father.
It is the children I have come to see.

BUTCHERS

Hooting from milk crates, outside
the back door, the butchers
with scarlet aprons like tongues
between their knees,
on break from the tedium of hacking
meat from bone, play mumbly peg
with cleavers in the high weeds.

After surgery for a tumor pressing
for years on the brain,
my grandfather told stories
of family never spoken of before,
his father and five uncles, butchers
in the same shop on Cheyenne
swinging their knives to the creak
of swinging meat.

Each with his chopping block and rhythm,
the 3/4 time of German stock,
for years raising axes over head.
"I remember, how those cows went down
splay legged," he says, "skin stripped down
like a glove." And inside
the ambling track of veins mapping
the simple animal inconsistencies.

When he is gone another thirty years
will be forgotten: my grandfather,
with hands that laid hold of rusted machines,
tearing metal from metal,
in the screech of lugs worn thread-bare
at eighty laying hold of me like I was ten.

And what is forgotten like dirt
folded under, like sleep laid over
the bones? Five uncles and a father
in their second-generation-immigrant

trade, and their father who whipped
the welterweight champ in K.C.
In Sand Springs, the grocery that burned
where only oil, like water,
seeped out of the ground.

Here in this small town where the meat market
and VFW Hall are all that remain,
like soldiers gathering
each Thursday night for sixty years,
Grandfather dozes on the screened porch
afraid only of dying in an empty room,
no starlings cackling an hour before dawn,
no brothers laughing, kicking stones
on the short walk home. Starched white aprons,
and the blood spray over all.

PHOTOGRAPHS

This is the one in which I look
demented, something about
the way the eyes focus.
It's like staring at someone else.
How many times have I caught myself
in a department store mirror
and thought I was another woman?
Once I even smiled back, absentminded.
And if my mind was absent,
perhaps it's here

in this photograph of me at five.
I would hate to look after that child.
Gerard took a look and said
You must have been a Real Child.
A child's child.
And here is a photograph of my mother
dressed like a Southern belle in a floppy
blue hat, letting us know she wants
to be beautiful.

Here are several of my father
hiding behind a newspaper.
Here he's ducking into the garage.
Here his arms collide with his face.
The same with my sister during her permanent
wave, head abuzz in pink curlers.

But my favorite is the home movie
where everyone tries to escape.
Lana wheels me in a wheelbarrow—fast.
Next we try to hide behind each other.
I put the hem of her dress over my head.
She shouts silently to the lens, *Go away!*
My mother buries her face in the dog.
My father runs around the side of the house.
It's almost like looking at someone else's family,
wanting to tell them,
Why can't you act natural?

PRACTICAL ARRANGEMENTS

There's always been the problem of getting people to stay. Twenty years ago David and Linda — my parents — set this place up as a free love community. At times there were as many as fifteen people, kids and all, but none of them stayed. You'd think they would have: one hundred and sixty acres of lush hilly country in southern British Columbia, goats, fruit trees, large gardens; but now only David, Caroline and Linda live here among the remnants of cabins built by people who thought they might stay, but didn't. Visitors still come in spring and summer, but they stay in tents, instead, and the old cabins, some of them only half completed, have been given over to moss and rabbits.

I haven't been here for four months: my first semester in university. Driving home through the floods that have hit the west coast this winter has convinced me that I chose California partly because it's so difficult to get back. It works the other way around, too. David and Linda have never made a habit of going back to the states, even after David was pardoned along with all the other draft dodgers.

They've plowed the road for me, and the old car bumps and slides through the narrow channel between banks of snow, evergreens rising on either side, the hills blue-gray behind them. It's all the same. I pull up in front of the six-sided log house they built before I was born, and I can see Linda moving back and forth in front of the window. She opens the door and comes out with no coat on, grinning.

"Amber!" She's been baking, and her floury hands leave prints on my shoulders when we hug. She doesn't bother to brush them off, and I know I'm back in the bush. I sit down at the table next to the stove and pull off my boots; I've forgotten that feet can get so cold.

"How about some cocoa? I'll bet you're frozen." She spoons chocolate powder into a cup and puts milk on to heat. "The car run OK?"

"The car's running fine. It only took two and a half days." She's making four loaves of bread at once, mixing in raisins and spices from glass jars coated with years of kitchen grime.

"Well, thank God! I thought we'd have to sell off most of the goats when you had that transmission job."

Linda is an immensely practical woman. She doses the goats when they're sick, she can fix anything, and I have never had a conversation with her when she wasn't doing something else at the same time. She knits the way some people chain-smoke, and has sold dozens of bulky sweaters, hats, scarves, socks and mitts, in addition to making them for every member of the community. She is so practical that she isn't aware of being that way; she simply doesn't pay attention to the things in life which do not demand response and action.

Now she lights the gas in the compact oven the community gave itself as a Christmas present years ago, and slides a tray of cinnamon rolls in next to the bread. The cabin smells of wood-smoke, cinnamon, and a row of colorful wool socks stiffening on the rack next to the stove. Hung from the rafters are string bags full of dried moss that pokes through the mesh like tufts of hair. She wraps it in cloth for menstrual pads; when I was a baby I wore moss diapers.

"I was hoping you wouldn't get stuck and miss Christmas," she says, coming over to put more wood on the stove. She bends down next to me, rummaging in the woodbox for a stick that's not too damp. She has a capable, comfortable body: strong legs in the tight jeans she wears, small breasts and broad shoulders under a rumpled turtleneck and her same old blue sweater with brown stains on the front. The gap between her two front teeth gives her a friendly and unselfconscious smile. She is not a pretty woman, but many men are attracted to her, and she's had more lovers than I can keep count of.

"No chance of that," I say. "I left the minute my last exam was over — I was already packed." Linda gets out the sweater she's knitting (one thing I did in California was to *buy* a sweater for the first time; my friends wear the homemade ones), and we talk. She tells me about the goats that came down with something she cured with extra minerals, about the old weathervane David found while playing Swamp Yankee at the dump, and she asks a lot of questions about school. I say I am tired of memorizing things.

"You should've seen what we had to memorize for nursing. It was incredible," she says. Linda was a nurse before she and David left Connecticut to come to Canada. "I had these mental blocks against certain parts of the body, you know, some of the bones? Until I learned how to picture them on my boyfriend —" She laughs at a past I can hardly imagine her in, back in New Haven. There's no indication that she senses my criticism of knowledge that must be written down and swallowed whole until it beams out like a slide show in your head. She's not unaware of these things, she just takes them for granted. If you want to get through university (they were surprised that I did, but couldn't really object once I got the scholarship), then you deal with whatever sham is there. She sees no need to debate a question once a solution has been found.

David says one of the reasons he went to live with Caroline was that Linda couldn't find the impractical part of him.

After a while I put my boots back on and walk up the hill to David and Caroline's cabin. The ground is covered with fresh snow, only occasional delicate tracks of deer or rabbits interrupt the smoothness on either side of the plowed road. The branches of the trees are piled with snow; their bark is outlined with it. Various trees along the way stand out, and I can remember the feel of their rough bark on my hands, or the length of a jump from an overhanging limb down to the ground.

About four years ago Caroline was one of the people spending the summer here, picking fruit, working on the buildings, painting in her spare time. She and David slept together in a tiny green tent she'd brought along, and Linda was with someone else, too. I was used to the way either David or Linda would move into a tent or one of the abandoned cabins with a new lover, and someone else would move into the six-sided cabin with me and whichever parent was left. I liked these seasons. There were more special hikes, canoe trips, dinners, more music was played than when the three of us lived alone in the cabin all winter, and they always came together again. It was part of the rhythm of our lives, the way the goats have to be milked morning and evening no matter what happens in between.

That particular summer, though, Caroline stayed until after the last cut of hay was done, long after the others had gone back to the city. Eventually David told Linda that he intended to keep on living with Caroline. That was the only time I've ever seen Linda visibly upset. After a few terrible days when we all picked apples in silence and I caught Linda crying and hurling the rotten ones at a tree trunk, she decided that she and I would stay on in the six-sided cabin. We were angry with David, but we've always liked Caroline, and afterwards things settled into the new pattern. David and Caroline fixed up a small cabin that another couple had started on the flat uphill from our cabin. David and Linda still come together at intervals: he'll spend an evening talking with her by the stove and then they'll climb up to her part of the loft, separated from mine by a woven curtain. Linda will still have one of her men friends, Jerry or Chris or someone new, with her for some months out of the year; the only difference now is that when they leave she's alone.

"Amber is home," David says softly, inclining his head toward the loft even as he is still hugging me. His straight, straw-colored hair and beard smell of woodsmoke and coffee; I catch myself putting my face down onto his shoulder and sniffing the worn musty wool—one of Linda's sweaters. The sweater is the same color as his brown eyes, which look me over as if I've either left something behind in California or brought something additional along without knowing it, like an obscene note someone tapes to your back in high school. Caroline comes down the ladder from their loft which, unlike ours, is big enough for only two people to sleep in. "Hi, Amber." She hugs us both at once, her long painter's fingers squeezing my shoulder. She has a lithe, delicate body, large dark eyes. Her short hair is cut unevenly around her neck, giving her a look that varies between sloppiness and sophistication, depending on her expression.

The three of us sit on chairs David made a long time ago, with cushions of brightly patterned batik material, and we drink coffee, which I rarely have except with them. A delicious smell comes from the corner where Caroline has ground beans on the handmill, and the cabin is warm. It is also much smaller and darker than the six-sided one, which has a window in each wall. Here, Caroline's easel stands in front of the one large window; on the opposite side of the cabin near the small window is David's work-bench. Tools, plastic water-carriers, magazines, and squeezed-out tubes of paint are scattered about, nothing at all like Linda's colonial New England neatness, her routines of floor-sweeping and putting books back on the shelves.

David sets his cup of coffee down on one of his inventions: a hanging table strung from the rafters by two long twists of rope. It can be moved anywhere in the cabin or stowed out of the way in the loft. He pats the large plastic-covered book next to his cup. "I was just starting to read about hives when you came in. The librarian seems to think I ought to be-come a beekeeper." The mail-order library that ships books back and forth between the city and the bush will often send a book at random if they don't have the one you requested.

"Might be a good idea," Caroline says. "There are only maybe two, three people in the valley who sell honey."

"I'd need a complete space suit, though." He opens the book to a drawing of the beekeeper's outfit, and holds it up, turning the picture first toward Caroline and then toward me, like a teacher displaying an illustra-tion of ancient Roman dress. When I was very young David would jump up from the table, go to the chalkboard he'd hung on the wall for me, and scribble pictures, diagrams, abstract squiggles — whatever was needed to explain what we'd been talking about. If he drew something especially nice, like the time he made an Apollo rocket taking off, I'd save it and erase carefully around it for days.

"Looks like an outfit for combat," Caroline teases him. She has a habit of crossing her legs and then twining one leg and foot completely around the other leg with gymnastic flexibility. It's almost a flirtation, except I think she does it out of nervous energy. As a matter of fact, she and David both seem nervous, harping on the bees like this. Maybe they don't know what to say to me anymore.

David laughs. "You know how I'm drawn to these sorts of things. Danger. Violence." David's violent streak is perhaps more noticeable in a pacifist than it would be in someone else. He has, of course, always had a gun, mainly because if you want to farm in the bush you will have to be willing to shoot a few ground squirrels and threaten a black bear or two. One summer, though, there were complaints around town about the community of people who could be seen from the road going around naked (you could hear the cars pull over and doors slam on the other side of the trees when they'd get out to look). The day a delegation of locals arrived at the gate, David took his gun from its place over the door and said he was going down to talk to them. He talked to them for a long time, but no one came any further onto the land, and the complaints stopped after a while.

He stops laughing now as Caroline gets up for the coffee that's steaming away on the Primus (only our cabin has a real stove). "You're all right?" he asks, directing a swift beam of concern at me. "Everything's OK down there in the south? You're still intact?" His questions are so sudden and fierce that they're almost a mockery of parental anxiety, except that I know he is concerned.

"I'm fine. Yes. Everything's OK." I speak the banal words with an exaggerated intensity that mimics his own. His eyes hold mine for a moment and then he is satisfied and leans back in his chair. This strange communication between David and me is actually deeper than my communication with Linda, for all the talking she and I do.

I can tease him now. "Sounds like you want to know if I've lost my virginity. Am I intact!" He laughs at that. I lost my virginity years ago in this cabin—before it was fixed up for David and Caroline—with Jesse, who lived here with his parents for a long time.

"Well, now, tell me this," David is saying. "Are they still teaching logical positivism?" This is a standing joke with him; he alludes to it in the long letters he writes me, which I answer only occasionally. He himself dropped out of university because all they were teaching was logical positivism, which he says is a method for tearing things down. Whether the course was history, philosophy, psychology, what they were really teaching was logical positivism. So he got out and became a plumber's assistant and attended anarchist meetings.

"I don't think so. I'm not sure I'd know it if they did, though." I'm just supplying him with the lines.

"Oh, you'd know it, if they were—"

Caroline comes back and pours us all some more coffee. To get David off logical positivism I say to her, "Hey, that's a nice one," pointing to the painting that's been hung next to the bookshelf since I left last summer. "I like that." It is full of subtle blues and greens—her paintings are all abstract—and has a kind of mermaid-shape in the center, floating through geometric water. Caroline's paintings produce the pleasant disorientation of waking from a long deep sleep: colors and shapes have not yet sorted themselves out into recognizable forms or precise meanings, but you have the comfortable feeling that in a moment it will all become clear.

"Do you?" She goes over and switches on the twelve-volt light next to the shelf. The light makes the painting glow like a window framing a sunset in a darkening room. At times I have thought Caroline shy and self-effacing, but then she'll do something like get up and turn on a light so we can better appreciate her work, and I realize that she is actually very sure of herself. "I've been working with that theme for a while now," she explains, and I notice that the canvas on the easel has a few similar blue and green shapes breaking up the white surface. Caroline has become economically important to the community: last year she got a Canada Council grant for painting. We grow a lot of our food, and there's money from David's odd jobs, carpentry, the sale of goat milk and fruit in summer — and of course Linda's knitting. But the grant meant we could get some new farm equipment, and I suspect it helped with my transmission job.

It is completely dark by the time I get up to go back down the hill to our cabin. David gives me a flashlight, which I've forgotten to bring, and hugs me again at the door. "See you tomorrow," they both remind. Tomorrow is Christmas.

The dense black cold of a northern winter night. If I stop walking and turn off the flashlight, I see the same thing whether my eyes are open or shut. I shine the light directly in front of my feet and walk carefully; in two hours the snow has hardened to an icy crust. Down on our flat the only light comes from the barn, which is about two hundred feet from the house. Without even thinking about it I find the path that gets worn in the same place through the snow in winter and the meadow in summer. The barn is an old building made of cedar shakes that have long since gone gray, and the rear section is partly collapsed so that it looks like it's melting into the ground. David says we'll get to it next summer for sure. There's still plenty of room inside for the goats and a few geese.

When David and Linda first bought this place, the barn was the only building on the land. Everything else — cabins, fencing, gardens, and orchards — has been done in the past twenty years. I think this is the real reason Linda and I stayed after David moved in with Caroline. She wanted me to be able to see him, but I think the work they'd done on the place was even more important than that. When they first came to B.C. they lived in the city for several years, saving money to pay off the land. During that time Linda was a nurse, a waitress, a clerk at an import-export firm, and a model for art classes at the university. (I asked her once wasn't it strange to stand around naked in front of a roomful of clothed people and she said it was even stranger to see what they drew). But I don't think she wanted to do it all over again. Even someone as practical as Linda has only so much energy for repetition in life.

The light is from her gas lantern, hung on a nail in a rafter so the goats can't kick it. She's milking, crouched on the plank floor, wearing an old green wool jacket that she's had since I was a child. I have the same urge now that I had when David hugged me: to press my face down onto that woolen shoulder and sniff it. Instead, I turn off the flashlight, shut the door, and crouch down next to her.

"Hi," she says, milking steadily. Her light frizzy hair is tied back, and it is beginning to be threaded with gray. "The other pail is on the shelf," she says pleasantly. David and Caroline milk in the mornings; she and I always did it together at night.

I've forgotten the taut beating warmth of a goat's body in the cold barn at night, the plunk of milk at the bottom of the pail when you first get it going. The barn smells of hay from the loft up above and shit from down below; where we crouch in the dim circle of light from Linda's lantern there's the sharp smell of goat.

"David's going to come down and cook Christmas dinner for us," she says gaily. "We'll eat at our cabin."

"Good." My fingers are cold. I press them against the warm hairy side of the goat.

"Everything OK up there?"

"I guess so. They seem sort of jumpy."

"So do you."

"I drank lots of coffee—I'll probably be up half the night." It's not only the coffee. I'm still traveling along at freeway speed, haven't really arrived yet.

"That's all right. I've been staying up sort of late, too. I'll play you the new records I got with my last sweater-money."

For some reason I laugh a little at the picture of Linda and me sitting up late listening to records on the old battery-powered record player, the way we used to when I was in high school and had to catch a bus a mile away at seven in the morning. "I'd like to hear some music," I say. I really would. It seems lonely in the large shadowy barn.

"Wow." I slip into my old place at the table made of thick scarred boards; the table, like the cabin, was built before I was thought of. "Real food."

David carries over the platter of chicken done in David's Ginger and Pepper Sauce. "Bet you don't get *this* in your cafeteria." Caroline has gotten out jars of all the vegetables that were cooked with herbs and put up last summer. I jump up from the table, remembering the jars of seasoned pickles I made last summer as well, and stored on the back shelves. Linda has baked three different kinds of bread.

When we're all finally seated around the table in the light of two striped candles, it looks like one of the Dutch interior paintings we saw in art history: everything piled up, sauces glimmering, colors mingled, so that you feel hungry not just for the food but for the whole scene, the candles, the dishes, the people. We all heap food on our plates, reaching across the table. In front of each of us is a glass mug of dark homebrew. David raises his in the air. He is wearing a new brown and gold sweater Linda gave him for Christmas.

"To us," he says, and we all drink. David's homebrew is the closest thing we have to prayer here. We eat hugely, then, until there are only remnants left — chicken wings, small tomatoes floating in their sauce. The pace slows until the rhythm of the meal matches the lazy wandering saxophone number Linda has put on the record player. This is the fourth Christmas the four of us have spent together. The homebrew is not like regular beer — David never measures the sugar — and it creeps up on you and then gives a terrific yank to all your laugh muscles. Linda and Caroline exchange a smile and then they both grin at me.

David says, with a quick glance at Caroline, "We have news."

Caroline doesn't wait for silence to drop; she turns to Linda and says, "I got the job — starting next month."

"Great!" Linda pours the last of a beer into her mug, careful not to pour in the yeast that settles at the bottom. She nods her head eagerly, the way she does for any good news, smiling her gap-toothed smile. "When do you two leave?"

The chill going through my body must show on my face, because Caroline says quickly, "Wait a minute. Amber doesn't know yet." She explains to me that she's been offered a job teaching studio painting at a college in Saskatchewan. They hadn't been sure it would come through because of budget problems. "It's only a year's contract," she explains, "but the pay is good — better than the grant, even."

"Of course, if they like her, they might renew — " David begins, but Caroline interrupts him: "Well, don't jump — no need to worry about that now."

"You're going, too?" I ask David, and he nods and says yes. I can hardly look at the two of them. Back in the old days, anyhow, neither David nor Linda would have left the community unless they had no choice. That happened only a few times, when funds were low and David had to take outside jobs.

"I can't wait to get my hands on that new generator you're going to buy us," Linda says happily.

We will have a new generator. Yes. Lots of new things. It will be excellent for the community economy. "We'll all retire," David jokes.

He will go along to Saskatchewan so he can keep on framing Caroline's paintings (which are selling these days), but they will both be back for summer. He'll come home ahead of her to help with the farmwork, most of which begins in spring anyway. I shouldn't be angry with them,

I'm in their category: I've already left. It's only now I see that I've depended on them to protect Linda while I'm gone, from the loneliness of the six-sided cabin and the miles of isolated bush that begin as soon as you open the cabin door.

There are only a couple of times I can remember hating Linda. Once, for insisting I wear the homemade clothes to school even after I was taunted by other girls (Jesse and I both had horrible homemade windbreakers that looked like torn balloons mended over and over again). And once, later on, for telling me about the abortion she'd done on herself years ago, before she and David wanted any kids. It wasn't the fact of the abortion that made me dislike her; it was the cold practical way she provided the details I didn't want to hear. I was fourteen then, and I was repelled by her, physically, for a while after that.

I didn't hate David when he left us and went to live with Caroline; I was more angry then. In fact, I've never hated David before, but I can't help it right now. We sit eating cinnamon rolls as if nothing has happened. Linda has put on her Great Men of the Blues album (the only indication of how she might be feeling), and I feel as though I've eaten too much and had too much to drink. I want to go outside and throw it all up, then lie down on the perfect hard crust of the snow. It is like a bad case of flu I had as a child, when I got delirious and kept begging to be allowed to go outside and take off my pajamas and lie down in the snow. I wanted to do that more than anything—I insisted it would heal me. But they kept me in bed, of course, tucked inside my down sleeping bag.

I sit quite still now and watch the swirling patterns of milk I've poured into a cup of coffee. I mix it and destroy the pattern. When I look up again the three of them are all smiling at me. I've missed whatever someone just said.

They look idiotic, smiling like that.

David has his glass raised again. "To Amber's first—well, to Amber—" It was probably something about *my* new life, away from here.

"To Amber."

I can't go out and lie in the snow. I'm here, with them. I raise my glass and drink the toast to myself.

Out trudging around in my snowshoes next morning, I let the cold wind blow in my face until my eyes sting and begin to water. I've climbed up one of the smaller hills that overlook the valley. Very little has changed in all the time I can remember: the same farms at the bases of the opposite hills, the barns filled with hay, cattle in their muddy mid-winter pens. Evergreens, outlined with slightly less snow than yesterday, cover the valley as far as it is possible to see. In spring the snow will melt and green plants will sprout up everywhere out of the thick reddish soil. Wild flowers will bloom, and the fruit trees will be rich and heavy by late August. In summer, you can walk into the bush and pick enough berries for a pie in just a few minutes.

This place is, really, too lush, too beautiful; too many life-sustaining things grow with no human help. Even now the hills are too magnificent, heaped with snow, the far-off peaks glittering against the blue sky like something out of a Sierra Club calendar. An environment like this changes people, it twists them. The beauty and richness of the land must have decadent effects like continual overeating. Look at all the human relationships that have flowered and spread outward like greedy vines, finally strangling themselves, right here on David and Linda's land, in the community where no one has ever had to do anything they didn't want to do.

When I get back to the cabin, Linda and I sit drinking coffee, and she says, "I'm thinking of writing to Pat, see if she wants to come up for a while next month." A friend of hers from the city who often spends the summer here.

"That's a good idea." I nod my head eagerly, the way she does. "She'd probably be glad to get out of the city for a while."

"And Chris says he's coming in spring, as soon as he gets back from Japan."

I nod again, and then there is silence. She doesn't mention all the months she'll be here alone. "You'll be all right? Staying here?" I ask tentatively.

She looks at me in a strange way and picks up her coffee cup. "Of course, I'll be fine." As though I've said something irrelevant. "Wouldn't want to be anywhere *else*." Only the subtlest jab at David. "Besides, the goats can't milk themselves."

"David should've thought about that," I say angrily. "Before he elected you as goat-sitter."

She shrugs. She won't rise to it.

So we talk about practical things: transferring the snowplow from David's truck to hers, the neighbors stopping by for milk and seeing that everything is OK. We talk about working on the barn, and about Pat, Jerry, Chris—all the people coming here for summer: another season, when everyone will come back and stay for a while.

FOR ONCE

Each day dropped the same ton of sunlight.
I had no mind for venture, my roadmaps
were cold as the capillaries in a dead foot.

Five reunions I passed up: I thought,
What if my wrong turns catch up to me?
What if my face sees how old it is?

But I went for once. I landed before dawn,
and mother's face yoo-hooed like the full moon,
and I felt the way I had once in the woods

when it was dark beyond bedtime—
the zing of it that made my lungs shake.
And the brother most like me had landed,

and he taped his arias and played them
seven hours on the road, and mother
perched like a smile at a school recital,

while I laughed inside me with no scorn.
And then we were so deep in Vermont
the green was black, the brooks lunatics

who've been saying they're cold for so long
they don't care who hears it. Still
a big clearing opened by the offroad;

my sister who'd seen to it and built here
was ready for us with her arms, her husband
like a French horn, and my memory snatched

their children's names who didn't fit
the baptism I was here for last time.
And then cars in the leaves became my sisters

from west and south, and my brother, too,
whose new wife none of us had kissed yet,
but did now as though she were always ours —

and his sons were with them, all the kids
like balloons flooding from the roof of a convention.
And it made no difference our sister who whined

like a tomb-hinge for the creep who'd left her
had mummy-sags for a face like father's
when he was trying on his own death —

we bumped into her too with our flatters.
And then we tore to the gluttonies of August
as though the surplus in a warehouse had burst

the bins and locks and we went woozy,
and the night that only wanted to be cold
had to take a beating from us instead.

And so next morning our brother who sang
sicced *Ave Maria* around the clearing like a hound
on a butterfly and we clapped and whistled

and dared each other to jump in the cold pool
and did. So the baptism had come for us,
as though we'd entered from-now-on like a creed.

Then we left, and next day I stood
where father and his two sons after me
were cut in stone while mother yoo-hooed

beyond the romance of the light rain there;
I touched the red lobelia on the grave
and felt if I sang now it would save them.

SIMPLE HOLDINGS

I own a pear
and two pecans

enough grass
to stuff three pillows

a ceiling
that weeps on my face in bed

plenty of nails
but no paintings

My mother
blames herself for this

Visiting us she frets
that my family will go hungry

How can I tell her
we no longer worry

whether we are happy
or unhappy

We have neither too much
nor too little

nails to hang our clothes on
when we tire of wearing them

the costless smell of grass
while we sleep

and when my son cries
and refuses to eat

I produce two pecans and a pear
and juggle for him

I am not very good
but he claps delightedly

Even mother
has to hold her breath

at the pecans
passing swiftly hand to hand

at the pear
weightless as a sun in mid-air

The Blood Remembering

You lick our wounds,
the salt healing,
the blood remembering.

—Herbert Scott,
"The God That Keeps Us Alive"

THE FLOWERING

There is something secret in the barn.
The corn husks whisper to themselves,
the horses startle in their stalls,
the stallion's eyes whiten as the
clover clings to his mouth. I am
all eyes and silence in the darkness
behind the wooden slats. I see

her now, young, shuddering excitement,
and I hear the little cries in her lips,
see how the sun shines through the barn
and glistens along her neck, flaming
between her breasts, while the wings of
her hair rise in the golden light.
Alone, and shaking with secrecy, I dream
of her long dark hair falling in my face
as she rides me home to the distant house.

I lean out of myself, away from the
heavy breath of the barn and taste the
warm tongue of the summer; something is
flowering in the green leaves, and
the stallion rears in the sun.

THE PAINTERS
for Sonya

You were startled to find me in the basement
when you came down to do laundry.
I was hiding from the painters and the heat
lying on the floor, with my hands
behind my head, thinking of nothing.
I saw you look out a window at the gritty knees
and splattered shoes of the outside crew.
And we both could hear the inside men
upstairs moving their rollers up and down
against the walls.
You hesitated, then put down your dirty work
and joined me on that floor.
How pleased we were by this—the busy men
outside moving ladders, tying back bushes
and trees, and above us, the placing
of drop-cloths on the furniture—so much
going on around us and soon even our cut-offs
were too much to wear.
When the heat went down we went upstairs
to the new walls of our old surroundings.
Our own love-sweat mixed with the smell
of the paint. It was a place we left
not long ago and had come back to,
but better than we remembered.
We didn't know then that our daughter
was conceived, how the mixing of liquids
inside you could produce such brightness.
And outside, the foreman waited for us
in his truck, taking care of invoices,
figuring out his next job, estimates
for the future.

LOVE LETTER

We've been sealed, filed
for winter like two
manila envelopes
thin with forgotten
business. We froze
separately in January.
February circulars
buried us deeper. But
a long weekend away
together starts a thaw —
kids in capable hands,
work done, we do nothing
usual. We dump all
news in the fireplace,
ski cross-country
on unmarked trails,
shake the whole second floor
with love. Then laugh.

In the middle
of our last night away,
my eyelids float up
like weightless spacemen,
the Dipper in the high window
draws me to my elbows,
my eyes slowly sweep
your sleeping body, the bay,
the wavery lights of Petoskey.
They meet the green beacon
of the Harbor Point lighthouse,
the ice in the bay
breaks up, I am
the first ship of spring,
and I bless insomnia,
roll sideways toward you.

COSMIC GENERATIONS

. . . —call it what you will, occultism,
the curse of the Pharaohs, sorcery, or magic,
there is some force that defies the laws of
science at work in the pyramid.
—Psychic Discoveries Behind the Iron Curtain

Near Cairo in '68
the IBM
1130 computer
whirred for a year (like those machines
of Dr. Frankenstein
on the late movie), storing,
recording on
magnetic tape (the way he kept
notes) the pattern of cosmic rays
striking the inside of
the Pyramid of Chephren.
I have never
phrased it before. But Dr. Amr
Gohed, like a man of faith, said
in the *Times* that "what was

happening defies all laws
of science and
electronics." Before that time
Monsieur Bovis, like
anyone seeking all, visited
the Pyramids of Egypt:
on the way up
in what was the pharaoh's chamber,
like a slap or a kiss a dreamer
remembers all his days,
the carcasses of stray cats
who had somehow
lost their way and lay there preserved,
exposed to the air like Bovis.
Caught by such power

in a language itself—
those late models
like Burton and Taylor movies.
One French firm, doubtful, mass produced
a scaled reproduction   .
and made much better yogurt;
religiously
the Cheops Pyramid Razor-
Blade Sharpener kept your blades keen;
now it is styrofoam.
I'd write out new inventions
for amputees,
and a pyramid condom: Ad:
Thrill Her Again and Again. It's
all in the shape of things.

What possibilities! And
there are other
applications: specially built
hospital rooms designed to please
today's schizophrenics
or lovers, and witches' hats
which, if worn, will
energize flesh the way your touch
wakes me. Charting wave fronts of sound,
scientists have proved how
the final chord of Handel's
"Hallelujah
Chorus" creates a five-pointed
star, looking like a pentagram.
Though I'm no scientist,

have never been to Egypt,
I'd imagine
such an art: stealing the design
I'd concoct a mad love affair—
your own trapezoidal
room like a bridal chamber,
that chord playing
on your stereo, styrofoam

miniatures, in a word,
something like black magic.
Then wearing the witch's hat
I'd visit you,
dreaming of how your breasts would sway
under your gown, these hands become
charged, living forever.

VALENTINE CONFESSION

All right. After all these years, yes,
I do not love you more than your fragile replicas.
I love you in another curve or design.
I admit, I cannot cleave only to you.
I get homesick for my mother's lips on my forehead
and the reflection I see in my father's eyes.

It's true while you pounded between my thighs,
I have let others tap on your shoulder.
How many? I never knew or counted.
And now that I've started and your tears pelt
my shoulders like stones, I'm glad
I opened this pressed heart.

There were times I blessed the blood curse.
Sometimes your demands stain me
dark-faced. And even this, I confess.
I have placed you in a casket and hid my smile
behind the black veil and it was not enough.

On occasion, I wiped you from my days
as easily as the kitchen sponge cleans spills.
Are you satisfied now that you've seen the uneven cut
of my heart? Can you grasp my lip-warm touch on the tip
of these words and believe I love you, as any woman loves
her man after twenty years?
And now that the air is strained by truth,
does my love sting your eyes?

JEALOUSIES

1.

My father wore a Homburg hat,
powdered his face with fine, white powder.
My mother raged when women spoke to him
on the street.

Once he threw the pictures
from his wallet into the snow.
Before he scuffed them under with his boot,
I saw a photograph of a dark-haired girl.
I was afraid to ask my father who she was.

Under the faded ironing board cover,
my mother still keeps a Valentine
he gave her in nineteen sixty-six.
On the front of the card,
a big-breasted girl poses
in a tight red dress.
My mother would not speak to him
for a week after.

2.

Sometimes I do not call first
before I come home early from work. I look
for changes in my lover's expression when
he thinks I am not watching him,
for scraps of hair in my comb
that do not belong.
Last night I looked
between all the photos in his wallet.

I count the little jealousies,
carry them with me, take them out fondly
and stroke their heads until they purr.

THE ORIGINS OF DESIRE

As the woman climbs to the top of the bluff
she can't see any ocean, only rocks
and a beached log. At the peak, she turns
embarrassed to find a man and a woman
stretched side by side on the shelf below.
He lifts his cup; she takes a bite
from her sandwich. The woman walking
over the rocks looks no more than a second
but she knows what it means to lie here
with a lover, how the stones slide
smooth as a mattress. Because she feels
envy and not a little lack, she assumes
they watch her step from level to level
until the slope deposits her on wet sand.

Down beach, two little girls approach,
clear plastic bags filled with shells
swinging from their hands. What if
the one with red mittens giggles or
sticks out her tongue? The woman prefers
to imagine them ducking their heads,
shy as she used to be. Drawing closer,
red mittens looks her in the eye, smiles
hello. The woman grins, disarmed.
If she had a child, she'd teach her
to gather shells and smile, just so.

A woman gets lonely when she knows
she means nothing to the man fishing
from the shore, his line forming a triangle
from a pole stuck in the sand. As she
circles him, he considers a flap of seabirds
out where waves toss their flirty heads.
If she tried, she could imagine longing for a stick
to tremble, the joy of line snapping taut.
When she looks back, she grins as she watches him
haul a mess of seaweed from the water.

Yellow and many-beaded, it sways from the hook
as he mouths curses only his poodle can hear —
a flurry of mad gray circles on the sand.

Pretending interest in the subtle tracks
of ebb-tide, she feels blessed as if
the fisherman, the child who said hello,
the couple who didn't mind her presence
after all were summoned to tell her something
she's almost ready to understand. In the tide-
pool, shadows play tag around submerged rocks
while she thinks something profound
about the origins of desire, wipes her nose
and heads home, not recognizing, for a moment,
her own prints in the sand, the huge round sole
of her boot, the impressive wedge of heel.

CLEANING TOILETS

There's a grace of rain
falling in the garden,
but I'm here on my knees
elbow deep in the bowl
scrubbing like a Puritan.

My husband hangs crucified
in the living room, nailed
to the wall last night by
a viciousness I save only
for those I love. He knows
me for what I am, knows I
treat strangers better.

He's a patient man. His head
taps softly on the wall, looking
down with the dubious regard
of one who has seen this
all before, while I go on pretending
I could wash away the stains
if I could just get deep enough.

FEVER

Father was to her, and to me,
like the wind—blowing through our house
on weekend leaves—and when we spoke to him,
he carried our voices away.

When he left,
and silence grew inside my mother like a child,
I would watch as she set the table for two,
then ate by herself in the kitchen, standing.

And she taught me this:
that silence is a thick and dark curtain,
the kind that pulls down over a shop window;

that love is the quick repercussion of a stone
bouncing off the same darkened window; that pain
is something you embrace, like a rag doll
no one will ask you to share.

Some nights, she allowed me in her bed.
Her skin was as cool as the surface
of the pillow the sick child clings to, awakening
from feverish dreams.

I would lay my head close to hers and listen
to the fine, knotted thread of her breath,
to her rosary of sighs,

her peace so deepened by sorrow, I know
it sustained me then, as the light
slipping past heavy, dark curtains might nourish
a small plant set, by accident, close

to the window.

ORDINARY LIFE

This was a day when nothing happened,
the children went off to school
without a murmur, remembering
their books, lunches, gloves.
All morning, the baby and I built block stacks
in the squares of light on the floor.
And lunch blended into naptime,
I cleaned out kitchen cupboards,
one of those jobs that never gets done,
then sat in a circle of sunlight
and drank ginger tea,
watched the birds at the feeder
jostle over lunch's little scraps.
A pheasant strutted from the hedgerow,
preened and flashed his jeweled head.
Now a chicken roasts in the pan,
and the children return,
the murmur of their stories dappling the air.
I peel carrots and potatoes without paring my thumb.
We listen together for your wheels on the drive.
Grace before bread.
And at the table, actual conversation,
no bickering or pokes.
And then, the drift into homework.
The baby goes to his cars, drives them
along the sofa's ridges and hills.
Leaning by the counter, we steal a long slow kiss,
tasting of coffee and cream.
The chickens' diminished to skin & skeleton,
the moon to a comma, a sliver of white,
but this has been a day of grace
in the dead of winter,
the hard cold knuckle of the year,
a day that unwrapped itself
like an unexpected gift,
and the stars turn on,
order themselves
into the winter night.

WHY I COULDN'T LOVE RICHARD

So here we sit, my father and me, in my husband's church. I'm in my usual place directly in front of the pulpit and my father is huddled next to me. He is in my mother's usual seat and it's strange — she used to sit so tall. He doesn't know it is my mother's seat — he never was a churchgoer — and I think it's just as well.

The casket rests on a folding contraption so close to my father he could reach out and touch it, if he had a mind to. Every now and then he leans toward it, then he leans back toward me.

There is an enormous spray of red roses covering the ebony lid. Two ribbons extend down over the flowers. One says in gold letters, "MOTHER," and the other says "WIFE."

The red roses were my father's idea. I said — well, no, I didn't say — I *wanted* to say, they'd look like blood dripping down, but he went on and on about how red roses were my mother's favorites — even though I swear I never saw her with red roses anytime, anywhere, except maybe in a hat — and certainly never from him.

I was never much of a churchgoer, either, and maybe I got that from him — from my father — and maybe we both didn't go because it seemed so important to my mother. And now it's hard to believe, but not only am I here in this seat way up front every Sunday, I'm even married to the man at the altar.

But the way I see it, the minister's wife *has* to be here. The congregation expects it — practically demands it — so Richard and I say fine. Let's just do it. It gives Richard a chance to rest his eyes on a neutral face, he says, and I have to confess I knew that's the way it was going to be when I married the man.

So I go through the motions: I stand up, I sit down, I repeat the Apostle's Creed and the Lord's Prayer. I open my hymnal and move my lips. But on those Sundays when I'm sitting here, my mind is everywhere but on God.

Richard knows that. We've talked. I tell him I plan menus and make shopping lists and think about the baby. (There's one on the way.)

But here's another confession: Sometimes I just don't understand the man. I mean, it's his job, isn't it, to try and inspire me. To convert me. And yet he never does. When Richard and I are alone, the subject of religion never comes up.

I don't know — this whole thing with Richard is odd, and sometimes, when I'm sitting here, I think about that.

I met Richard through my mother — and who else would it have been if you really think about it? Richard Arthur Westerfield — Pastor Rick to the ladies (Oh, yes)—was 36 years old when he came to my mother's church, and "very well educated" the ladies must have said a hundred times.

Well, those ladies fell all over each other to take Pastor Rick under their soft little wings. He went from place to place on Sundays for dinner, and for every chicken in a pot, there was an eligible daughter or granddaughter or niece (and sometimes just an eligible widow lady) at his elbow.

There was even a schedule, written out and copied at the 10-cent copy machine, if you can believe it. I thought the whole thing was a little silly, myself. I'd lived away from home for a while and nobody'd ever felt it their duty to keep *me* fed and happy.

He had been pastor at St. Matthew's for two or three months and was getting just the slightest pot belly when it was our turn to have him. I never did believe in having ministers in the house, so while my mother was in the kitchen, I told the man right out, before he had a chance to ask, that while I might believe in God, I thought church was the last place He'd actually hang out.

I told him about Madge Hendricks and her old biddy friends and how they whispered and snooted around all the time and made comments about who wasn't in church. I told him about the time Terry Roberts' mother's Easter dress didn't quite measure up and they let her know it by turning around in their pews and staring her up and down, even though they *knew* what a hardship it was for her. I told him to think about what kind of God would want to hang around people like that, let *alone* do favors for them.

He laughed at that, which I thought was a bit queer, and I almost told him about *me* in church, in another time and another place, except it was one of those stories that never got funny, no matter how long I waited.

We walked around the block after dinner and he got me to tell him about my job at Ben's Quality Realty. I was the secretary there and it wasn't such a bad job. It was pretty quiet, really. Ben and his crew of patent-leather-belted salesmen didn't sell many houses, and Ben, as nice a man as you could ever want to know, kept me stocked with Snickers Bars.

I told Richard I'd had my share of boyfriends (I don't now how *that* came up) but that was all I said on that subject. I went right on talking—I couldn't believe it—until out of the blue, he said, "You know, you're not dumb," and I said right back, "I don't remember saying I was."

He began coming to our house for Sunday dinners all the time, and Madge Hendricks snooted around about that, too. He asked me to call him "Rick" and I said I couldn't do that. The man has bushy eyebrows and bristly hair and just the slightest Jimmy Stewart stammer. He's short. He's not a "Rick"—though I didn't say as much to him. I said I thought "Richard" sounded better for a minister.

After about a dozen Sundays Richard asked me to marry him. I honestly couldn't have been more surprised. I hemmed and hawed and even though he hadn't asked, I told him I wasn't a virgin. He just looked at me with those eyes of his and pretended he hadn't heard me.

So that night I went in and talked to my folks. My father had no opinion whatsoever. But my mother! She praised the Lord and blessed Him for answering her prayers—right in front of me! And somebody told me my mother had actually giggled when she saw Richard in church the next Sunday.

I thought at the time that it was my mother who really wanted to marry Richard, but she wasn't the one he'd asked. "I want him in our family," she'd said.

I thought that Richard wanted to marry me because he needed a cook and a housekeeper and I was pretty good at that sort of thing.

I thought that I wanted to marry Richard because I was already 31 years old and a little tired of working at Ben's, nice as that man was.

Now I don't know what to think. My mother—my mother—died on Monday and I'm expecting her first grandchild.

My baby—no, *our* baby—is due in mid-summer and we already know it is a girl. She will be named Adrian Cora. We decided on "Cora" just this morning at breakfast and I said why couldn't we have decided sooner? My mother's name was Cora.

If my mother was thrilled at our wedding, you should have seen her when we told her about the baby. We were already making plans, my mother and me. She had already bought patterns.

When they found her at the bottom of the basement steps (an embolism—they're so unfair, those sneaky bubbles) she was still clinging to her wicker laundry basket and scattered around her like so many flotsam were my old, yellowed baby clothes.

It is still morning, and a cool one, but the sun spreads itself across the east windows and warms my side of the church. I can look out those windows and see that it is spring and everything on this part of the earth is coming back to life. I don't know—I thought about saying to my father that it just seems to me dying should be suspended during spring.

The organist is hammering out the first few bars of "Rock of Ages" to cue the congregation on the tempo and the key. It is my cue to find something to look at besides Richard. Richard tends to put his whole heart and soul into a song and sings it to the rafters, his arms going a mile a minute. It gets to be a real irritation, watching him.

The baby—*Adrian Cora*—gives me a kick and immediately I feel guilty thinking bad thoughts about her father up there doing his duty. Maybe I'm the only one here who thinks he could do it just as well with a little less gusto.

I look at Richard now, out of guilt, and this is what I see: His head is down so I can see only the ridge of his eyebrows. He is not singing, I can tell that. His hands grip the pulpit as though, if he let go, terrible things would happen. His skin is so gray you would think he was standing in shadow and not in sunlight. When he finally looks up, his eyes — *those eyes* — are filled with such sorrow I have to turn away.

I happen to turn in my father's direction and he chooses that moment to look me straight in the eye and say, "Wouldn't my Cora have loved this?"

There is a thud in my stomach and I don't think it is the baby. My Cora? Never in my life have I heard my father say, "My Cora." Never have I heard him say my anything. If he spoke of my mother to other people, it was always, "the wife." He'd say, "I told the wife the other day. . . . " and it would drive me crazy. "I fed the cow the other day . . ." It never seemed to bother her. Sometimes he would call her "Cora," but it was like this: "Corah!" Yelling.

And now this. "My Cora." He is looking at me, nodding, waiting for my response. I nod back, and suddenly I see my parents as Cora and Philip, together. Cora and Philip, who, away from the others — away from me — had a life together. Cora and Philip, who must have loved together, though I never heard them say it — rarely saw them touch except by accident . . . and now I want to ask my father if she knew.

The song is over. Richard rises to speak and I am saved from blurting out the question. He has lost one of his closest friends, Richard is saying, and he mentions my father and he mentions me. I sit up and monitor, just as I did the last time he got personal up there on the pulpit.

It was the time he announced that we were going to have a baby and I was as angry as a person can get at Richard.

"I have wondrous news to tell you," he'd said. "My wife, Amanda, is with child." He actually said, "with child," but that wasn't why I was angry. I was angry because — did the whole world have to know what we'd been doing together in the privacy of our own bedroom? The confession of fornication, the opening up of our most intimate secrets, was met with excited "Ooh's" and applause, my mother leading the pack as if she'd only just found out, and I could have strangled them both in a minute.

Later, when I tried to explain to Richard what he had done, he looked at me with those Bambi eyes of his, and, after he went to great lengths to explain to *me* that only unmarried people can fornicate, he just kept saying, "But I was so happy. I wanted to share it."

Here's the problem with Richard: When *I* think of family, I think of my parents . . . and the baby . . . and Richard, of course. Richard thinks the whole *world* is his family. It was all those early dinners, I'm sure of it, with all those women fawning over him. Plus the fact that his parents are dead and his only sister, Rebekah (yes, spelled like that), lives in Connecticut or somewhere and belongs to the Junior League.

It's the same with his students. There is a school attached to Richard's church, and he teaches grades six and seven during the day. He adores those kids, he says, and tells me while we're fixing dinner all the funny, clever things they've said or done during class. *Nobody* adores kids that age, I tell Richard. It just isn't done in America. He grins that grin of his.

Richard is one of those people who loves everything and everybody, even in the morning. My mother was like that. As soon as she'd hear my feet hit the floor, she'd pad over to the kitchen counter and turn on the radio. I like quiet in the morning—even the birds irritate me—but my mother would say, about the radio, "It does you good. It gets you ready for the world, and it lets you know the world is ready for you!" I swear.

I always thought people like my mother and Richard should be muzzled at sunrise, myself. I take after my father in that way, I guess. Mornings were when he yelled "Corah!" the most.

Things are quiet again here in church, and I could kick myself for letting my mind wander. What has Richard said? He is busy at the altar now, moving things around. He seems to spend a lot of time doing that—moving things—and I wonder why I have never been curious enough to ask what it is he does up there.

Church, even after all this time, is still such an alien place. When I lived in the city, Paul and I went to church—nearly every Sunday, without fail. Paul was in real estate, and what better place for contacts? So we went for contacts—and for laughs, I hate to say. Though Paul had great control. He'd laugh at everything there was to laugh at—usually at someone else's expense—but never in church. But I laughed. Boy, did I laugh. He'd nod his head at someone and suddenly they looked so funny I thought I'd die.

I was like that with Paul. I guess if he'd told me to barrel it down Horseshoe Falls I would have done it. But that was in another time, in practically another life.

Richard turns now and I realize he has grown lean. His hair is cut decently for once, and lays in Robert Redford fringes at his neck. It strikes me, as I try to remember who cuts his hair, that I haven't spent a moment with Richard without the thought of Paul peering over my shoulder, poking me in the ribs. Paul would have made mincemeat out of Richard.

"My Richard," I try out under my breath as I watch him bow his head, and it seems so strange I almost laugh in church. It is different than "my husband." Entirely different.

My father sighs and I take his arm in mine. He flinches. I haven't touched him in years. He smiles at me and settles back and his smile is so much like Richard's I stare at him long after he has turned away.

The baby is starting up again, kicking to beat the band, and I press my hand against my stomach to calm her. I get a picture of my mother holding her, calming her, and the tears come from nowhere again.

When Richard finishes and the "Amen" is finally sounded, I break away and stumble up the aisle and out the door. The perfume of warm roses follows me.

I pull in great gulps of cool air and when I turn around, I see that Richard has helped my father out of the church—has done my job—and is standing on the steps shaking hands with the men and women who knew my mother. Some of his students rush up to him, then hold back, suddenly shy. Richard smiles his open smile and welcomes them as though he'd been expecting them. They clutch at his hands in relief.

I work my way up to where my husband is standing and begin to rub his back as he talks. He is startled—like my father—and he slows and stammers and smiles my father's smile. When the color has come back into his face, I stop, give him a final pat, and reach for my father's arm.

As we head for the first car behind the hearse, my father falters and heaves a long, shuddering sigh. It is the saddest sound I've ever heard. It is music to my ears, coming from this man who loved my mother.

THE GOD THAT KEEPS US ALIVE

i.

Love, in whose honor
we grow towards the sky

in whose service
we diminish death

Love, on whose journey
we map ourselves,
the bodies of our mates

husband the grassy fields
where we feed
the pools where we swim

the shoals of bone
where we draw shelter

Love, we bend
to kiss you

becoming gods ourselves,
though not gods, and dying.

ii.

We mark our ascent
in kitchen doorways

in our children,
their shoes empty
as our lives would be.

Winter comes.
Trees die in this season

fall in the deep snows
unseen, unheard.

Beneath our feet
the earth shudders.

iii.

Love, brief father
who leaves us
orphans in dry rooms

winter heat
cracking our bones . . .

We are warriors
of loss

falling
in the streets
of foreign cities.

You lick our wounds,
the salt healing,
the blood remembering.

iv.

Love, you are
nearly great enough.

The myth you father
is worth the living.

HOOKS AND EYES

We take turns clocking the storm's approach
While the bread browns unevenly in the pans.
It would be one of those turbulent hours the wind brings
Changing directions fiercely. The whitest minutes are elegant
Hiding behind the laundry left on the line.
A christening dress: I've just sewn the tiniest
Particle of lace around its neck by hand
Sitting on the porch swing while wind rages through the chains.
The privilege of rage is the wind's only.
These are your hands, not mine, chaining hooks and eyes.
The cat leaps boldly to my attention. The cloud's dull stripes
Show places where the sky has stretched from gloom.
This long house depends on a hallowed silence.
We are merely women now, our men departed for the fields
Or the stream's running over mud and chaste stone,
To a distance beyond love, a semblance of what might be
Called a compromise between the maternal twins of our sexes.
I am sewing this white sleeve, torn from my wedding dress
While the flowers yawn, wind-prodded, awakened
From their individual, rainbow dreams here
And by the stream, where we lie naked as new gravestones,
Botticelli's women, in a shower of lily-colored light.
This delicate exercise of dress, elaborate, and to be worn
Once. Complete, the last knot of thread: What I feel
Is beautiful to see. If you agree then ask questions
Of yourself; if you disagree, then ask questions of yourself.

DRYING ONIONS

They hung in the cellar's dark all winter
untouched by wind and snow white as they are,
until long green shoots reached for light.
You helped me slice them; crackling
brown skins thin as dragonfly wings covered the floor.

Sweet bitter fruits of the earth —
spread on racks to dry, they became
more a part of us than we knew or wanted.
Our eyes began to burn. Our clothes took on the taint.
When we made love, your tongue and mine, this mound
of flesh and that, all flavors
disappeared in onion.
                                            All flesh is onion,
all sweat and juice part of us, fruit of our love.

Outside, the snow has melted, crusted,
sagged toward earth. We hack through it, peel back
layer after layer, searching for the white heart,
for earth warm enough to take our seed.

EARLY SUMMER CONCERT

All morning, behind her metal stand,
my mother practices violin on the back porch.
My father stops his planting in the field
to listen and clap his calloused hands,
this loud applause filling his veins with love.
And farther out the slow dance of a tractor
turns sod through music no almanac predicted.
Trees seem to waltz up hillsides,
birds open their wings like fans.
We are all conductors,
sun burning our bare backs like the quiet eyes
of an audience.
Even the two identical Belgians rehearse,
lipping their cold notes in harmony
from the clear surface of a wooden trough.

The Same Door

All enter through the same door,
wide open from above,
locked tightly from below.

—David James,
"Think Death"

PRENATAL

Preparing for you,
your mother and I spend one night each week
in a church basement with eleven other couples,
practicing our breathing.
Breathing's like this:
the ribs admit air, and settle,
the way a bush fills out with leaves.

All in good time. For now,
you and your lungs, those tiny,
twin sponges, go on repeating evolution,
just as the shore emerging from the sea
anticipates that very shore occupied
by a small boy sitting disconsolate in the sand
who's lost his castle to the tide.
The lungs make all the noises of childhood,
the songs and wailing,
company to our disappointments,

to the pleasures we hadn't expected:
last night, standing in line for groceries
behind a woman with a baby against her shoulder,
I couldn't help seeing you there instead,
startled, opening your eyes.
Little sandman, sleeper,
what a lesson it will be holding you,
your simple weight,
two hands long, breathing.

THE GATHERING BEYOND FOG

A large encampment, all women
giving birth:
I search for clean cloth
and bring boiling water
to midwives. Somehow
I should know what else to do

but, uninitiated,
I find a dress for one
whose after-birth won't drop—
the child's soul
in danger. It wants to follow
the mother who has refused
further help. The baby

folds with first pain—
smells of ginger and sweet basil
but when I look, its genitals
are hidden. Outside the camp,

trees sconced in fog.
If I could see in,
the forms of a different
matter would be visible, the after-
death we've been trying to bring

to that level
of mist: a silhouette
whose vaporous edge
nurses the child, fog which is slowly
descending on women

in a newly formed circle. We are all
cold, moving
closer. If there's longing
for men

we've forgotten.
To begin as one with us here,
they have chosen
to soar: like pain
the fog has no ceiling.

AFTER THE LOSS

I strap a twig to the cradle board,
feed the knothole mouth.
Two spurs reach like arms.
In the white cone of the teepee,
upside-down in snow,
the twig sucks my nipples.
Outside the camp dogs bark.
Even fleas bring their dead
to the surface.
The four-wall house
is a coffin,
the shape of a death-rack.
Under the yellow-hair moon,
I rock the twig to sleep.
Hairs shoot from my arms.
Behind the four-walls
wind breaks over the teepees.
The twig wails in the night
when soldiers pass.
I put my hand over its mouth,
hear the silence of our people,
the brittle snap of lives.

A MOTHER TO A DAUGHTER

Your daughter, home from college for the weekend,
tells you of the speck of flesh
that yesterday still grew inside her womb.
You brew camomile tea,
remembering how she began,
a fragile thing you hoped would hold.
You two lived as one, skin against skin,
until like a blood-sweet fruit
she burst from your body.

How shy she was among strangers.
You remember, too, those winter afternoons
side by side,
napping on her white trundle bed.
But now without you she waited
for the rush of blood between her legs
that never came. Lightheaded each morning,
breasts beginning to swell,
she let them scrape that seed away.

Your only daughter,
born in September's fullness,
you cannot keep her
from the pain of her woman's body.
Sunday noon she will pack her duffle bag
with books, groceries, the low-cut blouse
that shows off the milky curve of her neck.
You could say what you know of loss.
Instead you spoon honey into her cup.

SHIRT

When they unbraided you,
long curving muscle,
from my body
and laid you on my stomach
to breathe your own way
still smelling like my blood
I tried to stop my shaking,
to lie still as earth
so you could burrow.

your warm snout nudging
my breast until
the nurse took you from me,
washed you and pulled
the shirt over your head.
When she gave you back
to me, your face
clean, your shirt
and diaper white,
you were a citizen.

ANNA CERNIK'S DIARY:
OF SONS AND DAUGHTERS

Papa came in this morning
angry at the winter.
He had been with one of his calving cows
most the night,
had to drive her to the barn through snow to his knees,
and the calf's hind legs coming first,
the wet of birth freezing fast.
Mama in the barn held the lantern for Papa
as he worked.
I held the cow's head to calm and steady her.
But Papa could not pull the calf himself,
it was lodged so.
Then the cow fell to her knees,
rolled over to her side,
her great belly heaving and heavy with her death.
Mama, feeding little Tina who slept through it,
said Papa would not drink his coffee,
eat his breakfast,
but went out early to chore.
Then he came back in, angry at the winter.
Said over and over he wishes he'd had a son
to help him pull,
needed more muscle to do what last night
had to be done.
Over and over said he was angry at the winter.

WHAT'S DONE

My father stepped from the waiting room
when I was born, and walked the long hall
to the nursery where the babies, crying, all
looked the same; he held his tears and called
all the nurses "dear," aware he feared how soon

he'd see my mother, wrapped in her nicest nightgown,
propped on pillows, still in pain. A boy
he'd hoped for, but as labor came, he had no joy—
she pushed, he paced, for hours, sorry
this child was made and bound them now.

As I grew I never saw my parents kiss;
I thought this was how parents were,
until I saw my friend's father
touch his wife, sure, familiar.
And when my mother died, my father wept, missing

her now she was gone; and I, his grown son,
couldn't then hold him. He's remarried now; his wife
reminds me of my mother, frail, her life
maintained by her intelligence; she kisses him and laughs
at his reticence. When I kiss him I sense

him drawing into himself, feeling what's done is done.

SERVICES

First your tumor, then breast, then body
was gone. All we had left were grains in a bag
in a box. Then your mother and sisters, children and I
drove to the ferry and through Harsen's Island
where Bert has some land he said we could use.
And your children—what order! For a few minutes
no usual yells. You should have seen them.
Your John cut the weeds, sprayed for mosquitoes.
Mikey, hair flaring from under his cap,
did most of the digging. Pete, acting on cue,
took the small fir out of his clunker,
out of his trunk, and stood at the hole
while Jess on the sidelines told Pete where to slant it,
Mike how to shovel, John when to spray
and got no more back-talk than the warm blue spring air.
Then John took the box up to the sapling
and shook out some dust. With pieces of bone—
there were still chunks—with pieces of bone
he salted the tree, then passed things to Jess who
tilted the box, removed the bag, let more ashes
tumble. Mikey was next. He, taking his turn,
reached in his hand, pulled out a fist-full,
then sowed more of the earth by the tree with your cells.
"Hey look! I'm the first who reached in with bare hands!"
But that is when the grabbing began. And then the yelling.
Each showed the others how to strew ashes. Then
we climbed in our cars, out of the grave. On the way home
Pete's muffler broke. Bump in the road.

PARADE

Don't go. Something
is killing the trees.
Winter is a terrible miracle
coming fast.

You are so strong in the doorway
you could carry me home
in your arms. I can hear
your healthy heart from here.
You are solid when you say,
I'll be right back.

This is how my mother looked:
black hair and eyes
so much bluer than mine,
skin so much whiter, breasts
so much more beautiful.
When they brought me to her,
small and purple as a plum,
she was so lovely she must've thought,
This can't be mine.

I was ten when she told me
there might not be a god.
I argued there had to be.
It was a short lapse of faith for her.
I still believe in nothing.
The birds are a miracle
fleeing fast. Don't go.

This is how my mother looked:
pale and radiant
as winter on the way.
Luminous, like ice.
All those years so beautiful
but she didn't cry
when the cancer cut out her breasts,

when the chemo took her hair.
She said, I'm going to live.
She said I'll be back
when she left.

Oh God don't go. There's something coming fast.
She was so strong when she died
it took us both to hold her down.
She was angry
when I was only weak.

This is how she looked:
almost as tall as you, fervent
with appetite and life.
Like her you could hold me high
for hours to watch the parade,
but after I turned twelve
I never grew again.
I used to spend hours at the mirror
crying about my hair, crying
about my smile, dying
to be beautiful, and not.
She would roll my hair and hug me,
spend fortunes on my teeth
and say, You are, you are.

And still I couldn't be
because I'm not.

And you like a marble statue,
perfect, startling and spared,
and you don't even know it.
What will happen to me?

I will never see anything again.
The parade of fall is rising.
The amazing betrayal of birds
fit enough to fly to Florida
but too weak for winter.
This decline of the sun.

This swamp of snow on the way.
This hilarious memory of my mother
debating faith with a child.
Oh what do I know, she told me.
Sweetheart, decide for yourself.

DROWNINGS

From fifteen feet above myself unbreathing
there on the dock I evaluate those feet—
mine—splayed on the boards I painted.
The camp nurse bends over me to insert
the hard S-tube down my throat. My cool
eyes consider the restless boat,
the waterskis aligned, the tow-rope
a heap. No waves move onto the shale beach.
A benign Lake Champlain accuses me
under a Vermont sun, and I want to disappoint
all these people by dying out from under them
on such a smiling day.
                     Fifteen years
after my drowning, Jeff chases ducks off
a dock's edge. He sinks beneath the tidal
sheen of Five Mile River. I know he must bob
soon to the surface. I pass my son going up
on my way down.
                  Phillip's drowning
finds him clinging half swallowed beneath a dock
in the Fox River. At dinner in the cottage
I almost too late hear his cries above the voices
of aunts and cousins. I pull my dripping boy
from the suck of the lazy river.

In a film a child falls from a high window,
bounces to his feet, runs off. We can
do that on our good days: drowning
through a late spring afternoon held
to my desk by a student's whine, or
through the bed my wife in booze avoids
like my eyes, or through a drive
to scare the boys with my braking—
to be saved, emerging into changed air
and light—or to drown down through green
water into a deeper world where we breathe
through our wounds and join all the other
drowned children alive at last.

THE SURVIVOR

It was there all along, your nightmare,
like a body lost to the lake,
swept under like a child
and never given a burial.
Jim, could you feel the undertow
where the current took your father,
washed up, down in the basement,
the shotgun handed to you years after?

In the family stories you've told
it was there all along by its absence—
love, preserved at that depth,
has kept things in their place
like photographs to come home to.

No wonder, the other night,
you sweat in your sleep
when the lake washed him up to your door,
beaching him like a fish.
Why shouldn't you throw him back,
slamming the door in his face?
Today's paper does not report
a storm on the lake, a person found.

PACT

My brother would read my quiet sorrow,
follow me to our room and stand
at the door staring while I sulked
on the bed, head toward the wall.
When I turned to confront him, I'd catch
dirty shorts in my face. "Lighten up,"
he'd say, "you ain't dead yet."

I'd perform my leaping tackle
and he'd tickle me until I gave up,
half silly and drunk with anger.
We'd laugh at my teenage grief,
how goddamn serious I was about football,
U.S. History, and Becky Lewis. She dumped
me once a week.

At night he'd fart under the covers,
claim it was an earthquake, and the bed
shook like a life boat in a storm
while we muffled our laughter with pillows.
Camping at Price's Pond, he found
a black flint arrowhead which he would
rub at night before calling a host
of owls around our fire
loud enough to wake the dead.

These frames passed through my head
like coming attractions
this morning as I woke to the pastel light
of hospital green. My brother's vital signs
blipped across the screen and his lips
quivered for the words an aneurism
had stolen from his tongue.

I found myself saying, lighten up,
you ain't dead yet, you ain't
dead yet, saying it over and over
until the phrase became our secret pact,
as powerful as black arrowheads,
magic owl calls and his tight grip
on my hand.

TAPS

1

a guy from town died
in the war, 1967.
I was one of two
good trumpet players in school,
so the principal pulled me out
of shop one day & sadly
told me to get my horn.
Jinx was in the car,
we flexed keys & didn't say
much on the way to the funeral.
I thought, "this is for death;
this is bigger, a whole lot bigger
than a spring concert solo."

we were placed facing each other,
one on each side of the black funeral clump,
so far away I couldn't hear anything
until Jinx started playing taps & I fell
in, the echo, a bar behind.

as I let the last note fade,
I waited for some movement,
sound, toss of flowers.
nothing.
then the principal hustled us
to the car, said it was perfect,
patted us. I smiled
at Jinx & pulled at my tie.

2

a couple months later,
July 4, I played at the town's
tomb of the unknown soldier, alone.
flags hung, flowers wilted, color
all around: blue & gold

grim American Legion men, clean wives
in white, boy scouts in three-finger salute.
other boys, shooting each other, clutched
mock wounds, my perfect
taps dying in the heat.

LITTLE BEAR

Joey Malone found Pfc. Owens under a transport truck.

"You getting overtime?" Joey said.

Owens scooted out on his back. He held a black radiator hose in his hand. "They said it needed a new radiator. Look here." He bent the rubber hose to expose a crack. "I been lying under there a half hour thinking how stupid the army is."

He stood, skinny and black, threw the hose in a metal barrel, blew into his cupped hands. "Colder than Bejesus," he said.

Joey nodded. He looked out over the support unit and beyond it to the gray Korean landscape. When Joey had first joined the unit, the pointy canvas tents and six-wheel trucks, the single axle trailers and barking officers had reminded him of the circus that came to Michigan City in the spring, setting up in a field near the prison. Now, he could see only trucks, trailers, and temporary quarters.

Joey stuck his hands inside his jacket, under his arms. "Sgt. Anderson said I'm ready."

Owens stomped his feet to fight the cold. "I'm staying," he said.

Joey and Owens were the last of Master Sgt. Anderson's training detail, organized to make men who had performed badly in combat ready to return. Owens, they had discovered, was a good mechanic, so good he would stay with the support unit indefinitely. Owens had tried to teach Joey, telling him to picture the engine running, the pistons shooting in and out like the legs of chorus girls they'd seen in a camp movie. Joey couldn't see it. His head was too full of army regulations and meaningless numbers, images of Indiana and a great blank fear of dying. He would have to return to combat.

"I have to report to him in an hour," Joey said. "He wants to *talk* to me."

"That's lousy, Joey. I'd take combat over that." Owens pulled a cigarette from his pocket, lit it, and inhaled deeply. "Luckily, I don't have to do neither. You, on the other hand . . ." Owens chuckled.

Joey laughed with him. "I, on the other hand, get screwed coming and going."

Owens laughed, spitting out his cigarette. "That's the looks of it." He picked the white butt off the ground and blew on it. The end glowed orange. He twisted dirt off the lip end. "My last cigarette," he said, looked it over again, and tossed it back to the dirt. "This very earth is swarming with bacterias, I bet." He wiped the tips of his fingers against his chest. "Probably a thousand on your shirt alone." He pointed at Joey.

A circle of dirt marked Joey's chest like a target. He wiped and slapped at the dirt. Sgt. Anderson had made Joey shoot at burning barrels from a ditch as part of his training. "It's like I slid into home," Joey said.

"Always slide feet first." Owens took two steps, slid into the rear tire of the transport truck. "Feet first." He kicked the tire. "I stole fourteen bases once. In one game."

Joey had been a second baseman in high school, then a shortstop in Okinawa. "There was something I wanted to talk about," Joey said. "Really, something I want to tell you about."

"Michigan City?" Owens said. He was from Brawley, California; Joey, from Michigan City, Indiana. They took turns telling about home. "Let's get out of the cold."

They crawled into the cab of the truck. "I've been having dreams about this," Joey said. "It was when I was a kid." His words fogged the windshield.

"Yeah?" Owens said. He blew into his hands again, clapped against his shoulders, rubbed his arms.

"I was ten," Joey said. "My brother was six."

"My brother's six," Owens said.

"Nineteen forty-three, I remember that," Joey said. Eight years ago, walking to his friend's house on a street without lights, a night without a moon, Joey had tried to avoid the puddles. His little brother sloshed through them. *What's the point of wearing rubbers if you don't have any fun?* his brother, Dave, said. *Galoshes*, Joey said, *call them galoshes*. His brother shrugged, said, *Not what mom calls them*. Joey shook his head. *Trust me*, he had said.

Shelling sounded in the distance. Not really like thunder, Joey thought, louder, more explicit. To Owens, he said, "We spent the night at my best friend's house. Mickey Lawanda. His parents were out of town."

"Your folks let you do that? Mine would never. Not when I was ten." Owens slipped his hands under his legs to warm them.

"They didn't know Mickey's parents were gone. He lived across from the penitentiary." Three boys had huddled around the coffee table, reading newspaper clippings aloud to Joey's little brother, who couldn't read. They arranged the clippings in chronological order, passed around the seven pictures the newspaper had run again and again—blood on the tiled floor, the floral wallpaper, the bedspread, the ceiling, and Tomas "Pato" Rodriguez staring into the camera, his hands cupped over his ears.

"This guy, Pato Rodriguez, had killed his girlfriend with scissors," Joey said.

"Crude," Owens said.

"At least, they said he did. He didn't look like a bad guy."

His body had been no larger than a boy's, thin arms thickening at the elbows like the joints of tree limbs. Even in the grainy newspaper photographs, his brown skin looked soft. He couldn't speak English, which had seemed like crime enough. The boys didn't know what "Pato" meant or why he was called that, but they imagined it meant Tiger or The Knife. Mickey gave each of them nicknames. He labeled Joey "Mongoose" Malone. He called Joey's brother "The Spot" because of the large birthmark that covered part of his jaw and neck. He called himself Mickey "The Wonder" Lawanda. Joey's little brother's name had stuck. Everyone but family called him Spot Malone. Because of that night, Joey thought, because of Pato Rodriguez.

"We read the newspaper stories about the killing. We were right across from the prison," Joey said and crossed his arms against the cold. As midnight had approached, they had stared through the small squares of glass at the prison, a hulking concrete box, dark against the dark sky. Mickey had said it looked like a devil's food cake with barbed wire icing.

"We turned on every light in the house."

His brother had run upstairs, turning on the lights in the bedrooms, hall. Joey covered the downstairs, turning on the lights in the kitchen, closets, dining and living rooms. Mickey went to the cellar, switched on the remaining lights. Joey ran out the front door, a misting rain covering his face, to be sure they had not missed a room. The house had become an island of light.

"What for?" Owens said. "Why the lights?"

"I'm getting to it," Joey said. "We all looked at the pictures from the newspaper one last time." *Blood on the tiled floor, blood on the floral wallpaper, blood in the bedspread, blood on the ceiling.* "We sat in the front room." They had sat separately, each with his back erect, hands palm down on the arms of a chair.

"When they executed Pato," Joey said, "the lights in Mickey's house went dim." Two minutes after midnight, the state of Indiana pumped light through the arteries of Pato Rodriquez. Three boys sat in straight backed chairs with irretrievable smiles until the few dim moments passed and the lights surged on again.

"What'd it feel like?" Owens said.

The windshield was fogged over. *With my words*, Joey thought, imagining that the story could be read there if you knew how to do it. "It was thrilling," Joey said. *It was frightening. It was terrible, beautiful.*

Nearby, a jeep started up, idled. Owens pulled his knees to his chest, wrapped his arms around them. "Think our deaths here would entertain anybody?"

Joey shrugged.

"Idiots and dogs," Sgt. Anderson said, spitting into a pool of motor oil as they walked to the jeep. "Korea's full of them." Anderson jumped behind the wheel. Joey got in beside him, looked over his shoulder at Owens next to another jeep, oil pan in his hands.

"Every war is just like this." Sgt. Anderson maneuvered the jeep around a puddle of muddy water. "A shithouse mess." He began talking about World War II, how the units were segregated. Joey found he could let the noise of the jeep drown out the words. Owens' regiment had been segregated. They were the last all Negro unit, broken up after they had bugged-out. Owens said the unit joke was that they were "the asphalt crew" because the army wanted to pave the way to Korea with black asses.

The jeep bounced hard. Mud sprayed from both sides. "Mud'll be ice by midnight," Sgt. Anderson said. "Whole country'll be ice in a week." Joey nodded at the Sergeant. "Look here." Anderson switched on the headlights although the afternoon was still light. He pointed to the road in front of them. "A man's got direction, it's like he's got an extra arm. Army's built-in direction, like what bats got—your own personal radar. *You* can see that, Malone. *You* listen. Most the idiots here never listen to anything but mess call and the sound of money leaving their pockets. That Owens," he threw his thumb back over his shoulder, "wouldn't listen to his own black mother."

Joey followed Anderson's thumb back, half expecting Owens to be there. Korean children sat on a thin, gray mattress, stuffing hanging out of it like intestines. "Owens is all right," he said, and felt a rush of panic.

Anderson gripped the steering wheel with both hands, switched off the lights, accelerated. The jeep gobbled up the road faster and faster. Anderson's face, Joey realized, was light green, like the meat of a cucumber. The jeep swerved away from a spotted, yapping dog, but the rear wheel caught it. A crack, as if they'd run over a tree limb, and a short whistle. "Shit," Anderson said. "We kill it?"

The dog's head rose and fell slowly, rose and fell, like a toy dog in the rear window of a car. "Dying," Joey said.

"My brother hit a dog once in Italy," Anderson said.

Joey waited, but Anderson didn't add to the story. The dog's head finally dropped and stayed down, a dark lump on the road. The jeep continued. The sky, in a haze of dust from the jeep, turned khaki.

A half an hour later, the jeep stopped at a windowless, bare plank building just off the side of the road. Over the door hung a yellow sign with red letters: SUZIES SALOON. "Place is a pigsty. But so is all of Korea," Anderson said as he got out of the jeep. Squat, with hunched shoulders, thick neck, and arms too short for his body, Sgt. Anderson reminded Joey of a giant amphibian.

Anderson shoved a drunken private who blocked the door. Although

the ceiling was low, the building had the feeling of a barn. Joey could have
turned it into an Indiana barn if not for all the G.I.'s crowding around
wooden tables. Sgt. Anderson commandeered a table next to the wall. He
grabbed a Korean woman by the thigh. "Get us two beers." He smiled at
Joey as the woman walked away. "One time I was a kid and wouldn't eat
my stringbeans. Hated them. My father stuck a revolver to my head and
told me to clean my plate. Your father still living?"

"Yes, sir."

"I was mad at him, but I thought, Hell, he's my father. My brother
Paul come in saying, 'He's a son of a bitch.'" Anderson folded his arms.
"We both enlisted young." He leaned across the table. "WW2, Paul and
I spent a lot of time in Italy. Got more pussy there than we ever dreamt
of in the states." He reached across the table, cupped his hand around
Joey's neck, pulled him slightly closer, then let him go. "Got a girlfriend
back home — where is it — Michigan?"

"Michigan City, Indiana."

"Got one?"

"No, sir."

"Good. Man don't need a skirt home fucking the plumber while he's
gone."

Joey nodded, stared at the table. He felt uneasy, threatened, wondering if this were part of combat training, if he might have to fight a table
of drunks or make a weapon out of bottle caps and spit.

The Korean woman returned. Sgt. Anderson paid for the beers.
"Completed the training, Malone. Another day or two we're going to join
a unit at the front. The both of us. You're a soldier." He reached across
the table. Joey took his hand. Anderson gripped it firmly, looked it over.
"Important to know a man's hands," he said. They shook, then drank to
Joey's accomplishment, the army, Anderson's brother who had died in
Northern Africa.

"Best beer in the world is in P.I. San Miguel. Ever get the chance, go
to P.I. Heaven for a man."

Joey drank the beer, pretended to be interested. He thought he should
ask what P.I. stood for, or whether San Miguel was a place or a beer. He
said nothing. The whole evening seemed like a test.

"Basically, I don't like women," Anderson said. "They want you to
think you can't live without them. There's a lot you can live without. Sex
though." He ran his thumb and forefinger across the end of his nose. "The
thing about sex is you can't remember it. You remember the woman, the
night, maybe how everything worked up to it. But sex itself can't be
remembered. Like a shock or one of those dreams that never come back."

After an hour of drinking and talking, Anderson bought each of them
whores. Joey didn't want one. The Sergeant said it was an order. "Next

hole you'll be in won't be as warm as this one," he said and shoved a girl at Joey. "She's Suzie," he said, "all the whores are Suzie."

Joey took her hand, followed her through the bar and out a back door. Behind the building, a row of stalls stood like booths at the county fair. A cloth curtain covered the doorway. Inside, a dirt floor, a canvas ceiling ripped open into a smile.

Joey's whore was young and thin, and wore a tomato red dress with white buttons the size of quarters. She lit a kerosene lamp. "Cold," she said.

Joey nodded, blew into his hands, shoved them into his pockets.

She unbuttoned the top two buttons, pulled the dress over her head. Her breasts barely lipped away from her chest. She sat on a regulation army cot, smiled up at him with crooked teeth. She said her name was Suzie, then pulled his pants down to his knees. In the cold, his testicles and penis looked like nothing more than a shriveled apricot and stem.

Joey watched the crooked teeth surround his penis, looked above her at the wall, bare except for an ill-framed still life of cabbage and celery. He looked above that, through the tear in the canvas ceiling to the sky. He'd had sex only once before. He began thinking of that night so his penis would get hard.

He had made love with June Norris on the outfield grass in the school ballpark one night just before graduation. He remembered the sensation of being inside someone else, and afterwards, while he still lay on top of her, she lifted her right arm into the air, pointed to the sky, and said, "Ursa Minor, the little bear."

Joey rolled off her, looked up at the stars. She pointed out little bear, and squinting his eyes, he thought he could picture a bear cub. They lay on the grass and she pointed out other animals in the sky—a bull, a ram. The only one Joey could picture was the bear. June giggled, pulled her checkered dress, which was already pushed up to her chest, over her head. Joey ran his hands over her headless body. She pulled the dress back, bunched it around her neck. Joey thought her head looked like a bean, her lips a hilum. When he told her, she laughed, said he should plant the bean so she could grow another body.

June took his penis, rolled it back and forth in her hands like a child playing with clay. He remembered thinking she was beautiful but never telling her. She said she was leaving Michigan City to be free, that everyone in the city was in prison whether they knew it or not. She was going to college in the west where not one person in the entire state knew her name. She had promised to write, but Joey never got a single letter. He thought if he were to write her now he'd say, "Suzie was nothing like you."

Anderson talked the whole drive back about being stationed in Italy, how his brother had bought him his first whore. Joey tried to listen, but his mind was in Indiana with his own brother, his father, even his mother who had been dead for years. Joey was thirteen when his mother was killed crossing Water Street. In his last letter, his father had said the state was going to build a bridge over Water Street. This seemed to make his father very happy. His father taught science in high school: the way a cell divides, the position of the earth in the universe. He had majored in English at the University of Indiana, but never taught anything but science. Joey's brother was beginning high school even though he still couldn't read. They'd just kept passing him because his father was a teacher and because he was a good shortstop.

Joey had played shortstop in Okinawa. He had been a shipping clerk and played for the Green Foxes, one of the regiment's teams. Numbers had given him no trouble then. He'd even kept batting averages. During his first few days in Korea, his sense of numbers had become suddenly confused. Fatigue, someone had told him, he would get over it. Instead, it had gotten worse. His head was as much a jumble of meaningless numbers as the bingo cage at the Michigan City Methodist Church.

In the middle of the summer, his battalion had been told they were being shipped from Okinawa to Japan for six weeks of combat training. In the ship, they were told they would go to Pusan, Korea, for three days of intensive training. When they arrived in Pusan, they were sent to Chinju and combat.

Joey and the Green Foxes first baseman lugged a .50 caliber machine gun into position to provide cover for the other men. Neither had ever fired a machine gun. Joey was given quick instructions. He followed them, but the gun wouldn't fire. Grease coated his hands and forearms as he went through the steps over and over. The clatter of weapons became more regular, louder. They could not get the gun to fire. Nearby, a corporal shouted coordinates into a radio again and again, then slammed it with his fist. U.S. planes flew overhead, unaware. The radio man stood, screamed numbers at the planes until his face exploded from a round of fire. Joey and the first baseman ran. Joey ran faster. When the first baseman was hit, he called out, "Cinnamon."

Joey wrote to his father that he'd escaped with just some shrapnel in his arm. When the medic dug the fragments out, they were pieces of skull. Joey couldn't finish the letter. Later, he found out the grease was packing grease and the machine gun wouldn't have fired for anyone. By that time, Joey's head was a bingo cage. Since then Joey had been shuffled around Korea like the extra ace in a marked deck, until finally he'd been assigned for special training.

Back from SUZIES SALOON, asleep in his cot, Joey dreamed of

Pato Rodriguez in the electric chair, hands free from their straps, cupped over his ears. When the lights dimmed, Pato called out, "Cinnamon." Joey woke, stared into the dark. He was sure of two things, that he hated Korea and that *his* death was out there, patient, walking in regulation boots.

Owens told Joey to just sleep. Master Sgt. Anderson had left camp without leaving orders for Joey. "Sleep," Owens said. "Enjoy the scenery."

Joey couldn't sleep because he was sure Anderson would be coming to take him to combat. "I hate Korea," he said.

"Got to stop the communists here or they'll be at your doorstep." Owens smiled.

Joey tried to imagine communists taking Michigan City. "I still hate it," he said.

"I hate being here," Owens said, looking from side to side, pulling on his belt buckle with his right hand. "I hate the fucking food the most."

"I hate it all."

"All of it?" Owens asked.

"All of it."

"The clothes, you hate the clothes?" He looked at Joey disbelievingly.

"I hate this uniform."

"I like the clothes." Owens smiled, looked down at his khaki t-shirt, jacket, pants. "They let you keep the clothes. And the tags." He held his dogtags to his face, read his name, looked again at Joey. "I bet you a jimmy you can't guess my blood-type."

Joey thought the clothes didn't look bad on Owens, even though his t-shirt was inside out. "Bet a what?"

"A jimmy, you know, a favor," Owens said. "You win, I owe you. I win, you owe me."

"Type A," Joey said.

"It's O. Now you owe me one, Malone." Still smiling, he began to walk off.

"Owens, your shirt is inside out."

Owens stopped, looked at his shirt. "How can you tell?"

"Look at the collar."

He stretched the neck of his t-shirt out to look at it. "I think you're right." He looked back to Joey. "We're even."

Joey thought of Indiana like an alcoholic thinks of liquor. When he closed his eyes, he saw pictures: his backyard in Michigan City, the pitcher of lemonade his mother sets on the round table in the corner of the back porch, his mother in a yellow cotton dress, arms folded, smiling. He's playing catch with his father while his brother, only six, sits in the grass, rocking and watching. His father is teaching him to throw a curve, saying he is old enough now, his arm can withstand the violent snap of the wrist at the point of release. It's a warm day. The sun shines directly on his arms and face.

In Korea, the afternoon turned to a cutting cold. Sgt. Anderson had told Joey that winter in Korea was brutal. "Ever seen a man turn blue?" he'd said. Joey tried to block it out by thinking of Indiana, the smile that crosses his father's face as a pitch breaks a few inches. He couldn't make it last. Something always returned him to Korea: the smell of a rifle recently oiled, phosphorous clouds rising on the horizon. He wanted to stay back there with his mother still alive, his brother too young to know he can't learn how to read, his father squatting in freshly mowed grass, pointing two fingers toward a dish they'd taken to use as home plate. He knew the dream wasn't real, that it never had been. But his mind went there, and for a moment the khaki uniform became jeans and a white t-shirt, the flapping of the flag became striped sheets on the clothesline, the birds lining the top of the tent became cardinals perched on a telephone wire, and even the leaves, as they turned, turned toward home.

Late afternoon with no sign of Sgt. Anderson, Joey and Owens played cards in the cab of a truck with a burnt-out transmission. They played poker, but Joey had too much trouble keeping track of the cards, so they played Go Fish, talked about California, Indiana, food, women. Owens said the problem with Korean whores was that, basically, they were white. "White women don't fuck worth a shit," he said. "Good to look at but no good on their backs." After another hand of Go Fish, Owens retracted the statement. "Truth is, this guy in basic told me that about white women. I never really had much luck with women, really." A jeep rattled by. Owens watched as if it meant something. "Truth is, I never had *any* luck with women." He turned back to Joey, put the deck of cards on the dash. "Look at this." He pulled out his wallet, opened it, removed a photograph and held it up to Joey's face. The photograph was of a beautiful white girl with long, dark hair parted down the middle.

"Who is she?" Joey asked.

"Her name is Barbara. I met her in Geography."

"You go out with her?"

"You kidding? She gave me her picture when she found out I was going in the army." He turned the photograph to look at her again. "I hardly know her really. I seen her at school and stuff, but I don't know her mother or nothing. You think I'm stupid carrying her picture?"

"You mean everyone goes to the same school out there?"

"Yeah. Ain't no girls in your school?"

"Plenty of girls. No Negroes."

"Yeah. So this guy in basic told me carrying pictures of white women would either get me crazy or get me killed." Owens put the picture in his wallet, shuffled the cards. "He said I got the sickness of screwing black girls and pretending they're white."

Joey thought of himself with the whore, thinking of June.

"He's crazy," Owens said. "I never even been to bed with a woman, and he's telling me what I'm thinking." He began dealing the cards.

"Forget it," Joey said.

"What I'm worried about is getting shot-up or killed, and I never do sleep with a girl. We *could* get killed here. There should be a rule."

"For the army or for the enemy?"

Owens laughed. "You think the communists would cooperate?"

"You think the army would?"

Owens took the picture back out of his wallet. He looked it over again carefully, then began tearing it into pieces. "If they do pass that rule, I don't want any doubt about me being eligible." He threw the pieces of photograph into the space between them in the cab. The pieces fluttered to the seat and floorboard like disembodied wings.

"We really could get killed," Owens said. "Especially *you*."

"You have a seven?" Joey said.

Owens shook his head. "Think that's why Anderson took you to Suzie's?"

"What do you mean?"

"You know, the rule."

Joey shrugged. "I slept with a girl just before I left Michigan City."

"Really? You got a queen?"

"Go fish," Joey said. He told Owens about June Norris, the night on the outfield grass. He told him about her pointing to the stars, pulling her dress over her head. They played another hand of Go Fish, and Owens asked Joey to tell it again. Afternoon faded into evening, night. They huddled in their jackets, kept the flashlight pointed toward the seat. Owens made Joey tell the story five times. He liked the idea of animals in the sky. At midnight, they stepped out of the truck to look for little bear. The sky was too full of clouds. They climbed back into the cab.

"You think I could meet her?" Owens said.

"I don't know where she is. You have a five?"

"You just asked for a five. You don't know what college she's gone to?"

"Somewhere in Arizona or New Mexico. You have a six?"

"Fish," Owens said, shaking his head. "I been to Arizona once. Nothing special." He spread his cards, closed them. "She'll be coming home for summer, won't she? I don't want to hit on her. I just want to meet her."

"Okay."

"As soon as we get out of this shithole," Owens said.

"Yeah," Joey said, "as soon as we get out of here."

"You think your pop mind me staying with you?"

"You could fix his car," Joey said, laughed.

"What's he got?"

"A Pontiac. A big one."

"Probably a lot like a jeep."

"Doesn't look like a jeep. Looks more like a boat."

"I wouldn't tell your pop I want to meet June," Owens said. "He might get the wrong idea. Got a nine?"

"Go fish," Joey said.

Joey lay on his cot unable to sleep, trying to figure out why his brother could not read. He thought it might be his fault. When Dave was really young, Joey used to sit with him and hold open a picture book pretending to read, making up stories to go with the pictures. He wondered if his brother thought reading was some mystical thing having nothing to do with black letters on white sheets of paper. He remembered taking a head of lettuce, peeling off a leaf at a time, "reading" them to his brother. He'd promised to show Dave how to read stories on plankboard fences, cardboard boxes, photographs. The fogged window of a transport truck, Joey thought. He began crying silently.

He often cried in his cot. One night he'd cried because Pato Rodriguez stood with hands cupped over his ears as words he couldn't understand flew at him. One night he cried because they were building a bridge over Water Street years too late. One night he cried because he was worried about crying so much.

He was crying when Sgt. Anderson walked into the tent, squatted beside his cot. The gray stubble on Anderson's cheeks made him look ghostly. Joey tried to stop crying, couldn't. Sgt. Anderson said nothing, waited, finally spoke, "When I heard Paul, that's my brother. When I heard he was dead, I cried. Bawled like you wouldn't believe. Northern Africa's an awful place. Not as bad as here, but awful." He rubbed his nose with his thumb and forefinger. "McArthur probably spends half his time crying. Ought to, anyway." Sgt. Anderson waited again, but Joey still couldn't stop crying. "Tomorrow'll be better. Going to join a combat unit. The both of us. No more lolling around here."

He stood, then squatted again close to Joey, whispered. "Once, for a while, I heard this voice. Didn't tell me to do things, that was the frustration of it. I could hear it but couldn't make it out. I'd think, it's the wind, or it's my lungs, or those noises that go in the back of your skull. But it was a real voice and one night I finally made it out. It was asking questions."

Anderson whispered so close that his stubble brushed against Joey's cheek. Joey stopped crying.

"It asked, 'How is it?' and 'What of it?' and 'What are you waiting for?' " Anderson paused for a long time, then put his hand on Joey's shoulder. "We're soldiers. Tomorrow'll be like old times."

"What old times?" Joey said.

"I'll take care of you. Way my brother took care of me."

As soon as Anderson left, Joey cursed him, angry to have been caught crying over his brother. He wanted part of his life kept separate from Korea.

During the first day of the fight for Hill 409, Joey kept low in a bunker, shot his rifle at a large leafed tree in the distance. The drive from the support unit to the front had taken less than an hour. In minutes he was in the bunker. The hill was a long, gradual incline, wooded near the top. Some strategy was being played out, Joey was sure, but all he could make of it was that the North Koreans controlled the hill, firing from behind the trees and foliage, and the army wanted it. Joey thought of several alternatives to fighting over the hill—a trade could be worked out, graders could level the thing, citizens of Michigan City could pitch in and buy it.

Joey was ankle deep in icy mud. When the call came to withdraw, his feet were as heavy and awkward as bowling balls. He tried to run, slipped, fell, the icy ground hard as concrete. He flattened himself against it, crawled. Beside him a man yelled, "Jesus, my father," stood straight up, hands at his face as if he'd remembered something important. Mud covered his right shoulder and arm, his helmet tipped slightly to the left, his startled eyes the color of wet grass. Joey knew the standing man would draw attention. He rolled left, began running clumsily. He heard a burst of fire behind him and a sound like a baseball landing in a mitt. He didn't look.

That night, huddled around a small fire with a dozen other men, Joey tried to imagine pistons moving up and down like the legs of chorus girls. He thought about the Green Foxes first baseman calling out "cinnamon" as he died, as if he were trying to tell Joey something, to let him know what to expect. Joey had no idea what to expect.

Sgt. Anderson squatted next to him, put his arm on his shoulder. "We'll take that hill tomorrow," Anderson said.

Let them have it, Joey thought. There were thousands like it in Korea that had no North Koreans at the top.

Before the night was over, it had begun to snow.

During the second day of the fight for Hill 409, Joey muddled forward slowly across the snow covered ground. He was frightened, crawling on his elbows and knees. Snow soaked through his clothing, and he lost some of his fear in the cold. The crawling forced water into his boots. His feet grew numb. From behind, the firing stepped up to provide more cover. Joey believed he would die that way, from friendly fire, although the yellow flashes kept coming from behind the trees at the top of the hill as well. Suddenly the ground in front of Joey erupted. He flattened, unmoving, terrified. His right foot felt warmer. It took him a few seconds to realize he had been wounded. The boot was filling with blood.

"Malone," someone yelled. Joey had to resist the urge to stand. "Malone." To his left. A man motioning. A ditch. Three other men. "Malone." The air filled with sparks. "Malone." Joey started crawling, keeping his head low. His feet didn't respond. "Malone." He began rolling toward the ditch. The sound of mortar rose and fell like a scream heard through a revolving door. Suddenly he began flying toward the ditch. The impact of the explosion swallowed its initial sound, but the reverberations clanged in his skull. Hands pulled at his arms. Beneath the echo of the bell he heard a voice. "You ain't even hurt, bud." The blue of the sky rushed out east and west, leaving an enormous white.

A pair of feet, Joey saw them in the tangle of legs at the end of the ditch, thought they were his. He tried to move them, but the thick boots whiskered with frost and would not budge. He brought his right hand to his mouth, covered his fist with a cloud of warmth. He believed he was ready to die. The night was silent, dark, lit only by a quarter moon. He hoped his death would be like Pato's, that the moon would dim momentarily, then, with a surge of light, become full. Joey felt his eyes draw closed. "Cinnamon," he said, laughed. The quarter moon became dim, distant. He closed his eyes, opened them. The urge to close became more insistent. He opened them one last time, saw the full face of the moon near enough to touch. As his eyes closed, he heard a voice say, "I've found you."

The woman in the silent shoes with a dozen dogtags hanging from her wrist passed through the space between the beds. The man in the next bed tapped the floor so Joey would look at him. "I had the best treeing dog in Ballard County," he said.

Joey nodded.

The man pointed to his head. "The doctors here keep their heads in their hats, putting them on in the morning, taking them off before bed. They don't know what it is to be human."

"I had a dream," Joey said, "where the nurse had fingers strung around her neck."

"It wouldn't be so bad," the man said, "but I hate to leave before catching my limit."

They lay still. Joey listened to their breathing, believed the words had some value. He turned again, but the man had fallen asleep. Joey wanted to ask about his feet. Although everyone could see he had lost his feet, Joey couldn't help telling people. He wondered where they were. He thought the doctors might keep them floating in a large jar.

The doctors told Joey he was disoriented.

Dr. Perkins loved Joey's stumps, said he couldn't have had better care, that he was a showcase of army surgical skill. When Joey asked what he'd done with his feet, the doctor's face turned gray and he wouldn't say. He assured Joey they were not in a laboratory jar. "The army does not keep feet," he said.

Joey stared at the end of the bed where his feet should be. He tried to spread his toes, and could feel the muscles in the balls of his feet tighten, relax, threaten to cramp. "Phantom feelings," the doctor had said. Joey didn't believe him. Somewhere, floating in formaldehyde, his feet were dancing, he was sure.

Sgt. Anderson sat next to the bed in dress uniform, his back erect, his jaw set. He and Joey stared not quite at each other, one waiting for the other to begin.

"Proud of you," Anderson said.

"I lost my feet," Joey said.

Sgt. Anderson grimaced, tensed his neck. Joey thought he was holding something back as if angry. "I know, Malone. I know that." He looked over Joey's head at the wall.

They sat for several moments in silence. Joey felt he should say something. It dawned on him that he was going home and Sgt. Anderson couldn't control him now. Joey said nothing. Anderson's face was rigid, red, the muscles around his cheekbones thick and tense. Joey believed Anderson was about to burst into anger, say he should be proud to give his feet for his country. Joey looked away. It didn't matter, he thought.

When Joey looked back, tears ran down Anderson's face. "I searched for you. After the firing died down. If I'd gone another hundred yards, I'd found you. Finally did, of course." Sgt. Anderson cleared his throat, removed his handkerchief, wiped his face.

Joey again felt that he should say something. He had nothing to offer. Finally he asked, "What do you think they've done with them?"

"With what?" Anderson removed his dress hat, held it in his lap.

"My feet."

Anderson stared at Joey several moments, then crossed his legs. "Had to identify my brother by his hands. Most the rest of him was gone, just gone. I kept thinking, *This is Paul, This is Paul.*" Sgt. Anderson put his dress hat back on, uncrossed his legs, then took his hat off again. "My brother had big hands, like a boxer's." He made two fists, held them at his chest. "What they showed me were two little cauliflowers."

"I can feel my feet," Joey said. "I can wiggle my toes."

"Everybody gets things taken away from them." Anderson stood. "Got to make do with what's left." He shook hands with Joey for a long time, then left him.

Owens came late, had to wake Joey to talk. It was after visiting hours, but the nurse made an exception.

"You all right?" Owens said.

Joey opened his eyes, looked at Owens running his hands up and down his arms.

"You all right, man? It's colder than Bejesus out there."

"I lost my feet," Joey said.

"That's what I heard. I'm sorry, Joey." Owens took off his green wool pullover cap, dusted with frost. "I got a deck with me if you feel up to it." He sat on the edge of the bed.

Joey raised himself up on one elbow. "What do you think they did with them?"

Owens shuffled the cards once, then looked at Joey. "They probably got a whole warehouse full of them."

Joey nodded. They played Go Fish. "Anderson worked it out that I could come," Owens said. "He told me, 'You can remake a human soul just like you can rebuild an engine.' What do you think of that? I don't think he's running with all his cylinders."

"You have a four?"

"You just asked for a four. He told me they took that hill the next day."

"So the communists are that much farther from Michigan City?"

Owens smiled. "Something like that." They played Go Fish again and again. Owens asked about the Negro in the next bed. Joey told him he'd seen the man crying during the night, his left arm, just a stub, twitching around like a propeller.

Owens shook his head, dealt another hand. "Tell me again. About June and the little bear."

"It was the end of the school year," Joey said, and told about the baseball field, June pointing, how she pulled her dress over her head.

When he finished, Owens walked over to the window. "Damn, Joey, more stars than you can imagine tonight. I know little bear is out there, if I knew where to look."

"Let me see," Joey said.

"How am I going to do that?" Owens said. They stared at each other for a moment before Owens began crying. "This fucking shithole," he said. He walked to the bed, slipped his arms under Joey's back and knees. "Be quiet," he said. He lifted Joey out of the bed.

Joey heard the nurse calling after them in a hushed voice. Owens carried him to the door and out into the night. The cold air wrapped around Joey's throat like a hand. The stub ends of his legs ached. He could no longer feel his lost feet.

Joey looked over the sky, blurred his eyes until he could make out the round buttocks and chubby head of a bear cub. He lifted his right arm into the air, pointed to the sky. "Ursa Minor," he said.

"Little Bear," Owens said.

They stared into a sky blistered with stars.

DIRECTIONS

Father knew the graveyard
in the smell of the nursing home.
He knew the death watch.

His hands were thick with scars,
blued by factory dirt;
going in the door
he held my hand.

For six days I held his.

My father taught me water
flows in two directions
at the Great Divide.

I watched him quiet in the pull
feeling my own currents.

I held tight, begged
and begged
let go.

WATER LILY

One at a time so as not to rock the canoe, we
leaned to smell them, their wild cups offering
fragrance like blessing. You cut a lily,
hung it over my ear, took that snapshot I keep
with pictures of my life supposed to be over.
I still look toward you as if I can't believe this
is happening, as if I wanted to be a water lily only
for you and couldn't, knew it would take years of sun,
the lake levels rising, to make a climate right for
lilies with yellow hearts and snaky stems, flowers
out of Eve's tears in swaying that's almost like swimming.

The summer before your cancer killed you, we knew
it was going to kill you, and went home to lake country.
Fishing off the deck of the pontoon boat, I caught
the first fish, a bullhead with stingers. You can't
kill that fish, even with a hook in its mouth it multiplies,
stirs up the lake bottom. With his foot on the bullhead
your cousin forced its ugly mouth open, pried the hook loose,
knifed the fish in the belly, threw it back, sure it would
go on living. Nothing was biting. There weren't many keepers.
At dusk we turned off the motor, slid home quiet.

Close to shore a water lily moved on its stem
and I cut the flower, gave it to you. All night we
breathed it in, that beauty. Even now, holding what's left,
the flat petals thin as paper folded over the empty space
of the flower's heart, I find veins that look like gold,
a dry fragrance.

AT BESSEMER CEMETERY
for Diane

1.

I see you, bending over,
arranging flowers on your mother's grave
in that cemetery on a hill outside Bessemer,
with those stones and useless bodies
arranged in rows
next to that gray granite mountain,
shouting its immense loneliness into the sky.

And I see your father,
etching by hand those years
of brief life which Mary lived
onto a stone where her body
had lain unmarked, anonymous
except in the minds
of those who remembered.

Only last year he did that, you told me.
It is as if he,
as he begins old age,
before he steps into that unknown
where your mother lives waiting for him,
knows you cannot trust the mind of man:
important things must be carved
into stone lest we forget,
lest we leave anything undone
  or to chance, before it is our time.

2.

It is a nice human custom —
to bury families together;
to call such an activity
a symbol of our thirst for continuity
diminishes it.
It is our conviction of continuity;

our knowledge that we are
our family,
just as your father,
carving the memory of Mary's five brief years of life
onto that stone, is Mary
and the image of him doing it, is now me.

3.

I like your uncle's headstone best:
the picture of a trout
leaping and snapping at a fly
and the legend "gone fishing"
to commemorate the intensity of his passion.
Now, of course,
he doesn't come back.
He has been snapped up.
He is the mayfly
transmuted into God's
vast digestive system which no one of us
understands
and whose food we are.
We call it our purpose of existence:
to become Him.
Some of the churches have
it twisted around.
They think He became our food—
that He changes into us;
that we can eat Him.
Well, your uncle's headstone
clarifies that—
He has not gone fishing this time.
    He is the fish.

4.

Cemeteries are strange.
Who is who?
Because Mary lives in your father,
she is carved in stone
so that she will live in anyone

who passes by,
and now, through your telling me
this, she lives in me.

And when it comes right down to it:
for whom exactly did you arrange
those flowers on Memorial Day
at your mother's grave?
"Someone has to do it,"
you told me.
But it's more than that—
someone in the family,
you meant,
proving I think
that we all do live together
and cause death
to ourselves and to one another,
while God waits and smiles.

AT YOUR GOING

"Sons carry the name,"
my father said when I married,
"but a daughter carries the heart."

My first man, today the skies
will not cloud over.
We lay you in the soil west
of your country church, high noon
in the middle of July.

On a day like this I walked
to the fields to bring you a gift.
When you finally saw me
and the tractor wheels stopped turning,
I opened my hands and cried.
Melted candy, that's the best,
you said, scooped it from my palm
with one rough finger.

Now your eldest points
and directs, becomes you as surely
as if he'd put on your overalls
and begun peering at the sky,
demanding rainfall.

A small breeze brushes over
the stones, barely moves my dress
but nearly knocks me down. I reach
for my brother's sleeve. How empty,
weightless, drifting are my hands.

ORCHARD WINTER

To select death
is to uncrate the apples
of our mouths,
let them roll across
a blanket of frost,
the original,
eaten to the core,
lodged like a filling
in one tooth,
it was that hard.

To select death
is to shake children
from the crooks of our arms,
and let the wind
prune us to almost
nothing: a twig
for walking down
the narrow rows.
Surely, as Eve imagined,
the orchard ends!

If love is hard and crisp,
let rotting apples
soften the earth
from which we pull our roots.
The hole is not for burial.
Fill it with seeds,
then hang a smudge pot
from my waving hand.
I want to go in smoke
seeking the killing frost.

THINK DEATH
for Richard Shelton

I don't think Death
has much in store for us—
maybe a sale on silence,
a discount on all the darkness
we can carry.
Lowering ourselves into the ground,
blocking out any chance of sun or moonlight,
what do we expect?
Death is a hoarder by nature.
He keeps grabbing, pulling things
into him—dogs, insects, fish,
rhinos, trees, us.
A dark mass burrowing
under the surface,
his eyes are always open,
his hand forever clenched.

The idea that we live
a second life, or third,
makes for good science fiction
but no one really believes it.
We're born, we die.
In and out. Up and down.
Truth and truth.
In death,
the rich and poor,
the cursed and blessed,
all enter through the same door,
wide open from above,
locked tightly from below.

I don't think Death
has much to offer us
other than free cold storage,
a stillness close to infinity.
From birth, throughout our lives,

we create an enormous debt,
owing our parents, brothers, aunts,
neighbors, teachers, sisters,
husbands, wives, grandparents,
children, priests, strangers.
In death,
even someone who is a credit
to society gets tallied
in the loss column.

I don't think Death
wishes us any ill will.
He's got a job to do.
He adds up each life,
totaling each breath, each sin,
and when it's time,
he cashes in on us,
the ringing from his ancient register
like church bells
in the distance.

GIFT FROM ANOTHER COUNTRY

Grief was still wet on my cheeks
and wringing my dumb hands
when my father came back
to comfort me.

Do not laugh,
but he had wings
and the small black eyes
of a bird.

His eyes were not dust-blue
as the day he stood in the doorway
and told me my small son
would be the child to nick my heart.

"His eyes tell all," he whispered,
then turned and waved good-by
for the last time.
In Gdynia, the old people

used to sprinkle poppy seeds
on the graves of loved ones.
They believed the dead
returned as birds.

I do not know much
about my ancestors' country
but I know when my father flew away
that morning in the backyard
sorrow was lifted like smoke curls up to God.

That Foolish Flying

. . . laughing in spite
of the visions, grown old and ugly,
we glimpse what our play helped us flee.

—William Vernon,
"Freezing Weather"

TO THE IMPRESSIONABLE CHILDREN

(a pantoum)
From a warning inside a package of Superman pajamas:

"Dear Parent,
Impressionable children may think they can fly.
Please be cautious and warn your children that
people cannot fly.
                                                    Signature,
                                  Pajama Corporation of America"

Please grow up now.
Stop that foolish flying.
People cannot fly, children.
You must stop trying.

Stop that foolish flying.
We have tested our pajamas.
So please stop trying.
Dropping adults from helicopters,

we have tested our pajamas.
Even with their arms outstretched
adults falling from helicopters
landed with a thud.

Even with their arms outstretched
people cannot fly, children.
People land with a thud.
Please grow up now.

THE SOCIAL CONTRACT REWRITTEN

They know another dog
has been here. They can tell
by the cursive yellow
writing in the snowbank,

a word or phrase ending
in an absurdly-stylized letter Y.
It looks like one of the signatures
on the U.S. Constitution,

so highbrow and eloquent,
an educated man's mark. Still,
we all three stop to stare,
like tourists: me, bundled eskimo-

style in my coat, and them
in their furs. While I
see fit just to look
with that outsider's detached,

appreciative gawk, they go a step
further, adding their own—less
elegant but perfectly legible—
scribblings to the near-empty

cold white inviting parchment—
making history with their sincere,
steaming urine in the brisk
flush of early December sun.

FREEZING WEATHER

We run outside in shirt sleeves to
watch our skin prickle. Rub snow on
our cheeks till they redden. "Don't do
it!" girls scream, encouraging us. The nun
on duty seems blind and deaf, hands tied
to the rosary belt. Her black skirt
sweeps a dim trail, leaving a white

wake behind her. The muddy ground hurts
when we slide over puddles so stiff-
legged, the edges throw us down.
We kneel there, feeling the frozen, rough
earth bite our shins, chilled by the sound
of the church bells flung by the wind.
It straightens us, may mean the end
of recess—but no—there's still time to wet

our hair at the fountains. As it begins
freezing, we comb it wildly to set
in strange patterns, then look in low
windows to see patches of spikes,
Mohican brushes, horns, tails. Alone
in our oddness, laughing in spite
of the visions, grown old and ugly,
we glimpse what our play helped us flee.

FIRST DANCE

Black-haired Doreen —
the only girl with glasses in our class,
the only Catholic I knew,
the first child I ever saw dance.
We had heard that Catholics
danced, but when we snuck up
to their clapboard church at the edge
of town and saw the Virgin through
the window, we ran away — so young
we still believed all idols were devils.
We told brave stories of women
in long black dresses dancing around
a golden statue.
                              But when Doreen
danced at show-and-tell, when
those tiny black shoes clicked
so fast against the hardwood floor,
I almost cried. I wanted to dance.

TERRITORY

She has coffee bean eyes and nice hair, punk looking without being ridiculous. I meet her at Denny's Sunday night, my first night in town. Her name tag, printed by hand, says "Lydia." She catches me looking. "I'm just subbing," she says.

I like the liver at Denny's. That makes her laugh. "I hate liver," she says. She comes by a couple of times and kids around while I eat. I'm not the first guy she's flirted with. When she brings the check I ask whether the tip's included. "You leave anything," she says, "I'll faint." She looks to see if anyone is listening. "You leave a tip, I'll buy us a beer to celebrate?" I nod. "About nine," she says. "Out back."

My philosophy is people get what they deserve. But Lydia seems like a bonus. I'm forty-two. My wife Aggie says I look younger. Lydia looks twenty, twenty-two, but listening while I eat I know she's younger. It's been a while since a teeny-bopper gave me a tumble. I leave two bucks.

I wait for her out behind and take her to Wagner's. "Stroh's On Tap. The Friendliest Bar in Mille Lac." When the waitress brings the pitcher, Lydia pays. Actually insists, not faking it. "Come on," she says. "We made a deal."

Her talk's a little depressing at first. Her old man, an electronics genius, is on her case. "He can do anything with phones. Watch what you say, you ever call." Her old lady works assembly line and most nights drinks a fifth of vodka. Then Lydia looks right at me and says, "You're married, mister. Right?"

"A little bit married," I say. "Nothing I can't overcome, with help." I do screw around more than I should. Aggie is constantly pissed. But that's the way I am.

Lydia seems to relax once she knows I'm married. She jumps from one thing to another. I buy a pitcher, and when we finish it, she says, "Sunday's a school night, I gotta get home by twelve." Twelve's a good sign since it's only eleven. We stop halfway to her house. Jesus, kids!

At 5:15 Thursday I turn into the HoJo Motel. Something has been nibbling on me since I closed the deal at Bayshore Realty. It bites as I slide the key into the slot of 232.

Lydia! She'd come by HoJo's after school Tuesday. I promised then I'll call her Thursday before her parents get home. But I'm late. I find her number, dial. It rings once, "Yes?" It's her.

"This is me," I say, "I got caught in traffic."

"Who is this?" Lydia asks.

She knows who. Someone's home, maybe the electronics genius. But

I don't feel like being jacked around by a teen-ager. "Hey," I say, "sorry I'm late. You want to see me, I'll be at Wagner's."

"Who is this?" she says, again.

"Oh bullshit!" I say. "You can't meet me now, come by HoJo's later."

"I don't know what you mean," Lydia says. "Who're you calling?"

"Sure," I say. "Listen, I'll hang around Wagner's an hour or so, then get something at Denny's. I'll be back here by eight, eighty-thirty at the latest."

"Mister," Lydia says, "you got a wrong number."

I shouldn't say what I do. "OK, stop the bullshit, Lydia. Tell whoever's there you're going to the library. Tell them anything'll work."

I hang up and it hits me I've said her name. Up to then you could have made a case to anyone listening I had a wrong number. As for wanting to see me, she wanted to. We'd both had a good time.

I turn my Lynx in at "The Friendliest Bar in Mille Lac." I haunch onto the open stool and order a Stroh's. "Packers look like losers this week? Against the Bucs?" says the guy on my right.

Bucs. Tampa Bay Bucaneers. "I don't know. What do you think?"

"Hope you're not a big Packer fan," he says, looking at me as he tilts his beer, burps. "You a big Packer fan?"

"Aaah, I can take 'em or leave 'em."

The woman brings my beer. "You want another Bud, Rudy?"

"Yeah, bring me another," Rudy says. He waits until she's gone, then puts his face close. "I hate the Packers," he says. "My hobby, man. Packer hating. That slogan, too — 'The Pack is Back'? I see the bumper sticker, I rip it off. I'm crazy when it comes to the Packers. I hope the Bucs kick ass."

We're in the heart of Packerland. I hope Rudy won't talk too loud. He says the Packers ruined his marriage, turned his kids against him, and cost him his one decent job. I'm thinking if Lydia's coming, she ought to be here.

I buy him a Bud when he's ready. Rudy's a talker. I listen, nod, and ask a question or two. He says he had seven pro bouts as a light heavy. I believe it. His forearms are huge. He says he has family living all over the area, one an uncle who owns Mendenhall Realty in Menominee. I stay quiet on that one. Menominee's my territory, and chances are fifty-fifty I banged what could be Rudy's cousin. Ellen Mendenhall, or maybe Eileen.

Then he buys a round. I tell him I'm with the government, can't say exactly what. "Unnerstan," Rudy says. "No personal questions." Each time the door opens I look to see if it's Lydia. Our first time here all the guys were checking her out. Was I her father? I liked that.

Just when I decide to go to Denny's, another giant comes in. He looks around, adjusting to the light. He's wearing the jacket, green with PACKERS in gold across the front. He looks around again, chooses me. This guy's more mad-dog killer than any electronics genius.

I stand, checking the bills and change in my palm for a tip. He gets close. "Arnold Besser," he says. "You know the name?" Lydia's Lydia Besser. His voice is soft, his eyes very bright. "You waiting for Lydia?"

"Lydia?" I force my eyes down to my hand, find six quarters and put them on the bar. "Rudy," I say, "I'll see you."

"Yeah," Rudy says, "good talkin' to you." He's taking it in.

Arnold Besser steps sideways from the bar, so I can't get out without a real conspicuous detour. "You're the one," he says. "I can tell the voice." He gathers both lapels of my jacket in his right hand. That means I can't avoid his face. It scares me shitless.

"Let me lay something on you," he says, very deliberate. "Three, one, three. Seven. Six. Two." He has my attention. So far he's given the area code and prefix of my home phone. "Zero. Eight," he says. My knees are rhubarb. I mouth the next two numbers with him. "Four. Nine."

Arnold Besser has my home number. I'm a hundred ten miles from home and Mad-dog here has my number. I should never have called Lydia. "You know Lydia?" he says. I nod. "You know she's seven fucking teen?"

"My god," I say. "I thought she was twenty . . . "

"You know she's in high school, lover."

I tuck my chin down and roll my head. "Maybe you got the wrong . . . "

Arnold's shaking his head sideways. I don't finish. He opens my jacket with his left hand. "What do you think?" he says. There's an old-fashioned revolver stuck under his belt and into his jeans. From the belt a huge hunting knife in a sheath. "Whaddaya think, lover? A thirty-eight in the belly? Or just I cut off your cock?"

Oh God, I think.

He's still talking soft, but about to explode.

"OK, whaddaya think? Which one?"

Something burns my cheek. Arnold sinks to the ground, his eyes all white. Whatever hit him rolled his eyeballs into his skull.

It's Rudy's arm whizzed past my cheek. "That old boy talkin' mean, buddy?" he asks. Lydia's old man is half out, but stirring. "Take your time, pal," Rudy says to him, touching him with the toe of his boot. "Arnold's a wild man," Rudy says. "I seen him around. Pro'lly you oughta get out? This pecker's one a them Packer fans."

I touch Rudy on the shoulder with the back of my hand. "Thanks, Rudy," I say. I'm trembling. "Keep him here a minute, OK?"

"Hey," Rudy says. "You my buddy, or what?"

I pull out of Wagner's and head north. I don't even slow down near HoJo's where my suit's hanging in the closet. God knows what else. What Arnold couldn't get from my stupid call he could have got lots of places. The wimpy clerk at HoJo's, even Lydia. Jesus, I hardly know her.

But Arnold must know my Lynx. I imagine ten ways he can keep tabs on me. By the time I leave Mille Lac I feel sure he's got a bug on my bumper. Maybe a bomb. He had time. Now Mille Lac's another town to stay away from. My territory's starting to shrink.

You can leave Mille Lac two ways. I go north, away from home and maybe away from Mad-dog. Ten minutes north I have to choose between Interstate 96 and Michigan 81 North. I take the two laner, 81, and steady the Lynx at sixty. The cops'll give you sixty. I don't need any conversations with the cops with Arnold on my ass.

Nothing's behind me except a Dodge pickup I already passed. Arnold has the advantage, knowing my car. Outside Samara I pull into a Wendy's, thinking maybe death or something worse isn't absolutely inevitable. I park in back and walk to the phone out front.

I'm gonna call Aggie, get her out of the house. There's no reason she should get hurt. I'll rent a different car and drive to Chicago. Meet her at the Allerton, our honeymoon place. Maybe rekindle the old flame. Meanwhile Arnold might cool down. Murder's murder, even if you think you've got reasons for what you do. I'll give Aggie Rudy's name, the name of Wagner's, in case. There's beaucoup witnesses.

I stare hard at the number on the phone. Some outstanding citizen has doodled the dial with red, but I can make out the number. I dial 0 and my own—313-762-0849. I remember Arnold's voice saying the number.

Thank God Aggie answers. Sometimes she doesn't, even when she's home. The operator does her trick. "I have a collect call from Ham," she says. "Will you accept charges?"

"Where's he calling from?"

I can't believe Aggie says that. She never has before. Ever. "Don't say, operator," I yell. I feel Arnold's listening. "It's a surprise."

"My party does not wish to say," the operator says. "Will you accept charges?"

Aggie says, "Yes." The operator says, "Go ahead please." Aggie does. "You hiding out with some bimbo?"

"Honey, don't answer for a minute. I'm OK. Something bad's going on. Worse than last time."

"Holy crap, that's—"

"Honey, don't say too much, please. There's someone here wants my ass. He can tap phones just by looking at them."

"What about phones?"

"He's a genius. He can listen in on what he wants. Like here to there."

"Whose phone is he tapping?" Aggie says.

"Honey . . ."

"Don't Honey me. You're in some sleazy scene."

"This guy has a hand-gun, like a Luger? A deer rifle, a hunting knife. And hand grenades." I want her attention.

"Holy crap," Aggie says.

"And he knows my car, and where I live. We live."

"What?" She's pretty calm, as a rule. "Nice!" she yells. "Really nice! Some guy after your ass is gonna shoot me in cold blood?"

"He wants *me*, Aggie. He's, well, upset. He may be listening . . ."

"Some broad, right? You're playing around with this guy's wife . . ."

"No," I say. "Not that. Certainly not that."

"Then what? Damn you, Ham! After that babe in Milwaukee . . ."

"Aggie!" I shout so loud I look to see if anyone's heard. "I screwed up. I'll do something big to make it up. Swear to God I'll do something big."

"Another vacuum cleaner?" I gave her one for our fifth anniversary.

"You gotta help. For one thing, it could be your ass, too." I hear her whimper. "Listen, Babes, you help, I'll do something good." I wait. Our life hasn't been all honey and roses. "Babes, get a pencil, OK?"

I can tell she does. "Well?" She's still steamed.

"I'm going to give a message like in code."

"Who am I, that Little Orphan Annie?"

"Come on, Hon. In case someone's listening in."

"Listening in. Listening in! I should of left for good last time."

Good. It's more like Aggie. "I want you to call me at 8:30," I say. "Thirty-five minutes from now. Right? Check your watch."

"All right," Aggie says. "Five to eight. What number?"

"I want you to call me at a number you don't know. I'm going to give it in code. Anybody listening, they won't get it. OK?" Arnold had our phone at home, but he might be fooled by an outgoing call. I focused on the number on the dial. 517-247-5529. "The area code's the same one I've been in?"

Someone raps on the glass door. You heard where someone's heart stops in fright? Believe it. I look through the door.

A boy about sixteen. In a Wendy's uniform. If he was inside I'd kiss him. But he's outside, making I-want-in moves. He isn't too big. I raise my right hand as though I'll slap him. He gives me the ringer and turns away.

"Ham? Ham?" The phone's a foot from my ear, shrill even from there.

"Somebody wanting the phone," I say. "It's OK, now. The area code's where I've been working. You got that?"

"Same as that community college?"

Finally! "Babes, you're doing fine. The same, you got it?" It's also the same as Lydia's. I think, Jesus, what being just a little horny can lead to. "The next two numbers are how old I am, backward."

"How old you are backward."

"Yes. You remember I had a birthday." I look around outside.

"Who baked your carrot cake? Some bimbo?"

"I loved it, the carrot cake. Jesus, I remember. We'll take a couple days some nice place." She's flashing Carribbean, I'm thinking Chicago.

"I'll bet," Aggie says.

"The next number is how many pups Tinker Bell had in her litter." Silence. "Do you remember how many? Counting the one that died?"

"Holy crap, Ham, yes! Why is this person after you?"

"I'll give you the whole thing, Babes. It's not as bad as you think. If I'm dead, I can't tell you, can I?" Silence. "OK, do you have three numbers?"

"Area code and three," Aggie says.

"Terrific! The next number is how many cars Bob and Molly have. Including the Honda." An old Buick Riviera pulls past the booth.

"Tell me about it," Aggie says. "The new Honda's all they talk about."

"The fifth number is the same. How many cars?"

"Wait," she says. I do. "The fifth number is part of how old you are."

"No," I say. "You got it wrong?" Easy. You need her. "Oh, I see. The fifth number *after* the area code?" The Riviera's filled with kids.

"So it's area code plus your age backwards plus Tinker Bell's pups plus Bob and Molly's cars, twice."

"Perfect. It ends with the date comes the day after our wedding."

"Wait," Aggie says. "Like if we were married on the fifteenth, the two numbers would be one six."

"Those aren't the numbers . . ."

"Crapola, I know!" Aggie yells. "It's an example!"

Two raps on the glass. My heart dives like a stone. It's the boy. "Man, I got ten minutes left on my break. I gotta talk to my woman."

When he says "woman," I unbuckle my belt, put a goofy grin on my face, and give him a big wink. His mouth falls open. I reach for my fly. His face caves in. I watch him run into Wendy's.

"Ham? What's happening, Ham?"

"Things're OK," I say. "I just discouraged a local youth from interrupting us." Where was I? The last two numbers. "Now, Hon, you have the numbers for the day after our anniversary?"

"God I think so," Aggie says. "You better be able to explain this mess."

"OK. Two things more. I want you to leave the house soon as you can. Drive around. Make the call from a public place, a pay phone. Some place like a shopping mall, lots of lights, plenty of people. OK?"

"What the crap for?" Aggie says.

"My way, Babes, please. I screwed up. I'll make it up, I swear." I wait. "Some new clothes, nice place to stay?" Nothing. "Ok, give me what you've got for a number."

She repeats the whole thing in code. It comes out perfect — 517-247-5529. "Terrific!" I say. "Now one more thing, we're out of the woods."

"What's this *we*? I'm not playing around with anybody's wife."

I let it go. "Thirty-five minutes, OK? Actually, about thirty now."

"Holy crap," Aggie says, and hangs up.

Inside, Wendy's smells good, and I'm hungry. I order chili. The kid I spooked dishes out the chili. I watch to see he doesn't do anything rash. Then salad bar, and grab a thousand crackers. I eat fast.

I'm camped back in the phone booth in twenty minutes. At almost exactly 8:30, the phone rings. I pick up the receiver. "Ham?" Aggie says.

"Oh Hon, you're perfect," I say. "Where are you?"

"In the K-Mart mall," Aggie says. "Tell me what you've done."

"Hon, you gotta make one more move. Sorry, this is life and death. The guy wants my head is a real genius at electronics."

I can't hear what she says. Maybe "I don't believe this."

"He still may be listening, he's that good." The Riviera pulls out.

"Drugs," Aggie says. "You doing drugs again?"

"Hon, I'm trying to be careful. I don't trust anyone but you. Take this next step, I'll make you glad."

"Thanks, I got all the vacuum cleaners I need. Say what you've done."

"Swear to God, I'll tell the whole thing," I say. Pause. "If I stay alive that long. This guys wants me in pieces."

"Yeah yeah yeah. You must . . ." she begins.

"My way, Aggie, please!" She's quiet. "Now don't yell," I say. "I wanna call you back. But here's the thing. I'm going to another phone. It'll take an hour or so to find a safe one. And I want you at another phone, too."

"Oh God, Ham."

"Is there a phone book there? Yellow pages?" A Ford wagon pulls in on the far side.

"Yes."

"Now don't say the name of what I name now, OK? The restaurant

where we had our first date that changed its name?" The Ford's looking
for a spot. I turn to the phone.

"I don't get it," Aggie says.

"We talked about its new name. You said it sucked."

"Oh, yeah. What about it?"

"See if it's listed in the yellow pages. Under restaurants."

"Ham, I'm a grown woman." She's always saying that. I hear her
turning pages.

"I'm pretty nervous, honey." It hits me Arnold would *rather* use the
hunting knife, and I shiver.

"OK, I got it," Aggie says. "Under the new name. What a crappy
name!"

"Does it give the hours?"

"Open to midnight, if that's what you mean."

"Don't say the number," I say. "I'll get it from information. Go there.
Hon. I'll call until I get you. Then I'll tell you what's going on."

Another rap on the phone booth glass. I reach for the door handle,
figure I'll slap the Wendy kid's face. But everything's the wrong color.

The door's full of green. Green with ACKE in gold.

I drop the receiver and lean back, pressing against the phone. It's Arnold. He holds up a little electronic gizmo, grinning like a fan in the
bleachers showing the tv camera the foul ball he caught.

I flatten my palms against the booth. I see he's snugged his wagon
against my Lynx. "What's wrong?" I hear Aggie yell. "Are you OK, Ham?
Ham, are you OK?"

All that work! I think. Jesus, all that work for nothing.

OLD FRIEND SENDS A CHAIN LETTER

*"This prayer has been sent to you for good luck. It
has been around the world nine times. The luck has
now been brought to you."*

You open the envelope and people
begin to spill out on the kitchen table;
an arm, a leg, and poor Joe Elliott
who lost his four hundred thousand
all because he refused
to circulate the holy chain.
And worse there's General Welch
who lost his life only six days after
he failed to pass on the prayer,
the chain letter sent to you by a friend,
and begun by a holy missionary
from South America,
for those of us in need of a salvation
we could buy at the post office.

The list continues like a voodoo obituary.
You pour a second cup of coffee,
gaze into its dark circles;
all the small lives link before you,
people cutting up rosaries
at night in their garage,
snipping necklaces off the necks of young girls
as they wait in line for a burger,
large dogs set free
with one clean snip of the wire cutters.

Their chain fetishes gone mad
attract them now into armies;
they begin to hack down
rows of chain link fences,
work their way toward your neighborhood,

your fence, your dog, your daughter.
You rise to latch the chain
on your front door
and the old ritual rises with you,
taking you back to the kitchen table
where you take out your pen,
reluctantly, address the first envelope.

A SONG OF ASCENTS

You will ask in the morning if I slept well.
I will tell about this dream that has waked me,
left me smiling and confused, feeling
your arm beneath me like a fragile branch.

I had come home from a bookstore
where pamphlets with a guru's face on them
caught my eye. You fell asleep as I lay reading
of Lord Rama Krishna and his 25 Steps to Nirvana.

Twenty-five! I thought, more than Moses and A.A. combined!
But I read, and some of them were deep, like
"Consign yourself to the infinite," and others
practical, like "Carry an egg all day."

All of the steps were paired, except the last
—which I forget. There were two to each pamphlet.
I don't think I read them all. Perhaps
as I lie here the ones I didn't see are
under the bed.
                "As I lie here . . . "
I could throw my arms around you,
draw your curve near, but stillness
lies between us like a commandment.

I would be gentle, but am finite.
As I tug for a share of the blanket I ask
if my hand is gentle enough,
whether it needs practice
with eggs.

GOD BLESS YOU

or Gesundheit, if you don't like being blessed by God,
the eternal. I don't care either way, for I maintain
some wide-ranging belief that there is no reason to get
upset over such things since eventually the end, whether
through nuclear blast or judgment day, must be. My
particular belief is thinking the planet will end with a
meteor bashing us out of orbit, knocking a chunk of us
off right away while those still alive will cry and stare
unbelievingly at how dark space is without a domed sky as
earth rumbles and rumbles in our feet. Some may drive
their cars, chant over fires, pray for mercy, but there
will be nothing to do except hold hands and say I love you
one more time. Somewhere will be the ones who, in the split-
second and infinite odds of space, know the end of every
thought, word and action is with them in their bodies and
minds that are going, going, gone. Nothing left but the
cosmos, now sneezing without us. I apologize for getting
so carried away, but I feel much better now. Thank you.

THE SEMIDIVINE BEINGS

". . . in the early days of the human race,
the 'sons of God,' or semidivine creatures,
married the daughters of men . . ."
        Charles T. Fritsch, *The Layman's*
        Bible Commentary, Vol. 2

A thousand years before the flood
the helgs flew tree to tree,
like men but for their feathered chests
and wings of blue plumage.

Handsome, they clutched sturdy boughs,
guarding mankind, their wings clasped
in constant prayer, a kind eye
descending through the fall of leaves:
They'd wing over a drowning man
to extend a leg, or die in a panther's jaw,
wings cracking while a family fled.

Then the daughters of men unveiled
their heads: there was wild
unharnessed hair. There were napes
of necks, earlobes flicking
ivory and bone. Gowns flipped open:
"See those breasts!" teased a daughter,
raising them in her hands like drinks.
"And hips!" squealed another,
a strut born between her legs.

The helgs screwed their eyes tight
but soon one swooped for a closer look,
in a mishap knocked one girl unconscious.
He took her into his warm wings,
which tickled her ample breasts
with feathers. When she awoke,
giggling, "You Godly thing!"
her fingernails were deep in his wings.

LOOKING GLASS

the name given by the Strategic Air Command
to its perpetually airborne control center

"The President, he can fly several days up in the air,
but when he comes down, there's still nothing."

    — A man in the street, from a National Public Radio
    program on nuclear weapons, 9/3/83

Sometimes Alice forgets which side is up
and do people like turnips
grow with their heads in the ground?
Do stars like Polaris always sulk in the ocean?
Do flies like ointment
and which side is left
when the other is gone?
How is a red-tailed hawk like a ladder
or a raven like a writing desk?
What's the same backwards as forwards
like hopscotch and radar?
When is a man like the hands of a clock
and why o why is Wyoming?
Spell out a sack which is nothing but air,
a bee never born to a hive,
a sea that has neither coastline nor shore.
Make us into them by adding two letters,
make zero an option, make salt into paper.
What has three heads and a sensitive nose
and where does it go on Tuesdays?
If eight dull boys in the navy each took turns
counting by jacks down from improbable,
how many eggs could you boil before
all the king's men became vapor or gravy?

Ravens, like writing desks, give warnings,
but they are black from the first morning
that they fly, that they fly.

MID-LIFE CRISIS

You wake up one morning,
find each room crammed
with remembrances,
each closet a death cell.

In the kitchen, Aunt Sophie's waffle iron,
defunct for years, opens blackened jaws.
Aprons from your trousseau curl
like old leaves in a drawer.

The Red Queen milk pitcher
you used when you were five and finicky
stands by the telephone choking
on pencil stubs and inkless pens.

Everyone's china, cracked and yellowing,
is stacked in your cupboards.
Grandma's pots with round bottoms
roll off the shelves.

In your attic, cracked shoes in rows,
baby caps, beer cans in a crate
beneath the Christmas wreath,
the Easter baskets trapping bleached straw.

Unstrung rackets, photographs of relatives
you can't remember, of you, unencumbered,
knowing how to laugh, of soccer teams
whose players have dispersed and gone.

You wonder where you are
in all this chaos.
If you exist at all
except as keeper of memories,

caretaker of things too useless
to display, too meaningful to lose.

You wonder, would anyone notice
if you junked the past,

set in neat rows on the curb.
If you stood beside it,
round-shouldered from nurturing,
and thumbed a ride . . . out!

THE ASPARAGUS EATERS

then shall we eat asparagus
each of us
grasping spring's green spear
with fingers
a thumb

some of us thrust
the whole shoot into our mouths
and suck off the butter
before
we bite

others of us squeeze
that sweet pulp out with teeth
discarding
strings of asparagus

you are not one of us
you so neat
who slice with knife
and fork whose hands
remain clean

why, there are those of us
eating asparagus
who bite and
suck and sometimes even
stop
to lick our own arms
                        buttered to the elbow

at lunch
you may hear us whispering:
"asparagus, asparagus, asparagus"
as if the word
itself
could be eaten

you will know us
by our
green
smiles

GROWING A ROW OF YELLOW PEPPERS, REGARDLESS

I don't even like them,
their sly long fruit
hanging like
sheepfat candles.
I don't like the skin
peeling from my lips,
my tongue burning
defenseless,
the surprising outlining
of my insides
as they go down.
Yet each season I put in
a row,
near the tomatoes,
close to the beans.
By July I can see them
poke through
the abundant green—
the young yellow peppers,
the points of peeled
yellow crayons,
perfect as plastic,
the milkteeth
of summer.

ROSIE

Once, a woman filled this house
with her life of paneling,
a bed turned the wrong way
and the wrong color carpet.
There were oatmeal spills
on every stairstep.

Upstairs you could stand at the foot of her bed
and look through olive branches
at the red clay of Camelback Mountain.
The first day I saw this place
it was summer.
Rosie was not working.
She wore a bathing suit,
had print from *Cosmopolitan*
on the tops of her legs.

The realtor, a woman, looked at Rosie
to have her show me inside.
Rosie got up from her poolchair
with her coconut aroma and damp hair,
walked us through the place
choked with toys and ugly furniture.

Ever since I've lived here
men ring the doorbell.
Men ring the doorbell every day
and ask if Rosie's home.
Some have oil on their trousers
or tools in holsters
or lawn cuttings on their shirts.

From inside you can hear
the real world of planes flying overhead.
Rosie's life wants to rain
on all the windows of this house.

Men call for her.
I answer through the deep brown door,
tell them that she's moved.
There's no one here by that name.
Rosie? No. She's moved.
Moved a long time ago.
This is my house now.

FUGUE

The body replicates itself not quite perfectly
every seven years, the doctors say. When I
was twenty-eight,
four times my skin had shed,
four times the meat replaced itself inside, nothing
but a few nonreplicating cells remain—
the brain. The liver, maybe. I forget.
The hand that offended me at fourteen is gone.
Long gone the eye that screwed me up at twenty-one.
Where are they now? Have they
found coordination to peer, to clutch
from among the bricks in some garden corner?
And what of the rest?
The legs, now a half dozen, that wanted
only to run and never harmed a soul.
The hearts, the toes.
The intestines, veins and nerve bundles
unreeling by the mile through my past.
This bitter death, it neither comes nor goes.
It lingers, taking only little bites in passing,
as if I were a buffet.

"I'M CALLING ABOUT YOUR AD
FOR THE GOLDEN RETRIEVER."

You have a wrong number, although
it is true I'm retrieving, goldenly,
retrieving my life, for a start,
which I had fumbled like a choice bone,
still meaty, bloody, reeking
of nourishment and joy for strong teeth.

And I'm retrieving the gold itself,
that I left in the mine,
thinking it would mine itself
or that someone else would mine it for me,
never imagining the day
I would work bent over, as I do now,
with pickaxe and fingers,
enjoying the backache,
claiming as mine, as my mettle,
these veins that run
solidly every which way
like citizens rampant with virtue.

And I'm retrieving this phonecall
from the heap of discarded phonecalls,
and your voice, that is golden,
like that of all strangers,
full of shining possibilities,
and like that of our most intimate friends,
who deposit on our shores
as if by magic
nuggets not to be used
but to be saved as collateral
for all that is tender,
whether legal or not.

BRICKS

Chinese girl, 13, recovers from life among pigs.
. . . born to a mentally retarded mother and a deaf
father who had no affection for her . . .

                                                      The Plain Dealer
                                                      Aug. 28, 1987

Mostly she stank.
That's what people mainly noticed.
Her grunting didn't bother them much
nor the mud and pig shit matted in her hair.
Her hair was short anyhow;
her brothers and sisters chewed it off
over the years for some reason.
She walked all right and often stepped
over the low fence as she grew taller,
scavenged garbage by the back door,
her mother and father too blank to care.

When she was tiny, sucking was her only joy;
the heat of the huge soft sow comforted her.
The rubbery hooves of the step-mother
prodded her too much at first —
nothing wicked, you understand,
just the way it was —
and the brothers and sisters way too strong.
She was always bruised under the dirt
and had too many teeth missing.
But they played and played
(their tails made perfect handles),
and in winter the other pigs
made heated hollows in the straw
like little ovens where she slept.
She curled among her cousins,
kicked her own hard little heels
in piggy dreams, stayed mostly in the shed
while the snow fell, her eyes
seeming pale and small in the dim light.

Now she has been rescued,
taken grunting away to be washed,
dressed, and taught to read. They say
she may learn colors, how to count,
already recognizes 600 Chinese characters
but still squeals and runs for dark shelter
when the lightning flashes.

Child, I don't know
if you will ever love bathing
and wearing dresses. And you may always feel
too cold or too hot, for people are not given
to huddling or to wallowing in the sensible mud.
I can guess, though,
what your favorite story might be,
and hope that something deep inside
will tell you to build your house at last
from neither straw nor sticks.

DANCING IN THE DUNG

When I was thirty five
I wrote my first poem.
It was brief.
It consisted of three colors.
It contained forty-six words
and eight lines.
It concerned the action of memory
and was dedicated to tea leaves.

It answered more questions than it raised.
It had one hundred invisible branches,
three of which surfaced in a carport
in Jonesville, Michigan.

When read aloud
it made a sound like whales migrating.
When read silently
it made a sound like
five o'clock in the morning, New York City.

The first question the poem answered
concerned the meaning of Life —
in distant galaxies.
The next question,
Is there intelligent life on earth?
it answered with an appeal to reason.
One of the questions the poem raised
had nothing to do with Hamlet.

The poem was riddled with internal rhyme,
some of which founded a small community
in the Pacific Northwest.

The words in the poem
sometimes overflowed the page —
for economic effect.
Part of the overflow went

to a shopping bag lady
in St. Louis, Missouri.
She knew a bargain when she saw one.

The poem was written on a cardboard
  cylinder
so there was no way to tell where
it began and
one of the colors was blue.

One of the answers concerned
the apprehension of Truth. It said,
you approach truth by negation.
Another concerned the purpose of existence —
in this galaxy.
It contained six adverbs
and a reference to horticulture.
It pointed out that there are

seven letters in the word "purpose."
Somewhere in the poem
were three tiny characters
resembling nothing in any known language.
They were the best part.
They were tiny flaws in the paper,
which when closely scrutinized
induced a sense of wonder.

The poem had a secret title:
Ninth Inning, Bases Loaded, No One at Bat.
This seemed appropriate, combining as it did
the poem's sense of the dramatic
with the fact
that it had no beginning, no end.

The poem had two
revolving rhyme schemes
depending on which way you
turned the cylinder.

When I think of that poem
I sometimes envision
several million buffalo
grazing peacefully on history's
largest golf course
outside Topeka, Kansas.
The buffalo keep the grass
at just the right height.
They avoid the balls and carts
with ease.

An eagle circles high above
eyeing a prairie dog in the rough,
and the golfers don't mind
dancing in the dung.

POETRY READING

You must be invisible
and sit perfectly still,
legs crossed,
fingers out of your mouth.
How awful you could look
in the dead quiet of the room,
so you keep it all in,
the eructations, the yawns, the squeak
of your buttocks against the chair,
until the floor is a nail head
on which you must perform
a delicate balance.
The poet reads a poem about family
and you do not understand it.
You are the only one lost
in such a simple story,
the heads and necks in front of you
straight as pitchforks.
The poet reads another poem
about a famous Italian painting
and your mind is sweating blue peonies.
What a shallow little tramp
you are, you tell yourself,
sliming around art,
sucking on its ethereal walls
like a snail. You give up,
but just as you're dimming
your mental track lights,
you hear the poet say
wallpaper, and it's as if
he handed you
pictures small as comic strip frames;
first the dark outlines appear,
moving before you like a train,
then the deep primary colors
carrying articles of your
precarious wardrobe;

you're not sure
where the conductor is going
as he eyes you from the platform
but you hear yourself saying
here, take these, and this,
and this, nodding your head
yes, go on, yes.

Unlikely Shifts

---

*You are unlikely
and exquisite.*

—J. B. Goodenough,
"Dwarf"

. . . what terror the shift brings.

—Lila Zeiger,
"In the Luxembourg Gardens"

SMALL POTATOES

I make my own trail, not because it's quicker, but because there's more to see. I don't do it enough anymore, traipsing through with an eye for rose hips like puckered mouths or for the spider's snare with its lump of fluttering, tormented moth. As I bend branches, I'm comforted that there is still so much unfenced and untrammeled space. It hasn't come to that yet, that people here feel the need to mark it off and use it up.

Even as a little girl in Boston, I was looking for this. The day I learned about the westward movement—settlers trundling along in covered wagons—I raced around after school, drunk with the concept of first steps into unknown territory, stamping my feet into any unblemished patch of snow, shouting, "Pioneer! Pioneer! Pioneer!" When I came to Alaska, it was with the sure knowledge that here were places that, truly, no one had stepped. And it mattered, the sense of putting a foot down and knowing I was the first to look upon the world from exactly that vantage point. Every sight—of mountain or mouse hole—was a discovery. There was no end to new visions.

You said it was the same for you, growing up in the Midwest. When we met, it was as though we'd once been members of the same backyard club, sisters who shared a coded language. When you spoke, it was as though you were saying my own thoughts. I felt we were resuming a friendship instead of beginning one.

That first summer, working together in the cannery, I lived in my tent and you lived in your van. Days off, we mucked about in the bay after clams, caking ourselves with mud that dried to a ghost-gray skin. Other times we hiked into the hills to fields of camomile we picked for tea. I wonder if you still think about the day we walked the bluff's edge, weaving back around the ravines and then on out to the points of land where fireweed rippled in the sea breeze. Eagles rode the thermals above us, and we watched two at play, diving at each other and once locking talons as they tumbled above us. We agreed we both wanted to be birds in our next lives.

Now that the cold has come, causing the country to lie down and curl up around itself like a tired dog, it's easier to get through here. Only a couple of weeks ago, the trees and bushes were still lunging around, frothing with fevered leaves and seed, stretching, the high grasses dizzy over my head. Now the exuberance is gone, leaving jaundiced alders, berries fallen or pinched to skin, grasses pale and brittle as though the frost, sucking at them, drew the green resilience out their ends. Yesterday's wind has turned the remaining leaves to bare their undersides like submissive bellies; it's flattened the grasses so they all lie in one direction. I bully my way through, kicking loose the snarls that catch my feet. The morning's frost flakes off and sprinkles down.

It's only when I reach the highway that the sun clears the trees. Instantly it's warmer, and I pause to unzip my jacket at the throat. It's early and a Saturday; there's no traffic this far out the road. Most people are still waking up, drinking coffee beside stoked stoves and staring out windows at reminders of chores to be done before freeze-up: gardens to be turned, skirting to be nailed, wood to be split and stacked. The first hard frost, no matter how late, always comes before any of us is ready. In homes up and down the road, lists—the must-do's of fall—are being assembled.

You, too, will have your list, that you've brought from Anchorage: weatherstripping to stick to the bottom of the door, mouse traps to set, a load of firewood to arrange for delivery. Your list is different from the rest of ours, now that you come only on an occasional week-end. It's not the list of buttoning-up, of drawing shelter close like a wrap of sweater. Instead, it's a list of absentee fixes, of purchases. The mouse traps will bang shut in the silence, after you, catless, have closed the door behind you; the wood will arrive one day, heaved from the back of a pick-up to lie in a pile at your doorstep like a yardful of stumps.

Walking along the empty road, I think again of the eagles that tumbled with locked talons, the day we discovered the old log cabin. It stood just at the edge of the bluff, ramshackle, the roof partly fallen in and the windows broken out. I poked my head through an opening and smelled the damp rot that was somehow satisfying in its earthiness. "Move," you said in your eager way, and slung a leg over the splintered sill. We pawed through the debris and you dug out an old spoon, tarnished green. Later, we sat outside, chewing on chives we found clumped against a cabin wall, trailing them from our mouths like strings of licorice. We wondered who had lived there and where they had gone, and what it must have been like to have settled this land before the roads came through. As we wanted to be birds the next time around, we decided we'd been Indians, or explorers, or calicoed prairie wives before; we felt that much affinity for the open country.

This trip, besides your list of to-dos, you'll bring other things— groceries, cleaning supplies, new candles. You'll also have a second list— items you've decided you need in Anchorage and want to remember to take back. I've watched this ebb and flow between your two households. In comes the sack of groceries, out goes the smaller bag of garbage you'll drop in the dumpster as you pass through town. In comes the new broom. Out go the favorite chamois shirt, the binoculars, the game of Scrabble, the bread knife and the vegetarian cookbook.

When you made the decision to work in Anchorage, that's just how you put it—you would work there, but it was temporary, a job away from home. Home would remain here, and you'd get back to it on week-ends, as often as you could. You'd only be "camping out" in your furnished apartment, drinking out of jelly jars and browning toast in the oven. Your real, complete, household would be here, waiting.

I've watched it happen, though, the ebb of possessions. It's not like tides anymore, a wash in and out; it's like the flood of a river now. Every trip you take away more, emptying the house of those things that make it most yours. Load by load, you're moving away.

When I turn off to your place, I study the ruts, wondering if you're really here. You said you would be, when we talked. "This week-end for sure," you said, sounding guilty, regretful. "I want to spend some time with you. We'll pick cranberries. Plan on it."

It's funny in a way, how we've stayed so close through everything. Always, our friendship endured. We both looked for men to share our lives with, and we compared our ideals as we talked of the day that our Prince Charmings would appear. The men did come and go, for each of us. Some lasted longer than others, and each was a good man in his way, but none of them was a Prince Charming. Neither of us ever found one that was a friend in the way we were to each other, someone with whom we could sit and talk over cups of tea, saying everything without insult or doubt or misunderstanding and knowing what the other meant.

The ruts don't tell me much. The mud's frozen hard, tire tracks printed in it like waffles. Where it was wettest it's crystallized like quartz, pointed spears of brown ice radiating from each pit. They crunch under my feet, shattering. It's clear that no one has driven in or out this morning.

The low light has that luminescent quality, as though it were slipping under the sides of things, filling them from within. The bent grasses along the road glow yellow; frost melting to dew magnifies in beads along the edges. You always used to remark on it, summer evenings when the light slanted in from the north, washing the trees and fields with an underwater greenness.

When I reach the top of the rise, I can see the roof of your house. The shakes catch the sunlight the same as the grass, the cedar burnished like gold. But it's the chimney I watch. Straining my sight against the wall of spruce that rises behind, I look for the wavy distortion made by the heat from a dampered, smokeless fire. The trees stand still as a painted back-drop, and I know that you're not here after all.

You're busy, I know. Things come up. It's hard to get away. You would be here if you could, pulling muffins from the oven and pouring spring water into your kettle.

I keep walking towards your house. As it materializes, top to bottom, I think how systematically it went the other way, the summer you built it. I'm still amazed at the assurance with which you did it. When you

started you didn't even know the names of what you needed—joists or
studs, rafters or siding. They were all just boards to you. The times I came
to help, it was, "Cut all those boards to look like this" and "Use those big
nails over there." You knew exactly what you wanted, as if by instinct.
And when it was done, one board nailed to the next, it was one solid
piece—no holes, nothing extra sticking out.

Seven years later, there it is—still standing, still surprising me. With
time, the rough-cut spruce, once so banana blond, has grayed to distinc-
tion. It reminds me of a Wyeth painting with its patina of fog and
seclusion.

In the beginning, when we moved to the hill, the places we found
were simple and rough. Yours was a homestead cabin, with an uneven
floor that sloped downhill. A pencil dropped in the kitchen rolled to the
door, and in wet weather water seeped up through the floorboards. My
place was less historically pleasing—plywood, its walls lined with cardboard from cases of beer. I tightened it up with some ceiling insulation,
installed a barrel stove, and spent winter nights reading by a kerosene
lamp. Later, when you built your own place, I settled into my rental in
the trees. We joked about my electricity and your sheetrock. "It's real up-
town," we said. "We better watch out that we don't get citified."

Your top story stares at me first, the two south windows like eyes
flashing, the smaller one caught in a wink. Beneath it more windows, none
matching, line either side of the "L". The short leg thrusts forward, throwing a small shadow like a wedge of night against the longer. You did right
with the angles, capturing the best of the winter sun and avoiding the flat,
spiritless faces common to new construction. The porch, along the side,
adds an air of leisure and comfort, as though it might be hung with an old-
fashioned wicker swing.

As I get closer, the look of desertion looms larger. The road cuts
away, with the spur into your yard crowded from both sides by grass. The
center strip of weeds stands firm; months have passed since it's been
pushed over by the belly of a car. The yard, too, grows wild; nettles collapsed over the splitting block, a dry pushki stalk parting the legs of a
sawhorse.

I climb the steps, the sound of my boots a thudding of arrival. The
door is padlocked. I tug on the lock, testing. When it holds, I move down
the porch, nudging with my foot at a coffee can along the way. It's empty
except for a stiff paintbrush.

Framing my gloved hands around my eyes, I press against the window to see inside. Plates and cups are stacked on a dish towel beside the
sink, ready to be put away. There's a fancy cookie tin and a stick of marga-
rine on the counter. Beyond the wood stove I can see the edge of a chair
and some magazines—*New Yorkers*—scattered on the floor; their covers

are like fall leaves — one mostly orange, another green and yellow. Ragg socks lie where they were pulled heel over toe: a pair of sleeping gray kittens.

My breath — I've tried to hold it in — finally steams up my space in the window. The interior pulls away as though masked by a cloud.

It's part of your plan, I know, to leave it every time like this — odds and ends of food and clothing lying around — so that when you return, it feels like coming home, as though you've never really left.

"I can't eat the scenery." It's what you said when you took the job in Anchorage. You were joking, sort of — parodying what the business people said when they argued for more, faster growth. We both knew what the choice was — money and some professional achievement instead of the space and self-sufficiency and, yes, scenery that was ours here. Now you dress in suits and nylons and sit at a desk, reviewing plans and writing up reports. You told me that you don't even have a window in your office, and that the traffic after work is hell.

There's sacrifice either way, of course. Living here, I'll never be rich or influential. I'll never be quoted in the newspaper twice in a week; in fact, I may not even manage to read the paper twice in a week. Waking to knead bread and collect eggs from the hen house, my days will fill with mundane essentials. Instead of waiting in a traffic jam, I may spend an entire winter day chaining up my car and winching it through snowdrifts to the road. My words will fall into cliché, how-de-doo, and the sluggish thought that goes with chatter in the post office line or reporting to the cats at home. Work will be what I can find, always strictly for money as I support a lifestyle the way others support too many children.

Sitting on the edge of your porch, I let my legs dangle. I look back the way I came, across to the mountains. Snowfields divide the pale sky from the water below as though bleeding off the color, draining it down the cracked and broken glaciers to the concentrated, undiluted blue of bay. I never watch the mountains that I don't marvel that this is where I live, and I cannot imagine living where I couldn't watch the snowline rise and fall with the seasons.

And when I look around me again, I see the fenceposts of your garden. There it is, the old plot, looking small and indistinguishable from the rest of the field except for the gray posts that tilt like lightning-struck trees above the grass. Its chickenwire sags from one post to the next; moose, walking through, have pulled it free. In one corner, where it's still strung high, weeds — some climbing vines — have laced it together.

That's all that's left of the garden you turned by hand, layering in truckloads of horse manure and seaweed. You were so proud of what you grew — the early radishes, the chard, the heads of cabbage soft and leathery as medicine balls. I helped you dig potatoes when the plants lay limp over the hills and the soil was cold in our hands; they were small that year, the season short. Perfect for boiling, you said, content with what you had.

When was it, when all that happened—when the fireweed sneaked back across the fence line as though it had never been spaded under, when the chickenwire loosened and the posts were heaved out by frost? All that's left looks so old, I can't believe that it has anything to do with us. Somehow, we've become the ones who came before, as much a part of the past as the early homesteaders at the edge of the bluff or the later ones with sunken floors and cardboard walls.

Although you've left and I'm still here, the time when our lives were new and as brilliant as bright nails and fresh-sawn lumber is behind us both. Our first steps through—finding our ways along trails we parted, past rows we planted, up steps we hammered together—are history. I go on, holding to the vision, but I know now that you'll never be so satisfied again, with small potatoes.

I drop down off the edge of the porch, landing harder than I expect. I've sat too long, stiffening. I walk over to the garden and around one side. I want to see if the vines in the corner might be some surviving peas. They're not; they're nothing I recognize, the leaves scalloped and tinted red, as though they've rusted over. I step across the fence and kick through the grass, searching for some sign. It's all weeds, as far as I can tell, the same as beyond the fence. I step out again and start back towards your house, wondering where I can find something to write a note with— charcoal, wax, anything—but there's nothing here, in this yard grayed out, gone to seed.

Instead, half-way back, I stop and pick some weeds: stalks of fireweed still stuck with wisps of fluff; brittle mare's tail; a handful of grasses fringed with seed cases; the paperlike shell of a cup-shaped flower; a spiky pushki head, each pod spread like a parasol. I place them, inelegant, unar- ranged, in the paint brush's can and set the whole bouquet against your door. When you come—whenever you come—they'll be waiting, frozen in time. Although snow may have buried the country, smoothing this morning's rugged beauty into flat, forgetful obliteration, these will stay as now, a reminder to you of what came before.

MUSIC ROOM

Sunlight on a varnished floor.
A wooden chair. Your music stacked
like lumber. Missing you,

I sit among your stuff and think
how strange the cello is, all
wood and emptiness. You and I

worked hard, that's how we
stayed together all these years.
I used to think you most distant

when you practiced, woodshedding
the same phrase over and over.
Forgive me that I complained.

Today, with you gone, I sense
your absence most in other rooms,
shaking your head in the kitchen,

prowling shelves for a book.
Here's where you are, where you've
worked so honestly: a note

vibrating in a space that wood
creates, encloses and sets free.

THAT TIME AGAIN

Soon it will be that time again
to pack a suitcase of still shadows,
bid farewell to the sunroom
and leave for good.

Soon the neighbors will be new again;
the sunsets will look like lost faces.

My stomach will knot up
upon the occasion I drop
another name —
one that took me ages to remember.
I'll have other faces to learn
like strange letters of the alphabet.

They won't stone me I suppose;
I'm an unassuming sort.
I'll get used to introducing myself again,
answer the same questions,
and smile a lot.

All this fuss.
It will probably be a nearby town.
I will not pull another coast-to-coast job.
Today I do not want to try.
Today I will sit in the sunroom
and pretend to be a cactus in Arizona
by sitting very still.

HE SKATES FROM ME

Your father is disappearing
into yesterday's shadows,
skating backward into memories,
alleys with no way out.

He tells me
three, four times an hour
how he met his only sweetheart,
your mother,
on the ice at North Commons,
shows me two pairs
of rusty, clamp-on skates
hanging in the hall.

I watch him write down
what day is today
on little pieces of paper,
one in each room of his house,
islands he lands on as he glides
through his hours.

I watch him touch
a photo I've brought him,
his great granddaughter on a trike,
see him paste it
to the kitchen window already
overflowing to the wall, and beyond,
with snapshots, all faded
to blue outlines
like the veins in his hands
fingering the skates,
remembering your mother
of 60 years ago, every detail
clear as the open water
he slips into
where we cannot reach him,
cannot bring him back.

SUNDAY

Bristling after two days from the factory
and the knowledge that tomorrow
he must punch in at 6:58
or lose the farm,
Father would sit in his corner chair
to skim the classifieds
and read out loud about three-point plows,
auctions, and used tractors.

When he finished,
he'd go out to the shed,
re-set mouse traps, hone hoes,
then walk between the garden's weedless rows
until Mother called, "Dinner!"

Sitting at the head of the table,
he'd talk about the size of the green tomatoes,
keep an eye out the window for that damned hawk
that circled the chicken coop,
and wish Sunday would never end.

SAIL BABY SAIL

Now I sing to my mother, the lullabies she sang
to me as a child. Her hand trembles to her mouth,
as if to find the lips that once formed words, as
if to move them again with her fingers into speech.
She makes a face at me, and bounces her eyebrows
as she would when she sang, *Gunk, gunk went the
little bull froggy*, and I smooth back her hair as
I sing to her now, *Gunk, gunk went the lady froggy
too*. She laughs, and for a moment her trembling
is gone. She holds her smile like a note
sustained at the end of a phrase, like a child
waiting for another surprise. I tickle her
forehead, and remember a twilight over her
shoulder, or think I remember, and the creaking of
the chair as we rocked and the perfume she wore.
Sail baby sail, I half mumble, half sing, *Far
across the sea. Only don't forget to sail, home
again to me*. She cries, and I catch her tears in
a tissue, 'my tear catcher,' I call it, and she
laughs. Something is passing between us, something
I felt a dozen years ago as I talked to my father,
long after he'd stopped breathing, something that
holds us together, something like music, something
we might carry to another life, like the sound of
a human voice talking.

ANNIE

Annie folds her ninety-one years
into a wheelchair,
tilts to the left
away from a broken hip.
Every day she begs God
to take her home.
His bleeding picture hangs above the bed,
drips into her sleepless eyes
and flows through her body,
a transfusion
to bring them together.

The great-grandchildren have stopped visiting.
They're afraid of her eyes,
tired of listening to God programs
on the Atwater-Kent she brought from home.
The nurses tell them to be kind,
that she's old and melting
like a late spring snowball.
All the while Annie cries
and when empty
allows the nurses to lay her down
to be filled up again.

BEARWALK

Our house changes when Uncle Gerry comes to visit. He roars through it, head down, arms swinging at his sides like propellers as though he is pushing himself through the air. He is so big that our house shrinks until there is no place to hide from him. The air stops smelling of Dad's pipe or the bottles that make Mother's hair curly. Soon all I can smell are the horses Uncle Gerry keeps in his barn. He walks in short spurts through our house until he finds me. From where I sit I can see his flappy-toed sneakers coming.

When the older kids try to scare me, they talk about the Bearwalk. They open their eyes wide and scuff their homemade cigarettes into the ground. Then they whisper that it's like a ghost and that they've seen it on the highway outside the reservation. But I always think of Uncle Gerry as the Bearwalk. He walks the way a bear does, setting his feet down carefully, first on the toes, then settling down heavily on the heels. Sometimes when we go hunting I follow behind him, looking to see what kinds of tracks he makes, but they're never like a bear's, just like an ordinary person's.

I can hear him laugh, deep in his belly like thunder. He scoops me up onto his shoulders and carries me to the dinner table. I cling like a frog, my toes gripping the soft plaid of his shirt. My chin presses into his hat; it is thick with grease and sweat. He carries me like I am a trophy of war. On his shoulders I am weightless.

Mother serves the food, her mouth tight and sewn together. She has told my father that you can set your watch by Uncle Gerry. That's because he always comes to visit at dinner time. First he will stop just inside the screen door, his hands in the back pockets of his jeans, and he will sniff the air, just the way a bear does when it knows you're on its trail. Then he rocks a little on his feet, back and forth, back and forth. He'll say that it sure does smell good, aren't we the lucky ones, and that he wishes he had someone to cook for him. He pokes out his lip then and says not to worry about him, though. He can go home and open a can of franks and beans all by himself. Mother and Dad will look at each other and finally Dad will say, "God, Vera, he's on relief after all," and Uncle Gerry will end up staying.

I have to sit next to Uncle Gerry at the table. When the bowls come around to us, he puts food on my plate even though I already have enough. He tunnels into the mashed potatoes and plops the spoonful in front of me. He dips the gravy boat so that it floods over my plate. Whistling, he rolls up his shirtsleeves and eats. I always thought big men ate tough, splaying their elbows on the table, lifting the soup bowl to their mouths, but Uncle Gerry eats like I think a prince would eat. He takes small quick bites, touching the paper napkin to his lips. He is done before the rest of us and he goes to the refrigerator to get a beer. I look over at his chair while he is gone. The seat cushion rises slowly as if breathing in relief.

Uncle Gerry drinks loudly, though, slurping from the can. He rolls beer around inside his mouth, closing his eyes. Then, slowly, he swallows. He sits with eyes half-closed, watching my mother clear the table. She makes sharp angry motions as if trying to shoo an animal outdoors. He gets up from the table and beckons for me to follow. He hovers over me like a giant, swaying slightly on his feet. I follow him, walking where he walks.

In the living room Uncle Gerry sits me on his lap. His belly is soft and doughy like the bread I sometimes help Mother knead. Every time I see him he seems to get bigger, just like the way the bread rises when my mother puts it in a warm place with a towel over it. He bounces me up and down, the way the lady rides, the way the gentleman rides, the way the farmer rides. He pretends we are both riding horses. "Chh," he says. "Gitup." I squirm around on his lap but Uncle Gerry won't let me down. His arms are thick and strong, with veins running like highways through them.

Once when he was over, Uncle Gerry cut himself by accident with a kitchen knife. I was scared, watching the blood, but he pulled me up close, a warm hand atop my head. "Anishinabe blood," he said. "Not like white people's. This is one hundred percent Ojibwa." He took his hand with blood on it and drew lines across my face. His fingers were soft on my cheeks. When Mother saw that, she grabbed a washcloth and hauled me into the bathroom, but I couldn't help thinking that with his blood on my face I was more like Uncle Gerry than ever.

On his left arm is his prison tattoo. It is a bolt of lightning. Uncle Gerry says that our ancestors believed that beings called Thunder Birds used to throw lightning down from the sky. I used to think that prison must be a fun place if you could get tattoos there, but then he told me what it was like. Mother didn't want him to, but he said to shut up, Vera, because Indian kids should know what jail was like so that they could stay away from it. After that he took me to the zoo and showed me an old mangy black bear just lying in his cage. I asked him if that was what he did in jail. He threw back his shoulders and said that Nosir, he had been up all the time, pulling at the bars until they let him out.

He starts to tell me about the time he went hunting in the wilds of Africa. Every time Uncle Gerry tells the story, the number of lions and tigers gets bigger. Mother says that Uncle Gerry never really went off to

Africa, that he's barely been off the reservation. But he still tells the stories like he believes them.

I lean against him and listen. He sweeps off his hat and squashes it down on my head. It sits lightly on top of my hair. I am afraid to breathe because of the honor and responsibility of wearing Uncle Gerry's hat. I can feel the stickiness in it from the hair lotion he uses. When it's hot he takes a piece of paper and puts it inside the rim. It is strange to see him without the hat. His dark hair is flattened on top and sticks up on the sides.

After the story, we play tackle. I stand at one end of the room and try to make it to the goal, across the room. Uncle Gerry squats in the middle, his hands balancing himself, ready to spring. I move fast, but he is like a powerful animal. Laughing, he pins me to the floor. His breath is hot and spicy. I have to say "Uncle Gerry" before he can let me up. Uncle Gerry says he could have been a famous football player, if he hadn't quit high school. Whenever our television is working right, he comes over and we watch the games. Uncle Gerry takes a hand and puts it over the quarterback. "That could've been me," he says, every time.

Sometimes after tackle Uncle Gerry falls asleep. I move very close to him, watching. His plaid shirt rises and falls and his legs twitch. His mouth hangs open and he snores, his hands folded over his chest. I imagine his dreams to be bigger than life, the colors purple and orange. Though he is asleep I know that he is aware of me, watching.

Other times he goes and stands out on the back porch, his hands shoved in his pockets. I stand next to him, so close that I can feel him breathe. I try to match it so that we breathe at the same time, together. I concentrate, and I believe that everything we do is the same, that the blood moves through our veins the same speed, that our hearts beat at the same time. I want to open my eyes and find myself to be like him, big and strong and fearless, so that people will say: There goes the Bearwalk.

After Uncle Gerry leaves, the house gets larger again. Now there are hiding places, places dark and small and secret. Now the air is like leftover dinner and Dad's night pipe. The only thing we hear that can tell us that Uncle Gerry was here is the sound of his tennis shoes, flapping away down the road.

IN THE LUXEMBOURG GARDENS

Precision in the sunlight:
the symmetry of *parterres*,
painstaking statement of
the rules and tariffs
even at the playground,
children circling neatly
on the carrousel or
racing numbered sailboats
on the pond near
billows of impatiens
made to undulate
in perfect order.

A day of shining
after weeks of rain.
The pouter pigeon lover
entertains her friends,
a lone audacious pigeon
eating from her mouth.
A little blonde girl
right out of Renoir
in long gray cotton
runs up and hugs my thighs
and plants a kiss
upon my skirt.

And then I see him
sitting on a bench
beside his mother
but not near her
and not near anyone.
She is slender, *soignée*.
He is twenty, perhaps,
and holds a piece of
gray wool in his hand.
His thumb and forefinger
never stop moving.

The wool is frayed,
a tiny swatch by now.
I wonder how often
she has to replace it,
what terror the shift brings.
I pretend not to watch, but that
cannot matter to her anymore.
There is a life they live.
Outside, Vavin meanders still
toward Montparnasse.

Here in the Gardens
we may consider darkness.
The beak closes on crumbs,
a hull slits the
underside of water,
roots tat their lace
beneath the ground.
There is the place where
a child's lips meet the
red eagles on a woman's skirt
or where a young man's
fingers turn and turn
against a piece of wool.

Away from green,
the birds move out of reach.
Their down stiffens for
the ministries of air,
and the light is
always hiding
in the spines
of their feathers.

PEEPING TOM

Old Mrs. Munchback
flipped the bird to a cop once.
She yells at everyone
but feeds the neighborhood cats.
Doesn't like kids
but gives us money.
The bullies get double.
I asked my dad about that,
he said it's insurance against vandalism.

She drinks beer right out of the bottle.
Grandma won't talk to her,
says she used to be a flapper;
used to have money too,
before the Depression.
Never goes to church
but gave me a confirmation present.

She slipped on the ice this winter,
broke a hip.
I looked in her windows
to see if she was ok.
"Peeping Tom!" my mom said.
I was grounded
but I have a telescope.

She doesn't use her stove much,
eats a lot of buttered toast dipped in coffee.
When she gets careless with her cigarettes,
I'm afraid to fall asleep.
She used to watch Johnny Carson late at night
but now she listens to the radio and knits.
Sometimes she takes out her husband's old suits
and smells them.
Then she sits on the bed and cries.

THE MAN WHO WAVES

On Pothouse Road there is an old man
who waves, standing by his mailbox
in every weather. I have seen him
under an umbrella, waving through a downpour—
always the same slow back and forth
sweep of his arm from elbow to wrist,
as if he were clearing a space
in his life to see through.

On this gray December day, with its closed
sky, he stands in a green jacket,
offering himself to every car that passes.
When I wave back, he lifts both arms,
wiggles his fingers wildly,
hops up and down. But who could laugh
at the eager, beaked face?
He is so openly
what most of us are in secret.

Last fall my retarded cousin
gleaned a farmer's fields
for ten cents a day; if he could find
more than a wagonload of leavings,
he might get a quarter. In less
than three months, he could buy his aging aunt
a small basket that contained
such a weight of love she could hardly lift it.

I know what I am given.
The old man's stiff-jointed motion
speeds me down the road.
When he's no longer there, I will miss him,
miss some perturbation of the air—
a quickening, a stroke of luck,
a blessing.

DWARF

In a lower corner
Of a tapestry
You carry your hump
Across white flowers
From oak to oak.

The men, the maidens
Do not look at you,
They watch the hunt.
You go bandy-legged
From oak to oak.

They are glad to keep you
Among them.
You make them merry;
They touch your hump
For luck.

Pick these white
Flowers, and smile: in
The unicorn's bestiary
You are unlikely
And exquisite.

DECEMBER

Two nuns from Uganda
arrive
at Cincinnati Airport.
We drive them
the long distance
to our convent
in the country.
They cry out
at the landscape.
Who has sent them
to this place
where everything
is dead?

The ground, hard
and brown,
looks sterile
as the Kalahari.
Trees
like grasping skeletons
reach for sky
cold and flat
as river stones.

They don't know
that crocuses
and daffodils
wait
in shadowed hideouts
for their moment,
wait
till they can
spring out
on the world,
lovely
as their lost
green
Africa.

THE FLOOR

Sometimes I think I can't stand it any more. I know I did a dumb thing, not going to Easter services, and what makes me so depressed is I *knew* it was a dumb thing to do. Jody copped our cottage reports a few weeks ago, grabbed them off the screw's desk when she forgot to lock them up and went off to get something in the cellar, and we all hid in the toilet stalls and read them and found out what evil thoughts the screws are thinking about us. And right there on mine, so important in the screw's mind that she changed to a red pen to write it down, is: "Does not attend church services."

And now as I sit here with my chin in my hand staring at the goddam beautiful rhododendrons blooming under the goddam unbarred window of this goddam nonetheless prison, it seems unbelievable to me that I didn't go to Easter service, the only woman in this cottage not to go, so that Garth had to stay here and miss the service because they can't leave a prisoner alone in the cottage. I shoulda known I was asking for trouble. I don't know what came over me. It was almost like reading that cottage report made me more determined than ever not to go, even though I know those cottage reports are read by my parole advisor, and that's all she knows about how I'm doing. She's gonna base her recommendation to the parole board on those reports and one interview with me, and if you want to get out early you play the game and do what they want you to do. What a jerk I am. I maybe just blew it.

I manage to play the game better than most of the women, most of the time. I bow and scrape and say "yes ma'am" and never get in fights and when I go to work I actually work. I get good work reports. Some of the women think they're cheating the system by working as little as possible, but I see it as one way to get brownie points for getting out, and besides, goofing off actually makes the time go *slower*. When I get into my work the time passes much easier, though it doesn't make me too popular with some of the women.

But there's something about that goddam church service thing that gets to me. We're supposed to have religious freedom in here, including the freedom to *not* go to church, but in practice it doesn't work out that way. No one tells you to go, no one says anything if you *don't* go, but it ends up on your cottage report in red ink. What are you gonna think? That bothers me more than almost anything else around here, though I can't say why. I can put up with feeling degraded all the time, and being pushed around and bellowed at and having no privacy and lousy food and loneliness and depression and boredom and a thousand other tortures of this place, but something in me just won't put up with being forced to go to church when I don't believe all that crap, and I won't pretend to believe it, and I won't go even if it means I spend extra time in this hell hole. I can't even say why it makes me that mad. It's just going too far, that's all. Just going too goddam far. I mean even in prison you got to draw the line somewhere or you can't stay alive inside.

So when they lined up for Easter service this morning I stood out. Garth didn't say anything at all. When they filed out for church I went up to my dorm and Garth went in her office. I laid on my bunk, and the sun and the sweet-smelling spring air were coming in the open window, and something came over me that surprised the hell out of me: I wanted to wax the dormitory floor. I mean, it's a helluva crazy idea because of the way we wax floors in the joint, which is the hardest way possible.

But anyway I go down to the office and ask Garth if she'll open the supply closet because I want to wax the dorm. She looks at me like I must be up to something, because nobody ever volunteers for extra work around here unless they're promised some kind of reward, but she doesn't say anything, and she goes and opens the closet for me. I get a pail and paste wax and one of the old socks we use to put the paste wax in and some liquid wax and the buffer and some rags and the steel wool, and Garth watches me as I pick up every single thing, as if she expects me to pull some trick, and she stands there glaring at me as I lug all this stuff to the stairs.

There are five women in our dorm, sleeping on two bunk beds and one cot, and there's three dressers and three chairs and assorted junk. I push everything down to one end of the room and already I'm wondering what I wanted to do this for. Those bunk beds weigh a ton apiece, and the dressers, crammed full of stuff because they have to be shared by two women each, aren't any too light either. But I'm in it now, and so first I wipe up the loose dust with a soft cloth, then I pour liquid wax on the floor and scrub it down lightly with steel wool—that's how we clean the old wax off. Then I wipe it all up good with some rags, and take a cigarette break while it dries. I wonder if I should do the whole floor with liquid wax first, and then repeat the whole thing with paste wax, but then I would have to move all that furniture twice, so maybe I'd better do one whole half the floor to completion and then the other half.

I put a blob of paste wax in one of the old socks and start rubbing it in the wood. The heat from the friction and from my hand melts the wax just a little so it oozes through the sock and comes out just right. The floor glistens where the sun hits it, a glowing apricot color. This must have been fine wood they built these floors with. As many prisoners as have tramped over it, it still looks good. The air is cool and sweet like only early spring air can be, and there are a few birds singing. They can't help it, they don't know they're on prison ground. All these things, plus the motion of rubbing and rubbing, maybe the monotony and the rhythm of it, and maybe the unusual quiet in the dorm, make me feel peaceful. I don't often get to be alone in the daytime where it's quiet and calm. The more I rub the better I feel. Not happy, exactly, just not feeling the pain that usually stays with me. I'm not even thinking, just feeling the sun and the fresh sweet air and the smell of the flowers.

I push all the furniture all the way to the end of the room I just finished, and I go through the whole procedure again on the other half of the floor. Garth shows up at the door and stands there watching me a few seconds like she can't believe it. She goes away again without saying anything.

At last all the hands and knees work is done, and after putting all the dirty rags and socks and cans and steel wool out in the hall, I turn on the electric buffer and buff the floor down real nice. I'm in a state of mind I don't remember ever being in before, mellow to some Nth degree where it doesn't even matter any more where I am. The humming of the buffer seems like music to me, and the swinging movement of the buffer and the easy rocking motions of my body melt together and become one movement. We're swaying back and forth, back and forth, together in a rhythm I didn't even try for, but it's rhythm all right, and it's a dance. I'm sorry when I finish buffing.

Now I have to shift all the furniture again and buff down the other end. Then I put all the furniture back in its usual place and buff up the marks I made moving it.

That's it, I'm done. I didn't realize how hard I was working, but now my body aches and the fumes from the wax have made my head feel a little weird. Well, that's okay. The sight of the beautiful floor is very satisfying. I don't get to do many things here that I can feel proud of, just work well done, you know? I light a cigarette and lean in the doorway, taking a breather and letting my poor bones rest before I put the stuff away, and while I smoke my cig I admire my floor.

Garth appears before I finish my cigarette. "You can't leave that stuff lying all over the hall," she says.

"I'm just having a smoke," I say. I know she knows I wasn't gonna leave it there. She stands there glaring at me with her feet apart and her hands on her hips, like she always does. I know I better put out my cigarette now and pick up the stuff. I reach out my hand for the bucket and Garth says, "Pick up that bucket." I pick it up. I take a step to where the rags are lying, reach for them to put them in the bucket. "Pick up those rags," says Garth, at the very instant my hand starts moving downward.

Garth is a specialist at the power/humiliation game. She knows that every instinct in the marrow of my bones is rebelling. But if I stop reaching for the rags, if I even hesitate too long, that's it. I've been insubordinate and she can throw me in the hole, and there goes some of my time off for good behavior. There's no one around to witness that I hesitated only a second. But if I go ahead and pick up the rags she's won, too, because she's stolen my right to act on my own, like a human being. She's ordering my every movement as if I were a robot. I'm damned if I do and damned if I don't. It isn't a decision I can take time to ponder over, and the main thing in my life right now is to get out of here on the earliest possible day. If Garth doesn't get my self-respect today she'll get it tomorrow anyway so what's the use?

But when you're thinking survival, thoughts aren't necessarily in words and they can go through your head like a lightning flash. I've considered the whole situation and made my decision in a split second. Even so, I'm sure there's been a flinch in my movement, a hesitation that she can see and gloat over. I'm so enraged that I want to kill her, but another part of the game is that I mustn't let it show. Don't *dare* let it show, or she'll go after that chink and probe at it until she provokes me into something worse than insubordination. I gather all my will to hold on to my feelings.

I gather the rags together, start to pick them all up. "One at a time," says Garth. I pick up a rag and put it in the bucket. I reach for another rag. "Pick up that rag," says Garth. I pick up the second rag and put it in the bucket. I bend down for another rag. "Pick up that rag," says Garth. Oh god. There are six rags, and I see that we're gonna go through this performance with each and every one of them. Time seems to slow down. Because my mind is racing, I feel like I'm in a slow motion movie, or stoned, and there's time to think between every frame. I wonder if it would be better to just tell the bitch off and go to the hole. I've never been made to bend this low. It's like licking somebody's shoes. So what if I lose some good time? Some of the women do that. They figure it's worth it. You got to save your self-respect somehow. It doesn't matter about Garth, she's not gonna respect me no matter what. It wouldn't matter which way I choose, not to her. But it matters to me. If I just tell the bitch off and go to the hole at least I'd respect *myself*. I'm on the brink every second of making that decision, and yet I can't make it. I feel like I'm dangling from a tiny thread that's the only thing holding me from falling into a bottomless pit, and if I even breathe wrong the thread will break and down I'll go. I open my mouth to say something but I choke on my own panic. I can't do it. Yet the more I stall the lower I feel.

Another course occurs to me. I could act like I don't understand what's happening. I could pretend I don't see anything abnormal in what she's doing to me. I could just go ahead and pick up the stuff, piece by piece like she wants, and all the time be smiling and jiving and telling her how nice the sun is and how I enjoyed the quiet and how proud I feel about the floor. I could act like I don't doubt for one minute that she's enjoying the story. I could even say, *Gee, I'm sorry you had to stay in the dorm with me and miss the service.* If I don't take it seriously what would she be left with? Herself as a fool, telling me to pick up every goddam thing while I'm already doing it. After all, I don't have to *believe* what some twisted mind cooks up to make herself feel like God. It strikes me that the whole key is to not believe in *any* of it, to not believe in humiliation, to not believe that going to the hole can grind my spirit to powder. The trouble is it isn't that easy to change what you believe or don't believe. I *know* that if I don't give her the satisfaction of humiliating me she'll just go to more and more extremes trying to get her jollies, and I'll end up in the hole anyway. So I've come around in a circle right back to where I started from, yet I still have a suspicion that some kind of switching around of beliefs would set me free. But how to do that is just out of reach, like a word or song I can't remember. If I could just grasp it something amazing might happen. But I can't convince myself the humiliation isn't real. How can I not believe what I see and hear and feel? It's too scary. All I've *got* is what I see and hear and feel, and if all that isn't real, then there's *nothing*.

Now I realize I've picked up the last of the stuff and it's too late to change tactics anyhow. I've agonized all my time away. The game is over and Garth is in control. We walk to the supply closet with Garth right behind me, as close as she can get without actually stepping on my heels. Crowding me. I think of swinging the bucket right in her face. Garth opens the closet and I put the stuff away. "Stay in the dorm until the others get back," she says. I start to walk away without saying anything. "Baggliazo," she says. I stop and turn around. She waits. Then it occurs to me what she's waiting for. "Yes, ma'am," I say, being careful to say it with just the right amount of humility.

Whales and Nesting Owls

. . . there is
no place far from a nesting owl.

—Marc J. Sheehan,
"Owls

WHEN I'M EXHAUSTED

Sometimes when I'm exhausted
by the blank blue sky,
all the casual hatreds and death,
the reduction of everything
to buying and selling,
I dream about driving up to the Cape
and riding that boat out of the harbor into the feeding
grounds where the captain suddenly cuts the engine
and we drift into that huge silence
filled with expectation.
I want to stand at the rail, blood pumping in my ears
as he rises, slow and enormous, next to the boat,
see the massive back rolling softly above the water,
feel on my face the mist of his breathing,
see the flukes lifted like great wings
as he starts his homeward plunge
and know that for all my longing he's there
beneath the surface, moving serenely,
filling the dark depths with an ancient song.

SNOWFLAKE OR BONE

*The smallest of three California gray whales
trapped in the Beaufort Sea icepack*

He imagines his chainsaw's constant
high-pitched ring filtering down
through the icy sea like sunlight,
her great body circling below,
as intimate now with the percussion
of the pickaxe as a fetus
to the murmur of its mother's heart.

He stoops to tighten a mukluk lace,
examining the bloody ice where she
has chiseled her snout down to bone
against two narrowing windows of sky.

Another whaler suggests that they
put an end to the misery. He
half listens, recalling his first fish
floundering in the stern, his father's
hand firm around squirming silver, his
boyish heart pounding till the fishhead
rinsed over the crimson deck.

Tonight, new chain arrives from Seattle
but the yearling no longer comes for air.
A transistor blares in the distance:
"Whales possess the earth's largest brain."
The sun flares, algae photosynthesize,
plankton feed, bottom fish swallow,
whales consume. Snowflakes drift

over the closing squares, catch
in the wolverine hair of his parka,
melt into weathered crows-feet burning
at a glorious ninety eight point six.

He strikes a match to a Marlboro,
the flame fighting, then snuffed in the wind,
the charred matchhead blown like a tiny bone
onto the blue ice. He strikes a second,
the light as alive in his black eyes
as a boyhood memory,
as the spirit of the whale upon the wind,
no longer matter, but fact.

A PROFITABLE FISHING SEASON

"Can you tell the difference
between male and female kelp?" he asks me, sly.
The ridiculous is our adrenaline today.
We pursue hilarity like an argument.
Yesterday it was anger. Tomorrow,
in a storm, maybe fear. And
after that, only the silence
of exhaustion.
There is nothing left
but this work.
We have been
fishing for forty days.
No cushion now between our ribs
and the hard skiff sides
we lean on. Even
our fingers have thinned.
We are bones against the sea,
cradled in a craft just big enough
to sleep in—but never that—
only this stance, our booted feet spread
wide, backs braced against the wind,
arms dragging the net from
the ocean floor, and
the salmon, always
the salmon, quicksilver or dead, still
heavy in our heavy arms, stacking
like wood around us.
We can't go in, can't stop,
we just keep moving—
like coin machines in a bank,
silver flashing between mechanical arms,
except this silence,
the desperate jokes.

WINTER FISHING

It was my first shanty.
No wonder I left off the roof
and built a floor of nails.
When I stared up at night
the stars were schooled like fish.
I thought, this is what it must be like
to be adrift at sea,
to be a carpenter, an apron full of hooks.

I imagined the sky freezing like a huge pond,
something so deep I could lower a line forever
toward those open mouths.
Perhaps this is the way all fishing begins
or ends, the moon swimming by like a lure,
and me, tugging this line of light, pulling it closer.

WATCHING FISH

A lamp floats on the bedroom window.
Trees on the hill waver
like water plants. In the dark
I see my son, fists clenched,
feet apart, leaning again
toward the fish tank in our friends' house,
where a guppy mouths against the glass,
the bubbles floating up, clear
and indecipherable.
                        When I was small,
my cousin kept a tank
of the common roundtails,
one dot, black or orange, seared
into the body like a stone
whose weight they bore without effort.
I have been so far away
from the pull of those airy circles.

The other world is green. A glass
catfish undulates, translucent,
visible only as an eye
and a dark connecting line
fringed with bone. Black mollies hover,
flashing tender silver at the gills,
like glimpses of some mystery. A betta
darts among the water hyacinths.
My son confronts this fierce grace;
I watch his hands open,
gently fan the air.
                        In one
of his books, pelagic animals
like dandelions moored by threads,
anemones, and twelve-foot red worms
populate the Galapagos Rift.
In another, the fish are utterly simple,
triangles for tails,
no fins, the delicate breathing

invisible, in a land where
trees are green circles. He touches
the pictures indiscriminately,
from no distance.
             I remember
standing with my cousin once,
downstairs in the pet store, swallowed up
inside a cave-like dark, staring at tank
after tank, each lit from within
as if by random jeweled forms.
It's only now I recognize that
what I felt was joy.

Outside the window specks of pink
light begin to drift across
the ice-encrusted waves of snow.
As my son wakes in the next room,
he sings to himself behind
the closed door. What he says
is not yet in our language; syllables
waft into every corner
of the house — an iridescence
that sets the blank square
of the window shimmering.
                 I stand close
to the glass. Fish swim
through the needles of the pine,
and my son watches them avidly.
The wall between us is absolutely clear.
He has no fear. I can see
him entering the water.

RED IN THE MORNING

(sailors take warning).
  Split the lark — and you'll find the music —
  . . . Scarlet Experiment! . . .
  Now, do you doubt that your Bird was
  true?
                                    —Emily Dickinson

When the cardinal
comes to the empty feeder
which the squirrel with the broken leg
has just emptied onto the ground
I know it's time.

When, in this same morning
I see the large raw patch on the squirrel's haunch
near his dragging leg,
and he limps as fast as he can away
from my coffee-cup clad figure
down the path covered with creeping thyme just
beginning to bloom,

And, at the end of the path, I see
that weed with the small spade-shaped leaves
which is completely covered with a maroon-red blight,
I stop looking at the blooming and crimson
begonias, the flowers of
the scarlet runner beans,
the tiny-ribbed star-shaped red dahlia
and summer's frosting, the lush and grateful
red and white impatiens crowding over
their stone-edged beds.

No Rapaccini's daughter, I.
But I come here mornings for escape
from the inner rebellions of my body,
from the hospital red smears and knife warnings.
I come to think of nature
not red in tooth or claw.

With my morning cup,
this sailor's daughter gives up the Pacific
and accepts the midwest ground instead. She
does not need or want scruff and blood. Even the cardinal's
signal beauty seems ominous
as birds break their necks trying to eat from
empty feeders. And she not the filler;
only the Watcher on deck this morning where scarlet
seems at the least
a warning.
Certainly not,
an experiment.

THE SHOWING

Hunting for mushrooms, Agnes Dillon kept up a little counterpoint of prayer that she would not come upon one of her husband Keith's traps; it was sure to have in it a small corpse — a bog lemming or a meadow vole, a shrew or a mole or a whitefooted mouse. She never knew so kind a man to wreak such havoc. Since his retirement to the north woods, after years of teaching biology at the state university, he had fought the idea that his productive days were over by launching, in a frenzy of research, one experiment after the other. The snap traps, fifty of them, were set out in grids each night to determine something called "territorial invasiveness." Agnes wished the attractive little rodents had the sense to stay at home.

It was early May. There were still a few white rags of snow on the north facing slopes of the hills. The undecided spring breezes blew warm and cold. In the bright spring light, the blankness of the leafless trees gave an empty look to the woods. The patches of violets, in Easter colors of purple and yellow, were like bouquets of flowers set about an unfurnished room.

Agnes entered the woods of their neighbor, Mr. Selkirk, who appeared only during the deer hunting season when his enthusiasm and poor marksmanship confined Agnes and Keith to their cabin. Since Mr. Selkirk's land was not his to tamper with, Keith seldom went there. Agnes went often, hoping her repeated presence would send Mr. Selkirk's deer elsewhere.

As she bent to pick a little huddle of morels, her knees cracked and the binoculars strung around her neck thumped heavily against her chest. Close to the earth she could smell the rank odor of wild leek. The morels were cool and damp in her hand. A red spider scurried through the convolutions of one of them. She shook the spider gently onto the ground and dropped the morels into a string bag. As she carried the bag along, the spores from the gathered mushrooms would scatter productively over the earth.

There was shuffling of dry leaves. Peering through the binoculars she saw a bird with olive-brown back and pink legs. She was pleased. You often heard oven birds nattering at you from the hidden depths of a tree but you seldom saw them. She hoped it would stay where it was. Keith had left their cabin at five that morning weighed down with yards of mist netting. He was banding birds, anxious to get his hands on the little migrating warblers.

Looking up, Agnes saw what she thought was a mourning dove. She raised her binoculars. Mourning doves usually kept to town back yards. It was certainly the right shape: the ball-like body, the sharply pointed tail, the neck and head that formed a hook, but the bird was too large and the color wrong; instead of a pale mauve gray, its back was slate and its chest reddish. She knew the name of the bird, but was afraid to say it. In a moment it would fly away and she could pretend it had never been there.

Perversely the bird remained perched on the tree, its colors bright against the dark green of the hemlock. It was a passenger pigeon. Yet that was impossible. The last one had died seventy years ago, a pitiful captive in some zoo. Passenger pigeons once surged through the sky like great feathered rivers; then their nesting grounds, the forests of pine and birch, were cut down. The pigeons were killed and sold by the millions to fancy restaurants. Even the squabs were snatched from their nests. Then disease had come along to trouble them, and the passenger pigeon, beseiged on every side, had disappeared from the face of the earth.

As Agnes watched, the pigeon flew off. She sank down on a patch of moss and listened to the knocking of her heart. She felt she had been picked up bodily and shaken, but she did not doubt. Since there was so much that was not known, she believed anything was possible. On her morning walks she had discovered holes in the ground, tunnels across the road, a pile of feathers — things that had gone on while she wasn't watching. For thirty years she had wondered how the birch bark she found scattered about in the woods was pulled from the trees; then one day she saw the wind unwind a swatch of bark like a bandage. You could probe and dissect all you liked, but the important thing was to be there. Perhaps there were many passenger pigeons but until now, no one had been there to see them.

Keith would be astonished when she told him, but she made no move in the direction of their cabin. Last year an eagle had flown over their pond. She watched it grazing the tops of the trees and marveled at how much of the sky the bird took up. She told Keith, who, full of excitement, had called several colleagues. Fanning out through the woods, they had found the hodgepodge of the eagle's nest at the top of a pine tree. At once they set up an observation platform in a large maple near the nest. The men were possessive and secretive like boys building a tree house. They believed because of their research, eagles everywhere would be better off. They were against ignorance, even mystery. Between them they manned the platform twenty-four hours a day. The second week of the encampment, the harassed eagles abandoned their young and were never seen again.

Keith waved to her from the other side of the pond. He was a slight and agile man and looked engagingly boyish. He had stretched his net between two oaks. As she drew closer she could see, fluttering in the interstices of the net, small brown and yellow birds struggling to free themselves. Keith gently untangled a warbler from the netting and clamped a band around its leg. The bird, stricken, lay for a moment in Keith's hand, and then, seeing its chance, flew off.

"Aggie, dear, look here, a chestnut-sided warbler. We haven't had one in a couple of years." His face was sweet with pleasure.

"But it's dead," Agnes said. The diminutive brown and rust bird lay imprisoned in the net, its neck awkwardly twisted.

"Yes, it's a pity." He regarded Agnes more closely. "You look flushed." He laid his hand gently on her forehead. "Warm. Better go in the house and have a rest. I'll fix us a nice morel omelet as soon as I finish here."

Entering the house, Agnes was confounded by the familiarity of their living room: the rugs faintly soiled along the usual paths from one known room to another, the residual smell of Keith's pipe, the ticking of the grandfather clock Keith had spent months making for her. Everything conspired to turn the passenger pigeon into an illusion. As always the familiar overpowered the unfamiliar. She wondered how the saints clung to their visions.

Agnes, thinking of the birds struggling in the net, kept her secret through dinner. As usual she knitted while they watched the evening television news; knitting seemed to give the disorderly events a sense of tidiness. Could she possibly keep from Keith the ornithological happening of the century? He would report the bird, of course; it would make his reputation. His picture would appear in all the papers, perhaps on television as well. She looked suspiciously at the screen, remembering the rare shore bird that had been reported on the east coast a few years before. The networks had shown it hopping along the sand surrounded by hundreds of bird fanciers who had flown in from all over the country, greedy to add the accidental to their life lists. In the face of so many people, the passenger pigeon would desert its nest and any chance of its multiplying would be lost. Still, Agnes thought, it might be that she could win Keith over to secrecy.

"Do you remember," she asked him, "when we were in that redwoods park in California and we saw the quote from Walt Whitman?" There had been a display explaining the history of the redwood trees. The legends on the signs were terse and factual but the last one was the Whitman quote: "You must not know too much or be too precise or scientific about birds and trees and flowers; a certain vagueness—perhaps ignorance, credulity—helps your enjoyment of these things."

"I suppose by now his boss has seen the sign and given whoever put it up the heave ho," Keith said. "A scientific display is no place for romance."

"I don't think he was being romantic," Agnes told him. "He was talking about mystery."

"Same thing." He handed her a journal open to a picture of a hawk wrapped in leather straps. "Just look at that transmitter harness. If we did that with our hawks we could find exactly where they're nesting. All you would need is a mobile tracking unit and a portable receiver."

"What if they don't want you to know?" she asked.

"Animals are not creatures from the pages of *Winnie the Pooh*," Keith said. "They don't think about things. They just are. Besides the population of the roughlegged hawks has been going down. We need to know why."

At this she fell silent, for not long ago the number of robins had begun to dwindle. By banding the flocks that remained, Keith had learned the robins that had fallen off were the ones digging for worms in nearby potato fields. His discovery led to the banning of a pesticide. Now the robins were back in force. What had she with all her sentimentality done for those robins?

In bed that night she could feel Keith's reassuring warmth just inches away. It was hard to imagine him keeping a secret from her, or even having one. She considered her silence a deception and felt guilty. She did not know why she had been chosen to see the passenger pigeon. Her life seemed so ordinary: housework, walks in the woods, her daughter and the grandchildren. There had been days when she worried that the Lord had not noticed her in all that uneventful sameness. She had found herself wishing something exceptional would happen to her. This desire had frightened her, for she feared being pushed forward into the world where visibility would make her vulnerable. She knew there was safety in her inconsequence. Still, she had thought there must be more to life, or at the very least, she had not counted correctly everything she had. Now her singularity distressed her.

In the morning Keith emptied the refrigerator of several dead birds, fatalities of his previous day's netting, and took them off to prepare. It was a delicate skill which Keith did well. He had drawers full of little feathered shells of various unthinking birds. When she held the skins in her hand, Agnes was overcome by their emptiness.

Out of doors Agnes was glad to enter a world where things grew and moved. Reluctantly she breached the spider webs stretched across her path, someone's work gone for nothing. She scanned first one tree and then another, hastily at first and then slowly and more carefully. This time it was a beech tree. She followed the creased, wrinkled gray trunk two-thirds of the way up and found the pigeon shifting restlessly from branch to branch. After a while the bird flew off to a farther tree. When she followed, it moved farther still, and finally was gone, releasing her. She told herself that if she were to keep her secret she ought to find out if there were going to be more passenger pigeons. Each time she saw the bird she must mark the direction of its flight to help her locate the nest.

It was a pity she could not ask for Keith's help. He was experienced at finding the nests of birds and wrote expert papers on their location, on the number of eggs and when the birds fledged. The papers carried a caveat explaining the mortality rate of the nests he observed was apt to be high since a fox or raccoon sometimes followed his scent. She decided not to search out the possible nest of the passenger pigeon.

Agnes began to rise early. Each morning she went out to confront the bird. That was how she thought of the witnessing of its appearance. If *it* were there, then *she* must be there; it was the least or the most she could do. She saw it on dull days when its red chest seemed merely rufous and on bright days when its breast, touched by the sun, glowed brightly. By early June it was flying off with insects in its mouth. Carrying them to its young? In her excitement she could almost imagine how delicious the crisp green bugs might taste.

A morning late in June came when the passenger pigeon was not there. A white-throated sparrow sang. A flock of cedar waxwings with their black bandit masks stole from a Juneberry bush. Any other day these sights would have been enough. If something had happened to the pigeon, she accused herself, it would be her fault. As soon as someone gave you a gift, you were responsible for it. Agnes stayed in the woods all day searching for the bird, going without breakfast or lunch, returning home weak and shaky in time to make dinner, so Keith would not be suspicious. Luckily he was occupied with a loon he had caught in one of the floating bail traps he set out for ducks. He had been wanting to band the loon for some time but the loon was seclusive. Agnes had once seen it on a remote lake where it had gone to molt. Hundreds of its curled breast feathers had blown over the surface of the lake, coming to rest on the water like fanciful barques. Since the loon could not escape into flight during its molting period, she had neglected, at the time, to say anything to Keith.

The next day the pigeon was back. Twice that week she missed it. She began to attend daily Mass, appealing to a higher authority to tell her what to do about the pigeon. In those early morning hours even close friends slipped in and out of the church without a word to one another, their evasive, conspiratorial looks and cryptic smiles acknowledging the trials that lay behind so fervent a devotional practice. Although Agnes was regular, no answer came down.

In August, Agnes's and Keith's daughter, Carol, and Carol's husband, Robert, came to spend a week, bringing with them their sons, eight-year-old Blake and six-year-old Terry. The grass had faded to a gray brown, and along the roadside you could see the harbinger of a few red leaves. A cold rain began to fall and would not stop. Keith built fires to keep the damp out of the house. They stayed inside and played five-hundred rummy and watched old westerns on TV. Locked in the house together for days, Agnes felt their edges dissolve and meld. Occasionally one of them would disappear into a bedroom to write letters or read, but in minutes they would be back to look out of the window with the others, as though the storms were a command performance. Only Terry kept to himself. He filled the bathtub with pillows and closing the shower curtain, used the bath sponge to paste stickers in a notebook.

Agnes never stopped thinking of the passenger pigeon, worrying that the unseasonable weather might send it precipitously south. She had already sighted an early flock of snow buntings, a sure sign of fall, their white wings fluttering in the air like the blizzards to come.

On the last day of the visit they awoke to find the walls of their bedrooms kindled by the sun. Carol said at breakfast she felt light and might at any moment float off her chair. They planned a picnic for the afternoon. Keith and Robert went off to dismantle a beaver lodge to see what means the beavers used to protect themselves from invaders. The boys were invited but only Blake went along. Terry looked unhappy at the idea, asking, "Why do you want to wreck their house?" Carol suggested she and Agnes pick blackberries for jam.

"They'll be too full of water to cook up properly," Agnes said. "I'm just going out for a little walk. Terry, do you want to come along?" The boy followed her outside.

Everything glittered in the new sun. The wet tree trunks were slick black glass. On the leaves, drops of water flashed white and gold. Agnes pointed out a hawk working its wings, climbing higher and higher like a child pumping a swing. Terry paid polite attention. Unlike her older, more boisterous grandchild, Terry was reflective. Hours after you told him something, he would ask a question that showed he had been examining what you said, as he might inspect a shiny beetle to see if it were the biting kind.

When they reached Mr. Selkirk's woods, Agnes cautioned the boy to be still. "We're waiting for something," she said. He accepted her words and worked at trying to see what his grandmother was looking for. When the passenger pigeon appeared in a nearby beech tree, Terry responded to her excited signal. "There," she whispered, pointing, "there on the branch. Do you see it?"

The boy nodded, satisfied.

She told him how the passenger pigeons had ranged over the forests of North America; how the last great nesting of the birds had been only a few miles from where she and Terry were sitting; how their numbers were once so great the branches on which they roosted would break under their weight; how the flocks, passing overhead, would eclipse the light of the sun; how they sounded like a great wind rushing by; how the birds were unafraid of people and would hover about them, lighting on their shoulders and arms; how people followed the birds with clubs and nets and destroyed them.

When the bird flew away, Terry frowned. "You must not tell anyone what you saw," Agnes warned him. He nodded. She did not think he would say anything. If he did, she would explain she had been telling him the story of the passenger pigeon and his imagination carried him away.

Showing the pigeon to Terry had been a relief. The loneliness of the solitary witness was gone. Still, she regretted having to keep a secret from Keith. Perhaps it was this regret that stopped her from diverting Keith when he suggested a walk in Mr. Selkirk's woods; with the children's departure they had found the house ghostly. Keith had his butterfly net. "There used to be some *polyxenes asterius* over there," he said. "I might take a few home and breed them." He seldom went outside without a purpose.

The summer's last flowers were blooming. As they walked along Keith recited their Latin names: *Hesperis matronalis, Geranium pratense, Daucus carota, Pyrolaceae.* Agnes felt he was casting a spell. She stepped along beside him, silently giving their real names back: dame's rocket, cranesbill, Queen Anne's lace, Indian-pipe.

Keith was searching among the white tracery of wild carrot for swallowtails. Had she remained quiet he might have missed it, but in spite of herself she cried out, "Keith, it's the passenger pigeon." She longed to share her gift.

Startled, he looked up. There in the beech tree was the bird, its head tilted slightly sidewise, its chest ruby in the sun. "Mourning dove," he said absently, picking apart an oak gall to get at the curled white wasp larva inside.

"Keith, *look* at it. I've watched it all summer. It *is* a passenger pigeon." She couldn't bear his indifference.

He turned away from the bird. "Aggie, you're a hopeless romantic. *Helenium autumnale,*" he intoned, "*Mitchella repens, Lychnis coronaria.*"

For a moment his doubt was catching. Then, feeling a great sorrow for him, she slipped her hand in his. "Goldenrod," she urged gently, "sneezeweed, blazing star."

CROWS

1.

Last night a black bird
flew down the chimney,
fluttered on the floor
between us, broken,
then flew up into
your open mouth
which spoke on as if nothing
had happened.

"Are you all right"
I asked, and as
I spoke, a flutter
of wings in my throat
as my black heart flew back up
the chimney, into
the night and the snow still falling.

2.

There are moments when feathers
that aren't good
for flying or good looks
cover my body

and I must stay
inside, plucking
my feathers, licking
the small drops of blood.

OWLS

Keith says it, so it must be true: there is
no place far from a nesting owl. A mile
is the farthest that we're ever away.
Only our trafflc keeps us from hearing
the nocturnal down-rush-of-preying wings.

I can believe it, having heard that sound
in a swirl of taloned snow. What is it
that they hold in those claws? and what keeps me
from getting out of bed and preying? why
have I looked at *Like Wings* without buying?

I don't believe, Madame Tussaud, that these
wings are likely to help me fly, they're
surely no stronger than a pair of wax
lips which melt under their first real kiss—
even the moon would be too much for such flight.

Our bodies, I'm told, shed some gram of weight
at death, which leads the sham evangelists
to say the soul has flown this cage of bones.
But it may be nothing more than sorrow
having to migrate, being homeless again.

The owl's wings seem too light to keep aloft
a body more palpable than sorrow.
Yet it does, and with little ceremony.
I didn't know before I was told that birds
of prey must be desperate to scavenge.

CHECKING THE NEIGHBOR'S DEER

1

There is no need to check for death,
the eyes gone to the color of smoke.
The boy holds the deer in his arms,
pretends to make it come back to life.
They have the heart pickled in the refrigerator,
and on one of those long winter nights
in a whiskey dream
my neighbor will take it secretly
into his backyard,
reach into the jar
and pull the white heart
free of its juices,
eating it completely,
staring up at the moon,
listening to his own heart,
that voice he hears in his blood
pulling him farther into his darkness.

2

A man comes hard by this sweetness
of muscle.
In dreams he will watch the arrow
move in slow motion away from the bow,
and again and again feel himself
cutting deep, deeper,
down into the belly,
the steam rising from the carcass,
filling his nostrils
with a kind of mist.

3

I feel slowly along the mid-line
of my stomach,
knowing that somewhere in there

are the old mechanisms of staying alive.
I wonder how it would be to hang my body
in the garage,
the only sound coming from the friction
between rope and rafter,
waiting for someone to come in
and run their hands over thirty-three years
of sinew and flesh.
But this is the heart I want for myself,
this is the heart which senses
blue eyes turning to smoke,
this heart knows that death
moves through the body like a slow knife,
muffling the sounds of weather,
dulling the vision,
and sends the mind running for cover,
as if this running could still the heart.

DRAFT PONIES

I

These big draft ponies work all winter
instead of mechanical tractors
and skidders, from dawn

to mid-afternoon pulling
and pushing logs, fence posts,
piles of brush. Even when

nuzzling a human palm
they are harnessed to ropes
or the chains that pry

stumps upright and free.
By March the new growth
of fir and spruce is gone,

an old field ready for the new,
in the middle the old butternut
bearing every two years.

Then let loose near the barn
and limited by the battery
wire strung from stump to post

and back again,
the ponies forage beneath snow,
dull hooves pawing the ground.

II

On this Wednesday late after a spring
snow even the wire is grounded.
Two foot drifts and a white

sea. Out the window the yard
empty. They have gone, great
brawny giants whose tracks

are huge holes in the snow.
Their bellies sway.
Big hunks of ice and dirt

hang from their fetlocks.
Their huge balloon haunches
take them anywhere

they want to go, past
the mail box and the rutted
driveway, through stand after stand

of new birch and old,
over the hard earth they have rooted.
They clump across the airport

runway below the control tower
splashing in puddles
or stand in a white

backyard between two bungalows
as the sun goes down, like moose,
deer, creatures of another life.

HORSES

We left the camp and climbed the hill,
the fire behind us toiling slowly
as it boiled maple sap down to syrup.
I had been thinking about horses;
always laboring to pull the stump,
the plow, or the wagon.

We knew the neighbor's horses
would be standing beside the cedar barn,
heads together, straight-legged.
And as we ran there,
the moonlight pulled single pines
from the blur of forest.

In the paddock, two roans
came close to sniff our pockets.
We had saved apple cores,
and the horses took them,
their wide teeth crushing them.

The horses, too, yearned
for the snow to leave,
for the pasture to open up in green.
We stood together there for a while
under that heavy white light,
the horses locked in a kind of balance,
as if they braced against the ground
to escape the earth's mad turning.

And I knew something about transition,
the way that even people
who've shared campfires
end up walking for miles
in opposite directions,
leaning forward as if straining
to pull something large and heavy behind them.

MORNING MILK

In winter dark and cold
we went out at the urging
of my father
my sleepy brothers and I

to the low-roofed barn
and our makeshift stanchions
just as the sky was going
from purple to ruby
and those heavy gentle cows
came eagerly to our
young hands

they chewed their hay
standing in the new light
as we took our low places
and began with those heavy
udders the techniques
our father taught us
in love when he urged us
out of warm beds
in winter dark and cold

we had trouble at first touching
our hands always to that ripe
full roughness and almost
happy flesh giving us
warm liquid from our pulling
fingers like magic each
morning a mass we celebrated
and walked from the barn
with those heavy galvanized
pails like sinners absolved
into the white new day

*JULY 4*TH

Larkspur reaches
purple and pink toward
the hollyhock sun by the back door;
the pregnant tabby
pushes five greedy kittens
away from her dish.

Next to the barn,
shedding its gray skin,
three retriever pups tumble
over pretzled feet,
making the dust glow
around their mother.

Wheat spreads
the color of miracles,
corn rubs thick
against our legs,
and twenty brown cows
follow the afternoon home.

MY BROTHER'S KEEPER

The ape grabs me
with prehensile eyes,
asks me why I have
evolved according to Darwin
while she has not. Even
her hairy baby is
unevolved. For five
million years
she has waited in vain
to be free
to visit herself
at the zoo. She picks
nits off her baby
and stares at my feet
dodging Lysol

puddles near
a rusty cage where
a lemon-lime parrot
picks at day-old bread.
Plucked from the rain forests
of Brazil, he squawks his
bilingual sounds.
Parrot is his native tongue,
but in his Pidgin
English he strains
something like "Amazon
grass seed, raspberries,
cacao."

Away from the animal house
my feet chatter down the sidewalk
dodging ricocheting echoes
of my name.

OCTOBER WIND

Today the flies came out, to buzz
drunkenly against the screen. One lies
on its back against the floor and cuts
a mad circle every few minutes. Their bodies
dot the inside of my ceiling light.
No matter how many I kill there are more
that wish to die. I could feel them
sleeping all these months inside the wall.
They dreamed of awkward wings and shriveled legs
walking sideways, too crazed to fly,
even when I lift my foot and slowly
crush them. "Let us buzz,"
they whisper in my left ear. "Such is life:
A slow buzz interrupted by demented stillness—"
but I cannot help myself and my foot
crushes and they gasp. More wake
with a start
to the darkness I keep hidden in my walls. "Come out,"
calls the October wind. "There is overcast
and iron light beyond the screen.
Wake up and dash your brains
until you drive the social worker mad."
"Remind him," the wind goes on,
(and I sometimes think I hear it)
"That he has death in his soft, pink hands,
remind him death waits within his walls
and sleeps at midnight beside his wife
and wakes at dawn and is his own body."

MOTHS

The house begins to leak light
and they are with us, smudged
against windowpanes, or, folding themselves
inside, circling the wire of light.
The color of ash, of leaves, of
old paper, they swirl at the light's
edge, above us, a circle of hands
or scars, faces in a dream.
They would learn our names, our
histories, fasten their furious soft
wings on mouths to suck out
whatever we can't find words for.

It is not enough. They
rise against the ceiling like a hard
sky they can't get through,
begin to hit their wings against it,
over and over, before diving in to kiss
the bulb, the flame's small ache.
Tomorrow we will find them
there—sloughed skin, thumbnails—
piling up in corners like fluff
until we're unable to speak, to move.

Omens of Fire and Ice

Even in winter I open every window
against the smoke dreamed into my lungs.

—Jack Driscoll,
"The Love and Fear of Fire"

BROTHER FIRE

It took years. At first a gust
flared past — a week of smoke,
long rains with charcoal floods
across, and slow green coming back,

Then several fires a year. By then
the land appeared in its long lines
of hill and valley. Grass came
quietly, small willows, cottonwood
colonies, birds everywhere.

We have the world now, given back
from those tyrants who shadowed all
our paths. We have overcome. Our land
belongs to everyone; we can see it
rolling out, free. Fire did it for us.

NATURAL DISASTERS

Along June Street, winged seeds spun in long vertical curves, tapping the sidewalk and street, falling into puddles, or landing between blades of new grass. Red and white peonies, some large as soup bowls, bobbed on stems. The morning was already warm. Pretty day, Alec thought, avoiding a puddle. Nice time of year. Straight ahead, the sidewalk seemed to end in blue-gray cloud. Gonna storm, though.

As usual he had on work clothes, the same type of clothing he'd been wearing for over fifty years: dark gray shirt and pants, visored cap, steel-toe boots gray from the cement dust still embedded in the leather. "It don't matter what I wear," he told his daughter who wanted him to dress up a little now that he was retired. The shirts she gave him on his birthdays and Christmas were in the bottom drawer of his bureau, still brand new. He liked his work clothes the best, but he noticed something funny lately. His collars rode higher; the shoulders sagged, and the cuffs of both shirts and pants drooped more than ever. That morning he'd given them an extra roll.

Another three blocks, and he turned into the Blue Bird tavern. At nine-thirty in the morning, the place was as quiet as his parlor.

"*Jak sie masz*," he greeted two men at the bar. "How are you?"

"*Dobrze, dobrze*," Ignatz Zacharias said without any rise in his voice. "Good."

"How ya doin'?" Marvin Earle said.

"Oh, can't complain."

Not much to say after they'd worked all night, Alec knew. Just finish their beer, then go home and sleep till four or five. He looked sideways at Ignatz Zacharias. Getting gray. They had a saying at the plant: grayer you get, closer you were to that gold watch. Not youngsters like Marvin Earle, though. Not yet anyways. By the time they got Ignatz's age — or his, for that matter — you wouldn't be able to tell 'em apart from the gray scrub and roads around the plant. Even the lake curving in toward the plant had a coating of gray to it. He looked at his own hand resting on the bar. Gray as ash.

Ray, the new owner, poured Alec's coffee and pushed the cup into a square of light. "Say, Alec," he said. "That guy ever get ahold of you?"

Alec put his cap on the bar. His hand wasn't steady, and his heart started acting up. "What guy?"

Ray leaned against the shelf holding liquor bottles and folded his arms. "Hell, I don't know. Some guy from around Detroit was here looking for you yesterday."

"Detroit, you say?" Alec rubbed the bony knob behind his right ear. "Hell, I don't know nobody there."

"That's for sure," Marvin snorted.

"Well," Ray said, taking Ignatz's empty glass, "some guy was in here yesterday, askin' about you. I thought I better not say where you live. He was real jumpy. Spooked." Ray worked the tap for draft beer and set a full glass next to a circle of coins. "So I told him you come in here mornings and he just turned around and left. You know," Ray swept two coins into the palm of one hand, "if he wasn't so polite and dressed up and all, I'd say he was some kind of crook or something."

"Probably is anyways," Marvin said.

Ignatz laughed. "Those are the ones to keep an eye on, all right."

Alec watched steam rising from his coffee. "Well, boys," he said, "I guess someone finally found out who's who around here." His mouth twitched to show he was making a joke. He split open a packet of sugar and emptied it into his coffee. "And about time," he added. His mouth twitched again.

"Hey," Marvin said, "maybe it's for 'This Is Your Life.'"

"Hell, no," Ray said. "They took that off years ago."

After his coffee, a shot of whiskey, and a beer, Alec left. It wasn't much of an outing, but it was enough. When he got home, the day didn't stretch out as far as it had when he'd first opened his eyes in the morning.

The next day, Alec walked to the Blue Bird over a thick pad of wet seed wings and red tassels. After the storm there'd been a cold snap in the night, so he wore his red plaid jacket. In the yards peonies lay beaten down, their petals strewn over the grass. They should stake 'em, Alec thought. The wind and the rain. That's what had done it. The cold would be good for the blackberries, though.

"Al," Ray said in a low voice, when Alec took his stool at the bar. "There's the guy that was looking for you." He nodded toward a table.

Alec turned his head slowly, just enough to get a look. The man was staring at him. Alec turned away, his eyes going blank. He heard the man's chair scrape back. Jesus, he said to himself, and made a fist with one hand, wrapped it in the other, and held both in close against his jacket. In the mirror he watched the man moving toward him. Marvin and Ignatz were watching too. Alec looked down at the bar and gripped his fist more tightly. Then he felt the man's presence and turned.

The man—slight, middle-aged, worn out—had wedged himself between the stools. He had a face like the moon, Alec thought, all splotched. "Mr. Rukowski?" the man said. His thin lips parted in a shaky smile.

Alec studied the bright flecks in the man's brown jacket. "That's right," he finally said.

"The name's Walter Leska."

Before Alec could place the name, the man's hand was there at his elbow, and he had to take hold of it to be polite. A weak handshake, Alec thought. Damp, cold skin. He withdrew his hand quickly.

The man slid onto the next stool, brushed at his jacket, then drew a handkerchief from a pocket and dabbed at his face. "Cold today," he said. "Yesterday hot as hell and today cold." His hand shook as he put away the handkerchief.

Alec looked out the diamond-shaped window set in a wall of thick, cubed and rippled glass. Beyond the street, gritty with cement dust, beyond a field of scrub poplar, dusty and stunted, a gray shimmer of water rose into the sky. He couldn't tell where one ended and the other began.

"But they call it God's country up here, don't they?" the man said, tearing open a pack of cigarettes. His fingernails were bitten close to the skin, and he fumbled with his cigarettes and slapped his pockets, looking for his lighter, and all the while his leg worked like a jack-hammer. He said he'd come up to do some fishing, but in the next minute he said, no, not fishing—he'd just wanted to "take a ride up north." Holding the cigarette between forefinger and thumb and taking short puffs, he talked about a cousin—Stan Adamski on Third Street—and asked if Alec knew him. He waved his hand and ash fell to the bar, fell over his jacket. His wife Sophie, he explained, had told him to take a little trip—the change would do him good. But then he said she didn't know he'd gone; he'd just started driving and had found himself "way the hell north" and so he'd kept going. When Ray poured him some coffee, the man reached in his pocket and brought out a handful of crumpled bills and coins. His hand shook, and he spilled the money over the bar.

Alec wanted to edge away, slip out, but just when he thought he could, the man—Walter Leska—would turn to him, his mouth working like it wanted to get rid of something. But Walter Leska couldn't get rid of it, couldn't say what he wanted to say. Holding the cigarette, he bowed his head and pressed the bridge of his nose with the back of his hand. Alec worried he might set his hair on fire. "Better watch that cigarette," he told him, but he could see the man wasn't listening. Ignatz and Marvin said they had to go, and on the way out, they gave Walter Leska an odd look. He'd begun to laugh—a high-pitched woman's laugh—for no reason at all. Still laughing, he bent suddenly to pick up his handkerchief that had fallen between the stools. Alec lifted his whiskey glass, waited until fumes burned the lining of his nose, then tilting back his head, threw down the whiskey. He wished he hadn't come.

Finally Walter Leska stopped laughing. Taking a deep breath, he wiped his face, then spoke with care, as if repeating a lesson. "The thing is," he said slowly, "I was wondering if maybe you could tell me something about the Metz fire. The one in 1908. I was reading about it in some old newspapers. Ran across your name."

Alec brought the empty glass in close to his jacket. Clouds of smoke rose and fell in the mirror. His voice dry, cracking, he said, "You kind of hate to bring it up when it's done and gone." He set the glass gently on the bar and brought the cold beer bottle to his lips. After he'd swallowed half the beer and wiped his chin, he said, "Better to let sleeping dogs lay."

Years ago, Alec remembered, a reporter had come snooping around, asking everybody questions about the big fire. People didn't get enough excitement, had to go prying around everybody's business. Hell with that. After the fire, too, people had tried to get him to talk about it. He never did, and damned if he'd start now. He did have those pictures cut from his aunt's newspapers, and he knew right where they were. Down-cellar in a trunk. Probably all moldy. He saw himself walking down there — but that was *talk* for you. Already it was all coming back.

Walter Leska held the handkerchief half over his eyes, like a bandage. "My mother," he said quietly, "went through that fire."

"Your mother, you say?" Alec peered at the man.

"She was born near Metz, grew up there. Milly Ceslek was her name before she married. You might of knew her." He raised the handkerchief to his lips.

"Why," Alec said, "I knew a Milly Ceslek." The words were out before he could stop them. He rubbed the bony knob behind his ear. "Why sure." Long brown hair, he recalled. Always wore pretty bows. Lived three farms away. It don't seem possible, he thought, glancing at the man's ruined face.

Walter shuddered, as if cold, and took a deep breath. "I thought you might of knew her. You're about her age," he said. Then, resting his elbows on the bar, he brought his hands together and leaned his forehead on them. Finally, he raised his head. "She died, oh, a year ago."

Alec dug a fingernail into the beer bottle's label. Someone put money in the juke-box, and he was almost glad for the music, but it made things strange. Now all this seemed like a dream and back then, the fire, the only real thing. For years it'd been the opposite way around. His fingernail tore through the label.

Ray stood before them. "Anything to drink?" he asked Walter.

"Drink?"

"Something other'n coffee?" Ray suggested.

"Sure," Walter said. "I'll have something. Why not?"

"What'll it be then?" Ray held the empty cup and saucer.

Walter looked at his thumb, bit the nail, then suddenly laughed. "Hell," he said, waving his hand. "I'll have whiskey! It's a vacation, ain't it?" He turned to Alec. "Firewater, they call it, don't they?" He laughed like somebody already drunk.

He's crazy, Alec thought. He finished his beer and slid the empty toward Ray. "Again," he said, and Ray brought the drinks.

Walter stared at the wedge of whiskey, lifted the glass, set it down, lifted it again, finally drank it all at once. Sweat broke out, and he wiped lips and forehead, then talked about having to lay off drinking and smoking. "Doctor said, 'What's worrying you, Walt, money?' " But it wasn't money, Walter said, and told Alec how, after his father died, his mother "went strange"—not eating right and "craziest of all" starting to smoke, then dropping matches and cigarettes everywhere and burning pans on the stove. "So I says to Sophie, we got to do something."

Biting a fingernail, Walter told how everything was O.K. at first. They'd gone shopping for a bed to fit in the sewing room, found matching blue bedspread and curtains, and fixed up the room real nice. But the house was too small for all of them, and the kids started staying away, "God knew where," Walter said. And then it all started again—the matches and cigarettes on the floor, the burnt pans on the stove. But there was more. His wife Sophie would get these crying jags and look at him like it was all his fault.

The Blue Bird began to fill up; music played, chairs scraped against tile, men laughed. Walter, his leg pumping on the rung of the stool, talked of a sister—Marian—who'd married a big-shot dentist in Arizona. At first Marian said no when he called to ask if their mother could go there; then she'd changed her mind, but by then, it was too late. "Ma starts crying," he said, "when Sophie and me try to tell her about the orange trees, the swimming pool. Everything you could want, we say. But no. She don't want it."

Walter twisted the empty cigarette pack, then found a full one. He broke into the new pack, lit a cigarette, then tapped a coin on the bar. When Ray came, he ordered more drinks, but Alec didn't want anything, and Walter had to drink alone, talking of Marian. At one point his voice rose angrily. "And Marian says, get this, we have to live our own lives and can't be responsible forever. Jesus! Not responsible! Who the hell is, I ask her, if it ain't us?" Others at the bar leaned forward to look at him, then turned away. Walter went on, raving about Marian, telling how she said he was making himself sick, how he should take care of himself for his wife and kids, and how, finally, she gave him the idea of a nursing home and then sent a big check. "More goddam money than I make in a year!" He laughed, spinning out of control again, then brought himself back. Looking into the smoke-clouded mirror, he told of searching "week after week" for the right place. "Sophie didn't come along," he said. "It would of made her worse."

An argument broke out in the Blue Bird, and Ray had to step in. When it was quiet again, Walter talked about the place he'd found after a few months of checking out "dumps." Set back from the road, having a lot of trees, it looked just right. The manager, a friendly but snobby woman who smiled too much, showed him all around the big rooms. Walter thought his mother would like the sun porch the best, and that — above all — settled him on the place. When he told the manager about his mother's "spells," she assured him they were trained for "cases" like that. But it was too expensive. "So I call Marian that night," Walter said. "She has a fit but finally says OK, it might be worth it. For Chrissake, Marian, I says, I'll make good the difference. She just laughs, calling me big-hearted, saying I'd go broke. I hung up on her."

Walter stubbed out his cigarette, held his hands between his knees. Shoulders hunched, he rocked back and forth on the stool, talking as if to himself. "Two weeks before Thanksgiving," he said, "we had an early snow. Ma, I says. I found this nice place where you can live and be happy, meet people. I'm happy here, she says. I don't want to go nowhere else. Sophie runs out of the room, and then I hear the car starting up. I worry she'll crack up on the freeway — she's not such a hot driver. So I try again. Ma, I says, Sophie's not feeling good. But Ma's not listening. During those spells she'd stare at you like you weren't there. Ma, look at me, I says. Tomorrow you and me'll go for a ride, and I'll show you the place, just the two of us. But I can tell she don't want no part of it. That night she starts a fire in the bedroom. Sophie screams at me, the bedspread is ruined, and Sophie throws it outside in the trash, with the blankets and sheets and curtains. The whole house stinks of smoke."

Walter rocked back and forth, loud music suddenly filled the room, and someone yelled, "Turn that damn thing down!" In a moment, it was quiet again.

"So the Monday after Thanksgiving I drive Ma to Woodfern, that was the name of the place. Sophie don't go on account of her nerves, so it's just the two of us, like I said. Look Ma, I says, when we turn into the drive. The trees are real pretty with all that snow. But Ma won't look. She's just sitting there, staring at nothing. The manager meets us and takes Ma and her stuff to her room. I already seen it, so I wait downstairs for them to come back. I want to show Ma the sun porch. The sun was coming in the windows and everything looked nice, but nobody was talking or laughing or nothing. Then one old guy in a wheelchair just leans over and spits on the floor, and all of a sudden this nurse or something comes and wheels the old guy away. Then somebody starts laughing and then they're all laughing, like at me or something. They stop as soon as they see the manager coming back. Ma ain't with her, and the manager says Ma wanted to rest and could I come back the next day? Sure, I says, that's fine.

Then I go and sign the papers and pay the money and leave. When I get home, Sophie wants to know how I made out. Fine, I says. Just fine. Then Sophie says, "Well, I'm glad that's over, aren't you?"

"I'd shoot myself before I'd let anyone put me away like that," Alec told Walter.

"I know," Walter said, rubbing his eyes. "Christ, don't I know? But what the hell could I do? I kept asking myself that all the time. At first, when Ma was still living with us, I used to tell Sophie it'd work out. But Sophie would start crying and then she wouldn't talk so what do you want me to do? I'd ask her. Tell me! But she'd just look at me like it was all my fault and I should know what the hell to do."

Walter finished his drink, then his cigarette, and wiped his mouth with the handkerchief. "At Christmas we take the kids to see Ma. Sophie don't say nothing when we get to the place, but I know what she's thinking because she has to check her lipstick. Then she says, kind of mad, You didn't tell me it was the Conrad-Hilton." Walter tried to fold the handkerchief, but it was too much for him and he stuffed it in his pocket. "At first Ma seemed good. She tells us about this beauty shop there, and I say she looks nice. She does, too. Sophie takes a good look at everything in the room and sees all these presents on the bureau. Where'd you get these, she wants to know, surprised like. And Ma says, Oh, I have friends here, but won't say no more. That's fine, I says, but then Ma lights a cigarette and drops the match on the carpet."

Walter rubbed his face with both hands before continuing. "At Easter Ma was in a different room. Smaller. Not so nice. I get there, and the manager tells me Ma isn't supposed to smoke in her room. I go up to see her, and she's just sitting and staring in this little room, no carpet or nothing. Ma, I says, and try to give her the nice Easter lily I brought, but she won't look at me. I stay for maybe an hour, telling her about the kids, about Sophie. I ask her what she'd been doing, but she won't talk. Her hair is straight and sticking up over her head, and I know she didn't go to that beauty parlor or whatever it was. So I go down and talk to the manager. What the hell's going on, I says, but the manager just smiles and says they'll need more money for extra care. What extra? I says. I don't see no extras. Then she gets on her high horse and asks if I want to take Ma somewheres else. I might, I says, mad as hell. Then I slammed the door, got in the car, and just started driving. Another place? I was thinking. What's wrong with that one? Ma liked it in the beginning. So the next day after work I go over with a check from the bank, and the manager smiles and tells me not to worry. The next weekend Ma has her hair curled, but she's still just sitting and staring. Why the hell can't you do something? I says to the manager, getting mad again. But the manager just gives me this funny look."

Walter closed his eyes. "And then . . . then we didn't hear nothing until we got this call two weeks or so later. It's a Sunday morning, early. Who in the world is calling at this hour, Sophie wants to know, and all of a sudden I'm scared. I go answer the phone, and it's the manager. Can you come right away, she says. What's the matter, I holler into the phone, but she won't tell me. Just come right away, she says. Jesus Christ, I think to myself. Sophie! I yell, get something on. Get in the car. It's Ma! When we get to the place, I see all these cars and firetrucks. Jesus Christ, I says to myself."

Walter leaned on the bar, his head against his hands. Ray lifted his eyebrows but said nothing. Alec brought his hands in close to his jacket. Finally Walter raised his head and turned to Alec. "You want to know something? Ma started that fire. Maybe an accident, maybe on purpose, I can't say. But you know what I think, I think it may as well been *me* that done it."

"No," Alec said.

Walter turned away and looked into the mirror. "It's a hell of a thing. I can't eat. Can't sleep. I've been having these dreams. Terrible dreams, you can't imagine. I'm falling apart." His lips trembled, and he covered his mouth. "You see?" he says, when he'd gained control. "Go see a doctor, Sophie says, and gives me this look like she knows. Take a trip, she says to get rid of me. Then I got to thinking about something Ma always used to talk about when she was getting into one of those spells. Something about a big fire. I thought about it for awhile and put two and two together. And then just to see, I go to this library one day, and sure enough — there was a big fire where she grew up, that's where I saw your name and I . . . I thought . . . Oh hell, I don't know anymore what the hell I thought." Then he poked Alec's arm. "Why the hell should I live? Tell me that? Why the hell should I? It was my fault, wasn't it?"

"I don't know," Alec said. "It's hard to say." He was trying to listen to the man's words, but his mind was sliding somewhere else. He saw a wall of fire rising up, rippling the air and reaching to heaven. He and Willie were headed straight into it. *Let's go!* Willie was hollering at him. *Let's go, Al!* And holding hands, they were running straight into the flames. Alec grabbed hold of the bar and in the next moment he saw the beer bottle again. He moved the bottle an inch to the left. "I was in that fire," Alec said before he could call back the words. Then, to his horror, he was telling the man about the pictures.

"You mean photographs? Could I see them? Are they at your house?" Walter was gathering his cigarettes and lighter. "Let me give you a ride."

"No," Alec said, and thought for a moment. "You wait here. It's just a couple blocks away. I need to stretch my legs."

"You won't come back," Walter said. "I know."

Alec thought of Willie pulling him forward, dragging him through the fire. He stood, felt the cramp in his legs, and waited until he could move. "I'll be back," he said finally.

Walter looked at his wristwatch. "Almost noon," he said. "I'm not hungry, but could I buy you a sandwich or something when you get back?"

Alec opened his retirement watch, held it near his face, then snapped it shut. "I guess you could," he said. "It's about that time."

Half an hour later Alec carried a wrinkled brown packet into the Blue Bird. Walter was waiting for him at a table in the back, near the pool table. After Alec finished his sandwich, he pulled out a pack of newspaper clippings, each glued to a piece of cardboard.

"These here pictures," Alec said, "were taken by my cousin Dwayne." He hooked bifocals around his ears and spread the pile like a pack of cards. Black shapes merged with brown backgrounds, as if the paper, too, had been charred.

Beer in hand, one man came over from the bar; another followed. They stood near the table.

"Boys?" Alec said, looking up. He recognized both men from his years at the plant. The Sobek brothers.

"You gonna tell about that fire?" the older brother asked. "Mind if we just listen in?"

"Pull up some chairs," he said, the words just coming to him now, like he was supposed to be saying them. Coming out of the blue like swallows.

When the men were settled, Alec poked at the pictures. "Like I was saying," he told them, "my cousin Dwayne took these when he worked for the newspaper. We kids always used to be after him to take our pictures in them days."

Walter turned one of the clippings toward him. "Don't tell me these are railroad tracks," he said.

"Let's see." Alec took the clipping and held it before his eyes. Wavy lines. Smoke. And them ties all burnt out. That's right, he thought. That's how it was. All them trees burnt up. Hemlocks. Cedar. And then they'd jumped.

"Are them railroad tracks?" the younger brother asked.

Alec placed the clipping on the table. "They are," he said. "Them rails outside Metz just melted all to hell." Above the pool table smoke curled through rays of sunlight. "Nothin' green left anywheres," Alec said. "And the tracks got so hot they just melted and fell apart. Just melted like butter and fell apart."

"Jesus," Walter Leska said.

"They say people saw that fire all the way from Detroit," the older brother said.

"Hell, that's over three hundred miles," said the other.

"Well, that's what they say anyway."

"I wouldn't know about that," Alec said, "but I do know it was real bad. A whole county burned right up."

A stranger to the bar—skinny in levis and t-shirt, with brown hair to his shoulders, headband, moustache—began setting up balls at the pool table. Alec watched him for awhile but then remembered the clippings. He looked down and poked at another until it was clearly in view.

"There," he said. "See that?" He paused and the picture blurred. Human bones, he thought. Sixteen people died in that car. Before he knew it, he was saying the words aloud.

"In that railway car?" Walter asked, and wiped his face with the crumpled handkerchief.

Alec was silent. "They was called gondolas," he finally said. "Open cars made of steel. The metal got real hot."

"Holy Christ," one of the men said, leaning to look more closely at the clipping Alec held.

"The only things that made it," Alec said, putting the clipping on the table and pointing with a trembling finger, "was these brass bedsteads and this cash register. Folks said they found some jewelry and such in the cars, but I wouldn't know about that. I suppose there was, with all them women there."

The stranger at the pool table bent his thin body over the ledge and braced his legs. Alec watched as the cue stick slid backward and forward in one smooth, swift movement. After the sharp, sudden crack, balls clattered and thumped into pockets. The stranger sized up his next shot.

"You were on that train then?" Walter asked, after the racket of the pool balls. Smoke rose into layers of fine cloud over the table.

Alec stared straight ahead and spoke slowly. "We was just kids at the time. Me and Willie. Willie Malin—used to be Malinowski. I'd say we was just eight, ten years old." The words came faster. "It was in the fall. October an' hot. Indian summer." He paused. "Course Willie's dead now. They say the cancer got him." He rubbed the knob behind his ear. The men waited. "But me an' Willie was pals in them days. We used to walk to school together." Alec saw the weathered gray clapboard school near the cedar swamp, the piles of stone in the fields, the big timber stand. "Willie lived on the next farm an' that day I remember we took a short cut over the German's wheat field. All stubble it was. Go right through your feet if you didn't have shoes on. It was a real bright day. Hot. Sky blue as cornflowers at first. We could see pillars of smoke, like, over on the horizon, but hell, everybody knew they was just clearin' fires. Timbermen had some work in those days. It was real rough country. Swamps with cedars that thick." He pointed to tables pushed together. "And hemlocks. *Boze Kochany!* God in Heaven! Hemlocks big as houses."

"Two in the corner," said the stranger to no one in particular. Click, thud went the balls.

Ray cleared their table and brought beer.

Then, like the stranger leaning over the pool table, Alec leaned toward Walter. His hands touched the edge of the table. "All mornin' long we was antsy, like before a storm or somethin'. Miss Verda, she was our teacher, she couldn't do nothin' with us. Settle down, she kept on sayin'. Settle down. Those're just clearin' fires, you know as well as I. But they was growin' we could see. We started seein' them pillars in all directions and by noon or so the wind picked up an' it got real smoky. Then pretty soon Mr. Rousseau, the postmaster over at Metz, stuck his head in yellin' about some fire. Then old man Jensen came for his daughter, an' then a bunch of folks came clamorin' for their kids. I don't know where my folks was. Gettin' stuff ready to go more'n likely. By 'round one or one-thirty, the teacher couldn't hold us no longer. We was rarin' to go an' we bust right outa there. The air was real heavy an' smoky by then an' we got scared an' just started runnin'."

"Twelve in the side," said the stranger.

Alec drank from his bottle, then removed his glasses to rub his eyes. He put the glasses back on and began again. "Hell of a thing it was," he said. "Folks was runnin' all up and down the street carryin' stuff, yellin', and closin' up the stores. Train's comin', they said, headin' for Posen. That was a couple miles from us, away from the fires, seemed like. Get your valuables an' load up, they said. Then we saw the big D & M train comin', steam engine churnin' to beat the band. It pulled up to the sidin' an' we saw men loadin' up cars of tan bark. That was hemlock bark they used in those days for tannin' leather. Other folks started loadin' household goods. We run home — about two miles or so — to tell our folks, but they already knew. Ma was runnin' round the house, cryin' and tryin' to figure out what to take. Pa was buryin' the old safe we had, an' he started throwin' cans of food, pictures, an' even forks an' knives into the hole. I remember throwin' in two school books an' I said to myself how I hoped the worms'd get 'em. Pa loaded up the wagon an' we started for town. There was six of us, not countin' two dogs. My Ma and Pa an' my three sisters. One of them was just a baby no more'n six months or so. On the way we met up with Willie's folks. We was all real scared we'd miss the train. I remember askin' my Pa what we'd do with Dan an' Red, our horses. Pa said we'd let 'em go in town an' maybe they'd get somewheres we could find 'em later."

The Blue Bird had filled up with men from the plant, and Ray moved back and forth behind the bar. Someone played a Johnny Cash record on the juke-box. "See that train a-comin'," sang Johnny. "Comin' round the bend."

"Nine in the corner and eight in the side," sang the stranger, in tune with the record. Thump, thump went the balls.

"Set 'em up again," said an onlooker, slipping a five-dollar bill under a beer glass.

"It's the Orange Blossom Special," sang Johnny.

"Anyhow," Alec said, looking away from the pool table, "we got there an' the train was still standin' by the sidin'." He leaned back in his chair, and his bony wrists swam out of the gray cuffs and rested on the table. "Folks was loadin' everythin' up on that train. Beds an' clothes an' livestock. I remember your ma was there, cryin' to beat the band. Seems she lost her pony on the way to the train an' she wanted to get off and look for it. Folks was holdin' her back. An' all the time the sky was gettin' darker an' darker an' you could hardly breathe the air, so bad it was. One man, Mr. Tertzel the butcher, he kept on hollerin' how we had to go, how the train better start up, but someone always was beggin' it to wait for somethin'. Finally, the engineer, a big German by the name of Ruchauser — he died a long time ago — said he was pullin' out no matter what. Folks jammed into them open cars then, an' the big wheels started turnin'. Where's your pa? Ma hollered at us. Her hair was hangin' down, flyin' every which way. We didn't know where he was. We thought he might of been helpin' folks load stuff. The train picked up speed an' we never did see him again."

"One-ball in the side," sang the stranger, cue stick pointed at the ceiling.

"You'll never make it," said the onlooker.

"Wanna bet?"

"How much?"

"Ten bucks."

"You're crazy."

Thud went the one-ball into the side pocket.

"Son of a bitch," said the man.

Alec hid his wrists under the table and leaned forward again. "It was just a ways out of town when we hit the big woods that we saw what was happenin'. Sparks was flyin' all around us in the air, cracklin' round the fir trees an' overhead. Some of them landed on the tan bark in them open cars an' little fires started right on the train. Folks was brushin' themselves an' hollerin'. The engineer kept on pushin' that train. Pushin' it an' pushin' it right on through. He wouldn't stop for nothin'. Then we come on a stretch of woods where big hemlocks were burnin' like signs of God. Crown fires we called 'em. Them big trees was burnin' like giant pitch torches. God almighty! Ma was holdin' the baby an' coverin' it up with a blanket. She hollered at us to keep down under the blankets we brought. All the time she kept on lookin' down the train for Pa. I remember thinkin' how hot that car was gettin'. You couldn't hardly touch the side without gettin' burnt."

"You bastard," the onlooker said when the stranger sank the eight-ball and shoved the ten and the five into his jeans. "Set 'em up again."

"It's your funeral," said the stranger.

"D-I-V-O-R-C-E," sang Tammy Wynette.

"I don't want no gamblin' in here, boys," Ray called from the bar.

"We ain't," said the stranger.

Alec looked at the men playing pool and then took a drink of beer. "My throat seems all scratchy and ragged," he said. "I guess I ain't used to talkin' so much."

"Take your time," Walter said.

Alec set the bottle on the table. "Well, that engineer kept pushin' that train. Pushin' like it would bust outa hell any minute. Tan bark in the cars was burnin' good an' folks stopped tryin' to put out them fires. Mattresses an' such things were flarin' up, too. Even the wool on the sheep was burnin' an' you could hear the bleatin' an' smell the stink. We got through them crown fires an' into a section of woods with more spark fires. It looked like we was gonna make it. But all of a sudden there was this crash an' the train fell right off the tracks. Holy God almighty! Those rails melted right under us like wax. Stuff was burnin' off on the side an' brush an' trees was burnin' all round. And there was the train, stopped dead. Folks got real scared an' hollered for each other. Willie an' me jumped out of the car together, holdin' hands like we used to when we jumped into the lake, summers. My straw hat fell off an' soon as it touched the ground, it flared up in flames like tinder. When I hit the ground an' turned round, I lost my balance an' fell on that melted steel. See here? See this?" Alec undid one button with a trembling hand and pushed up his shirt sleeve. A puckered scar blotched the gray of his inner arm. "Devil's brand, I used to say later, jokin' like."

Alec looked at the scar for a while and then pulled down his shirt sleeve. "I don't remember seein' another soul around us," he said, buttoning his shirt. "I thought Willie an' me was the last to get down. We had a blanket each an' we covered up as we ran. Hell, we ran down the railway bed a ways an' all's we could see was flames. We was crazy, I guess, an' had no plan. He was hangin' on to me, and when he dove into a wall of flame, I had to go, too. Crazy, like I said. But it wasn't so bad on the other side of the flames an' pretty soon we come on this clearin' in the woods. We just lay down there in the middle of that clearin' right in a bank of ferns that smelled clean and sweet. That clearin' was maybe four times this here room. We stayed under them blankets, breathin' in the dirt, an' could hear the fire all round. Stumps was flarin' up an' a little line of fire came cracklin' an' crawlin' toward us, like a snake or somethin'. We had no choice but to let it come right up to where we was layin' an' then we rolled over it in our blankets an' flattened out on the burnt side. Trees was crashin' down in flames, only you couldn't hear them fall. There was just a big roarin' sound like wind all round. I guess that's what saved us in the end. That clearin'."

At the pool table the stranger shoved another bill into his pocket.

"You dirty son of a bitch," said the other man.

Ray stepped in. "Boys, I think that'll be all the pool playin' for now. This is a friendly bar. We don't like gamblin' here. You'd better be on your way."

"Go to hell," said the stranger. He slung a denim jacket over one shoulder and took his time walking out of the Blue Bird.

"You'd better clear out, too, mister," Ray told the other.

"That son of a bitch," said the man. "You shouldn't let him in a decent place like this."

"I don't suppose there's much more to tell," Alec said. "The papers called it a real natural disaster. But I think there was more to it than that. Them fires seemed alive, if you know what I mean, like they wanted to eat a man right up. I can't hardly explain it the way I feel, though. Lots of folks lost their lives. My ma and sisters died in that gondola. Too scared to leave the train, folks said. My pa was never found. Lots of folks got lost like that for good. Not even any bones to bury." He paused. "Some folks was found, though. In one place where cedar burnt and turned the stones into lime, the body of a man and child was found. He was still holdin' a lantern in one hand, an' in the other, the hand of the child. She was holdin' a china piggy bank with some coins in it. Some folks was found layin' on their backs an' their bodies was roasted brown, like marshmallows."

Alec gripped the table. "They say them fires raged over three counties in all, goin' right up to the edge of Lake Huron. There's one story of how a family over on the other side of Metz just drove their wagon into the lake an' sat there watching the fires come right up to the edge, playin' with the grass an' driftwood, like. Another story tells how the fires chased a man an' his family in a wagon goin' down the old swamp road. He just whipped those crazy horses an' drove 'em off the road an' into a swamp. They all stood there in the mud. An' they had to get a team of mules to pull 'em out after the fires passed, but they was all saved. Wagon, too. Most folks burnt out altogether. Houses. Barns. Stock. Even the village of Metz. There's a sign there about it. Everythin' burnt up. Right after that, I came here to town an' been here ever since. My aunt took me in. Wouldn't ever have anythin' to do with that land up there any more. It does somethin' to you. For awhile there I couldn't sleep hardly at all. Thought those fires was gettin' close an' there was no clearin'. Course, if you go out there now, they say there's nothin' to see. All growed over. Scrub an' rocky fields. A few farms. Not like it was before, though. It does somethin' to you."

Alec stopped talking and looked at Ray's clock over the bar. He was surprised. It seemed he'd been talking in his sleep, and he wasn't sure if he was good and awake yet. He dug in his pocket, and when he felt the warmth of his retirement watch, he knew he was awake. "Funny thing," he said, putting the watch on the table, "I just don't know how I remembered so much. Surprised myself even."

The two brothers shoved back their chairs, stood, nodded to Alec and Walter, then left the table. Alec stared at his watch on the black surface and saw the sun floating behind ragged veils of smoke. "My ma and my sisters died in that car," he said. "My pa died somewheres on the train probably, and I—" His voice sank. "I jumped." He rubbed his shirt sleeve. "I got the scar that says so." Walter Leska was staring at him, his face like the moon close up. Alec gripped the table. "All my life I thought it was my fault." He tried to get up.

Walter said something Alec couldn't hear, then came around the table to help him. Alec felt himself being lifted; his legs banged into the chair like anchors swimming on old ropes. When he stood clear of the table, he caught his breath and felt blood rushing back into his legs. "I believed that for many years," he said, straightening his shoulders. "Then I forgot for as many." He paused. "Now I have it with me again."

"I'm sorry," Walter said.

Alec considered the scuffed black and white floor tiles, then raised his eyes. He reached for Walter's hand and gave it a good shake. Then he slipped the watch into his pocket, put on his cap, and slid the clippings into the packet. Finally he got his glasses off and into their case.

"See you later," Ray called, as Alec left the Blue Bird.

Alec walked down June Street, all sun and color, but he was still seeing straight through those clippings into that other time, when only the dark shapes of things were left. When he reached his house, he gripped the porch railing, slowly climbed the steps, and walked through cool, empty rooms to the kitchen. He made himself a cup of instant coffee and drank it, standing near the sink. Then, still wearing his plaid jacket, he went into the parlor and sat in his chair. The room was just as his wife had left it: lace doilies everywhere, a prickly sofa he never used, and tinted religious pictures on the walls. But shaded by old maples outside, the room was tranquil as a lagoon. He unlaced his boots, slipped them off, and raised his legs to the hassock. The day had been too much for him; his legs were shaky and aching.

When he opened his eyes, it was dark, but robins were chirping in the yard. Could it be dawn? he wondered, and tried to read the clock face across the room. It was too dark; he had to dig in his pocket for his watch. He opened the warm gold disc and held it close to his eyes. Eight-thirty. Not dawn, then, but evening. The robins fooled him; they were chirping as they did early in the morning.

Feeling rested and awake, Alec put on his boots and stood. He was surprised to find he was wearing his red plaid jacket, and when he thought about it, everything came back to him: the Blue Bird, the man named Walter Leska, the fire. But had he really told the story? He walked unsteadily into the dining room, turned up the thermostat, for the rooms were chilly, and then saw the brown packet on the dining room table, next to his cap. He stared at the packet a moment before picking it up. It seemed heavy.

For a long time Alec stood there holding the packet, then went into the kitchen where he stood as he had in the dining room, listening to the birds and the new sound of crickets. Fireflies sparked the tall grass near the garden. He watched the tiny signals for several minutes, then turned on the lights for the back stairs and carried the packet down into the cellar.

Kneeling alongside the musty, black leather trunk, he found what he wanted. He pulled up a straightbacked chair, put on his glasses, and carefully opened a fragile, yellowed newspaper.

Long into the night he read through columns of fading print, from time to time puzzling over complicated sentences and difficult words. Mumbling, nodding to himself, reading passages aloud, he held the brittle paper in gray fingers and read each word, each line. Several times he stopped to rest his eyes, close them against the glare. Once the hairs on his neck rose and chills passed over him like cold wind. Once he stood, rubbed his legs, and checked the furnace. From time to time he had to wipe his eyes with his blue handkerchief.

When Alec came to the lists — *Those Surviving, Those Burned* — his heart fluttered. Starting at the top, he scanned the first column and saw his own name burning on the page. Then he went back to the beginning of the list and read slowly through all the names, remembering faces, seeing farms. He stopped again at the name Milly Ceslek and remembered Walter Leska. Then he took a deep, uneven breath and began the list of the burned. It was all there: his mother, his sisters, and at the end, his father.

Finally Alec read and reread the last paragraph, telling of financial aid and new construction — a depot and post office, a store and saloon, a blacksmith shop. He lowered the paper to his lap and saw once again the black smoke blown by the wind, the charred clearing and smoldering stumps bursting into flames like tongues.

When Alec opened his eyes, he was surprised to see gray laundry tubs and concrete walls. Outside, rain fell and spattered the cellar windows with dirt. He checked his watch: long past midnight. Then he saw the newspapers on his lap and on the floor. He gathered the papers, folded them carefully, put them back in the trunk and rose stiffly. With one hand on the back of the chair, he waited until blood flowed into his legs, then he left the cellar, turning out the light behind him.

Sometime before dawn Alec dreamed he was trying to stake up a bed of peonies when the stranger from the Blue Bird appeared out of nowhere.

"Want to shoot some pool?" the stranger asked.

"I knew you'd be comin' one of these days," Alec said, and the peony he held burst into flame.

The dream scared him awake. He got up and shuffled through the house in bedroom slippers, turning on light after light and checking locks and windows. He even checked the stove and oven to see if everything was properly turned off. He looked out the kitchen window and heard a steady rain in the garden. Before he fell asleep again, he remembered jumping from the train as if into a lake and his hat catching fire just like that.

In the morning Alec heard robins chirping and a cicada buzzing somewhere in the distance. A real summer day, he thought, putting on his gray pants and shirt in the sunlit room. Then, sitting on the bed and lacing his boots, he had a sudden thought and waited, letting it grow. Finally he stood and unbuttoned his gray shirt. He went to the bureau, pulled open the bottom drawer, and saw enough shirts to last him another lifetime — plaids, yellows, whites, pale blue. He liked the blue, but considered each in turn, lifting them one by one to the light. In the end he chose the blue.

On June Street water ran in gutters, and peonies lay in wet grass. Light fell everywhere — on grass, shrubs, trees. A breeze fanned puddles and shook rainwater from maple leaves, and Alec felt drops on his head and arms. Then something Walter Leska said came to mind. Alec stopped — another dazzling peony bush catching his eye — and then heard it again, the man wound tight as a clock, saying, "But they call it God's country up here, don't they?" *Ja, ja,* Alec thought, glancing up at white clouds round as tree-tops. That was it. After a while he continued down June Street.

AUTHOR'S NOTE: Although the characters of "Natural Disasters" are fictional, the story Alec tells is true. The "Metz Fire," as it is known, was one of many fires that raged through Presque Isle County, Michigan, on October 15, 1908. The details of the fire in "Natural Disasters" are reasonably accurate and are based upon newspaper accounts, notably excerpts from the Presque Isle County News and the Presque Isle County Advance. In addition, the author gratefully acknowledges the account of Henry Hardies, whose recollections of the fire appeared in the July 2, 1976, edition of the Alpena News, as well as the account of Mrs. Clara Wojewski, the author's mother and a survivor of the fires.

THE LOVE AND FEAR OF FIRE

This is the danger of sleep,
the body drifting towards its weakest pulse,
unaware of the moon as it smolders for years
in the bedroom mirror.
Even in winter I open every window
against the smoke dreamed into my lungs.

Some nights I wake shivering,
my reflection staring back a long time
from the dark glass.
My father is never there
lighting his last cigarette for bed.
There is only the wind,
my white breath rising to the ceiling alarm
I test with a single match.
I always put it out in my mouth.
There is no trick to this—
my throat burns and burns with each small flame.

FIRES SHE COULD HAVE DIED IN

You read about fires.
You are not always careful
not to be in them.
You wonder at how clever you are,
and why the other
woman in you gets burned.

Why she always cooks alive
in her blue peignoir.
You see her trapped in smoke
in rooms begging you
to save her. Her screams
remind you of music,
a parade you once marched in.

You try to forget her,
wrap her in blankets
to hold back the dancing.
Swallow her ashes, or
stuff them in pillows.

But, oh you know
she is too real to die.
You leave her flying
alive in the flames,

her hair loose as memory,
diaphanous and full
of her last lost fire.

INSIDE THE CLOUD

On the fortieth anniversary
of the bombing of Hiroshima

1.

Before she walked to town,
the girl my daughter's age
stood by the garden gate
for a moment, looking up.
That high the plane looked fixed
like an iridescent beetle to the sky.
She saw the house collapse, the air
turn hot and white. She tasted dirt
and spat out teeth and stones. Blood
stained the baked earth beneath her head
where she lay pinned by the heavy gate
on her back. Splinters of wood
hemmed her dress to her skin.

In the months following, she turned
icy cold and thin. Too weak to feed herself,
she sucked juice from tangerine sections
her mother lifted to her lips.
On New Year's Day, her mother helped her dress
and forced her to walk a few steps
because they believe a person will spend
the whole year the way that day is spent.
In a while, the girl began to mend.

2.

Away from home, visiting
a family in France, my daughter writes
she had a terrible nightmare,
the first she remembers in her life.
How difficult it was to explain
to her hosts, in French. She couldn't
find words for the hand at her throat,

the demons that whispered her name.
She couldn't move or shake herself awake.
"It's only a dream," I write back.

But I know my daughter has entered
the other side of childhood
where the random events of an August day
can burn into unconsciousness
like the cloud years ago
surrounding the girl, the sunlit yard,
her mother coming down the path
to remind her to close the gate.

THE BAG OF STONES

Winters, I wake up partly to forget the story
a friend handed me when it got too heavy,
a bag of stones I'll have to carry till I die.
Sometimes I would do anything to relieve its weight.
Watch me open my bag to lighten it.
Don't read. Don't read.

It's Viet Nam. 1971. A hut outside of town.
The father's walked to town to buy supplies
and won't be back till nightfall.
In weak November sun the mother hangs up wash.
Twin babies crawl beneath brush
and several children forage for dead wood
where pines breathe, at the edge of the clearing.
A dark child whittles clothespins.
He doesn't see the Marines creeping toward him.
They have him tied before he feels their hands.
And the oldest—they thong her to a pole
and start a fire.
                    The mother hurries
the others inside, bolts the doors, shutters
the windows, piles chairs, heaves tables—

"Come out," the white men call. Their voices
walk in boots. They'll let go
if everyone comes out. But the mother counts
her children. She has to save the ones she can.
Flames fold Nama, blackening, into them. Watching
between boards, the mother weeps. She weeps
and weeps. Then Sim runs weeping,

bleeding toward his mother's door. He pounds.
Let me in! he screams. She slumps
against the latch, head swimming.
                    That's when
I invent the door that stays open while it's closed,

the fire that burns everything but children.
That's when I pretend on both sides of the door
they realize they're holding pieces
of the same puzzle and it's the face of God.
That's when I pretend you can end a story
any way you want to.

LOTTERY
for Naomi Shihab Nye

Because she seemed interested,
and her dark felt hat was tilted back
like a confident wager,
I was trying to get across
to this Central American
woman how our North American system
of gambling works, mostly
the state-wide type: Pick-The-Right-Numbers-
And-Be-A-Millionaire-For-Life.
It's just blind chance, I was telling her.
I said it's the luck of the draw.

Oh, she said, in a kind of Spanish
that picked through empty pockets, like when
some soldiers come suddenly at night
through a village, with the soft pad
of animals, as though night
grew red eyes weaving from the jungle
where reality has become
altered, overruled,
and the first person who hears them
wakens, cries out slightly,
stirs their attention
so that they turn to that hut first
and throw open the shaky door —
but are the welcome soldiers
her whole village waited for, and knows,
so this person sighs,
offers the one with the worst uniform
a drink, a cigarette, some talk, whispers
Good Luck, hums her child back to sleep.

Yeah, I said, it's just like that.

OMEN

This morning five crows speckled
Harpers Ridge like coal chunks
thrown against snow.
They tilted and dove,
jostling and cawing as they flew.
I knew that they would fill
the thorny haw limbs
to complain and preen
in the morning sun.
It was a sign that winter's here again
and deeper frost will
still orchard roots and turn
unpulled turnips into mush.
A late December thaw
had maples budding red
but now it's January fourth
and a frozen hush has filled
the air. Quiet is broken
only by a falling branch
or a sudden snow devil
whipping down the road.
Last night you said
your stiff joints felt
bad cold coming on.
One of many signs you've
come to trust. Twenty years
ago I scoffed at omens
such as that and now
our daughter's almost grown
and it's been six years since
Jack broke through pond ice
and drowned. No omen would
have saved that child.
But I've been with you long enough
to know, that through the meanest times,
the hardest lessons learned,
you come to heed what
feelings say is so.

THROUGH THE ICE
OFF BINGHAM LANDING, 1878

In Memoriam: Jack Hadfield and Sons

The dray team felt the cracking first
Through the blue horn of their hooves.
They halted short, listened
Away from their own pulse.
The hollow fear in rapid ears
Drew the rumble up their legs
To show it to the lumbermen
In the wide profile of their eyes.

Accidents happen slow, really —
Like milk snakes coming undone
On their slivered loft beds.
Once they start, they have
A confidence about them.
They are sure to finish.
Your tension is useless, then —
It leaves you because it knows that.
You stand watching with retinas
That are stuck to your brain
Like dewed petals to a silo dome.
There is no blinking, no shun.

The horses fumbled into themselves,
Tested the harness, then lost their tension
For all their knowing. The men
Were not held submissive by the leather.
Their heads, full of wives,
The ton weight of lumber,
Christ on the water,
And the moan in the arch
Of a felled beech tree,
Sent them off and running heavy
With the hope that is bound in men.

The ice exploded in a gash,
The tension drained off,
Everything slowed in the coming undone.
The horses' legs buckled, splintered,
As the wood dray begged them back
To all the solid it offered.
The dark sinking let the horses' tails
Float and spread on the water
To test well the cold
Before it took down their rumps,
Bit wet their black hide,
Then stiffened their soft eyes
As the bodies followed their anchor
Into the rumor of the lake.

WOMAN ON A SLED
on my 40th birthday

This is her last ride,
the one flat on her belly,
face first into stinging whiteness.
She is arcing over the rise
before the river where all sleds
stop short of the broken ice.
After the flat stretch she hears
the runners she waxed so well
crashing over the frozen waves
and cheering
somewhere up on the hill.
She knows the river
never freezes over
but she will not drag her feet.

SNOW: A LETTER

Facing the wind, I glimpse the far edge of hills
along South Fork River. Ridges,
smothered in white, push hard against a low sky.
Fox prints in snow lead up a trail
rising to high bluffs. I walk back to the cabin
under starlight, an arch of bone in cold air.

You wake in that warm harbor town where the waves
smooth the sand you walk on, and cliffs
hold the sea back. Here, snow
falls and gathers into continents of white. You lived
here once, in winter, and saw with me
the barren field where the wolf sang.

Tonight, the fox and the wolf, like you, hunt
in another valley. You watch flecked wings of gulls
diving for fish off High Rock Point. The sea,
you tell me, seems incorruptible, like a waterfall
beating down and rising, changing itself
and coming back as pounding and steam.

You walk into groves of palms.
Scattered among ferns and leaves, you find
rotting husks of coconut turning black,
their odor like milk, water, and earth;
and you gather what you can
and carry them to salt water.

Snow creeps up the cabin's side. Frost glazes
the windows with strange foliage. With my breath,
I part it, and I see the path to my door covered,
my reflected face hovering in the cold,
and remnants of a lake that went up
into clouds and has come back as a vast, white sea.

Tomorrow, under the ice, a Northern Pike
will swim into the dark reeds
and find its way without sunlight.
I will snowshoe to South Fork.
You will return
into the ache and curve of the sea.

NIGHTS OUR HOUSE COMES TO LIFE

Some nights in midwinter when the creek clogs
With ice and the spines of fir trees stiffen
Under a blank, frozen sky,
On these nights our house comes to life.
It happens when you're half asleep:
A sudden crack, a fractured dream, you bolting
Upright—but all you can hear is the clock
Your great-grandfather found in 1880
And smuggled here from Hamburg for his future bride,
A being as unknown to him then as she is now
To you, a being as distant as the strangers
Who built this house, and died in this room
Some cold, still night, like tonight,
When all that was heard were the rhythmic clicks
Of a pendulum, and something, barely audible,
Moving on the dark landing of the attic stairs.

CUTTING WOOD: VERMONT, 1977

The fire, which had died in the night,
almost taking my heart with it,
warms the kitchen at 5 a.m.
I drink coffee with cow's milk
drawn just yesterday.

I'm here as a favor to a friend,
and spend the day working
his brother-in-law's farm.
We cut birches and pines
for the fire that will make

cider of apples, syrup of sap,
which he'll sell in Boston,
or to the tourists who make it up
this way for the foliage.
The work makes me forget

the cold of the day and the cold
of the night ahead, the frost
I'll find on my woolen blanket
in the morning. My breath smokes
and I suck in air

that almost burns my throat.
But I feel good, I feel good.
I'm doing it the way they used to,
and that, as Frost might say,
makes all the difference.

Listen!

*I can believe in the deliberate bread you
have worked and served to me, the imperfect
flesh we have borne, the doubt we have benefited
from.*

—Phillip Sterling,
"The Forgiveness of Sins"

SCRIPTURE

O future, unimaginable God.
— Allen Ginsberg

In the middle were the stiff pages,
Family events listed, such as they were,
Between testaments. They seemed more holy.
As secret to me as women's underwear,
Marked with silk ribbons no one ever used.
Late at night I would take it under my covers
And look for my dead sister's little presence
And try to imagine her now lost
In the thin scripture on either side,
Those pages to the left where legends
Lived, those to the right thinned
With red melodrama. I would suppose
She was somewhere round and shiny
As a bullet arcing across a Jesus-calendar-blue-sky,
Above the sheep and palm trees,
The bearded men and aching women, the calm.

You live on, here, three names, two dates,
Beside the curlicued, Technicolor letters:
B for births, D for deaths, G for guests at your wake,
In a cardboard-bound Holy Bible my mother left me.
Tiny grain of sand, tiny leaf, brief guest of this world:
They say you were so deformed it was a mercy,
Face split open to the storm of this life, brain-dead, dead.
What's God like?
I can't imagine, anymore than I can conjure up
The crime of your nine days of pain, the howl
Already unearthly, not of our kind.
Mistake, error, carved from our mother
Like a mortal blemish, hidden away, denied.
Whose bright idea were you?

MY SON EXPOUNDS
ON HIS THEORY OF CREATION

In the beginning,
before the birth of God, there was nothing. No word,
no sound, not even silence. Just a vastness as deep
and empty as the desert at night.

The first man
and the first woman came out of this vastness, rising
from the dirt like some wild, deliberate dust storm:
bone, muscle, an arm, a leg, teeth, hair.
They began their lives like ageless clocks,
with no sense of the past. They began their lives
together, reflecting nothing but the present —
the imagination of the other.

And with this
imagination, they created all manner of living things.
Cactus and Queen Anne's lace. Tree frog and toadstool.
Chartreuse moray and gray trout. Ruby-throated humming-
bird and masked shrew. Triceratops and cave man. All
manner of living things they created.

And then they
created death (so life could continue) by giving birth
to a pale girl who could neither hear nor speak but only
stare as she collected the dying souls like small, rare
postage stamps from a foreign country.

The first man
and the first woman then rested, because they thought
by creating life and death the universe was complete.
But something was missing, something invisible yet
tangible. The man and the woman could not imagine angels.
Pure spirit eluded them.

So they decided to take all
the dead animals that anyone ever loved and make them

angels. The old collie that died in Mrs. Blazek's arms —
a seraphim. The green parakeet that sang for Mr. Kivela —
an archangel. The small turtle that lived in a box
in the corner of Joey's room — a cherubim.

                                   Listen well, Mother.
Because when I leave you to create my own life in my own world,
and your heart breaks because I am no longer yours,
and your body aches for the child who has left it,
and your mind can do nothing but stay in the same empty room:
do not worry.

                    My guardian angel will be with me always,
as real as he was when he walked among us: Sam, our Siamese
cat, protecting my every move. His blue eyes will be calm
and omniscient like that one day you held him in your lap
and he felt the baby kick inside of you. The complete
and utter improbability. The shock of new life.

THE FUNDAMENTALIST
ARGUES AGAINST DARWIN

Saying that human beings are more like frogs
than they are like monkeys anyhow.
You boo him, of course. But you wonder
about this—if maybe he's right. There
are times such as when you're making love
and a thick sound way back in your throat
crouches not unlike your body and you
repress it just as you repress at moments
this desire to jump. To see how high off
the ground you can escape, and maybe
how softly you might come down.
You've read of how the male frogs in spring
will screw coke bottles, each other, even
poisonous mushrooms; how these frogs share
with you this problem of distinctions. You
question whether Darwin ever listened
carefully enough to the story of the
frog that was changed into a man
by the kiss of a good woman.
By now you swear that the largest vein
in your arm is green. Your eyes shade
dangerously away from the blue you claim
is yours. Suddenly you are afraid
of ponds. Afraid. Of waking some night
to the sound of others, their knees to their chins,
all of them croaking Jesus in their sleep.

VILLANELLE OF THE CRUCIFIED
AND THE RISEN CHRIST

Almost identical, nearly Siamese; more than twice
the tongue of Mother Church, imbedded firmly in a rock,
has preached the crucified and the risen Christ.

After the crowns backed out of the manger, little brother quietly
fell like another star in Father's eye into Mother's.
Call us irrational, merely conspirators: More than twice

was brother Jesus taken for brother Christ: he, a knee-slapping, feisty
rabblerouser; and me, a rabbi, a real thinker, always turning
the other cheek of the crucified and the risen Christ.

We walked slowly on my shoulders across the water,
    forty days and nights
applauded our Holy Father's repartee with the fallen angel's
violent, most identical speech. More than twice

as hungry as ever in our lives, Beelzebub's surprising
illusion of bread rising out of cactus
almost reached the stupified and the suspicious Christ.

Under the table at the last supper, little brother gave me crumbs
on his fingers dipped in wine. I lifted him down into the outcome.
Almost responsible, nearly at peace, more than twice
alive I reappeared and preached the crucified and the risen Christ.

THE GOD IN WINTER: A LECTURE

Anaximander and Xenophanes
wanted to know what properties the gods
must necessarily possess — not just
what Hesoid and Homer overheard.
Could gods be liars, thieves, adulterers,
jealous women and conniving men?
There cannot be a Zeus and lesser gods,
Xenophanes observed, because a god
by definition cannot have a master.
Out-reasoned, Homer bowed to principle
and human gods withdrew. To take their place,
Anaximander posited the Boundless
that circumscribes all things and steers them all.
Xenophanes called up a god whose form
and mind are unlike any human thing.
He does no traveling: it would not be
fitting for deity to go about
now this way and now that. So god became
a principle inhabiting the furthest
rim of thought — until in Ephesus
young Heraclitus called him home again.
Now the god himself heats up the pot
of mutton stew or lights the altar lamp.
A sudden puff of breath can blow him out
and a coal lifted from the hearth can bring
him back. What's elementary is most near.
The god that conjures up this winter cold
himself is cold, fallen to ashes in
the grate — or else, fed with some thorny brush,
he cracks and flares to warm our frozen hands.

A BERLIN OF THE MIND

A young East German soldier watched Turner through binoculars from the window of a tower that rose behind the other side of the wall. Turner stood on the iron platform staring back through his own binoculars over the wall's rolling lip, across the desolate zone of emptiness to the tower window. He could see the German's clean, scrubbed cheek, his blond hair, the rough grey wool of his uniform. He could see the young man's lips, pictured him going off duty in the evening, home to kiss the mouths of wife and children in a simple apartment in the clean city.

The soldier lowered his binoculars. His eyes were blue. The sky behind the tower was blue. Turner felt an attraction to the young man which was almost carnal. He nodded. The soldier made no sign. Turner nodded again. He understood the young man's hesitation. He climbed down the platform's metal steps to Pottsdamplatz. The wall furled out in either direction like a ribbon, scribbled and stained with graffiti—a solid mass of clashing, overlapping, underlapping color, wayward strokes, scrawls, scribbles upon scribbles, a mix so interdigested as to become even drabber and more depressing than bare grey concrete. It seemed such a mindless disrespect for this functioning symbol of division that Turner felt ashamed of freedom, of the idle, foolish use to which it was put on this side of a wall designed to enforce its denial.

He started moving again through the late afternoon sunlight, following the wall, surveying the splash of images that unrolled along it: a broken skull beneath the caption *Big Skull Science*; elaborately block-lettered mottoes: *Our dream is your disaster — Dead Kennedys*; a bizarre-winged creature paring its toenails in a horseshoe wreathed caption, *The sleep of reason produces monsters*. Side by side at one stretch on the rim of the Kreutzberg were a pair of contrasting images: a huge grey face peering hungrily from behind a grey chain link fence with one link severed; the zipper of an enormous fly tugged halfway down to reveal the green idyll of a garden where the pubis would be.

Turner paused to study the last one, the unzipped garden. It occurred to him the zipper was not meant to be on trousers, but on the wall itself.

Behind him, a voice whispered, "Hey, you, *Deutscher*: You fick mit Trallala."

Turner glanced, saw a dark man, a Turk perhaps, with full lips, black coily hair. Turner ignored him, kept moving, but the man circled round to cut him off.

"Hey. *Deutscher*."

Turner said, "I'm not German. And I'm not interested, thank you."

The lid of the man's right eye sagged beneath the weight of a shiny red growth. "*Deutscher, Deutscher*: big kicks, *nicht?* Big Sexyland. Nonstop kino. Club You unt Me. Zpezial wishes, look!" The Turk drew a photograph from inside his jacket. Turner looked at it: a toad-eyed dwarf with an enormous erect phallus sat astride a corpulent, blackhaired woman whose mouth was bridled. The woman's eyes stared out above the leather and metal between her teeth; they looked like some other creature trapped inside her skull; their gaze entered Turner's mind.

The Turk grinned.

Turner said, "Put your damned pictures away. I don't *want* them. I don't want them in my mind."

The Turk giggled and palmed the photograph into his breast pocket. His fingernails were long and polished, though rimmed beneath with dirt. Turner began to move more quickly. He sensed the Turk hanging behind him, closed his eyes to block out the image from the photograph, the woman's eyes, Eileen's eyes, his little daughter, the children who had to grow up in this filthy world.

As he moved in away from the wall toward Kreutzberg, he watched the road for a taxi. He passed a cinder block apartment house, a red brick church with twin towers, its dome topped with green copper angels; stepped over a single, rotted shoe, abandoned in the muddy gutter, stiletto heel cracked; heard or thought he heard the Turk's nasal whisper. "Hey *Deutscher*, you fick mit Trallala. Sexy, oh! Big meat, *nicht?*"

A taxi cruised past, but did not stop at his wave. Turkish music drifted from an open doorway. He passed a shop window heaped with smashed-in television sets. A naked-armed man with green hair and nose jewelry leaned against the doorjamb, watching him pass. Turner's heart felt like meat.

A silver Mercedes taxi idled at the corner. Turner lunged for it. "The Grunewald, please. Brahmstrasse."

He watched the Turk grinning from a street door after him as the cab made a U-turn and reeled away. Turner leaned back against the fabric-covered seats, blotted his forehead with a square of handkerchief, saw the driver's eyes watching him in the rearview mirror, shifted, saw his own face there: self-portrait of excess: map of drink down his scholar's nose, bleached eyes weary of desire.

"You like Berlin?" the driver asked.

"I'm resting. I'm here to rest."

The driver smiled into the mirror. "You don't got to rest here until you an old man."

Turner shook his head, closed his mouth, watched the cab glide past the Metropole, saw above the entrance a frieze of lovers or naked wrestlers, he couldn't tell which. His intention had been to stay clear of the city's belly. He wished to avoid the distractions of the Ku'damm, the flesh-houses and dragshows, the sex shops and whipping rooms and slender young German women with their soulful eyes and skintight leotards.

He was here for the wall. He was here to see where east and west lay nose to nose, to know this place of jumping over, to be within its reach and look across to the Other.

As the cab turned into Brahmstrasse, his nerves calmed. He lowered his eyelids and heard lullabyes as they glided beneath the sheltering trees of the Grunewald to the Schlosshotel.

He took his evening meal in the hotel restaurant, sat afterward sipping the last of his sec and gazing at the carved wood sylvan figures banded along the molding of the high ceiling as the light outside faded hue by hue to darkness. He felt safe, decided to order more wine, looked up and saw an elderly gentleman approaching. He nodded politely. Turner returned the greeting, and the man stopped before him. "May I choin you, sir?"

"Of course. Please." Turner motioned to the chair across the table, but the man sat beside him. His hair was grey and wild, the shoulders and lapel of his dark jacket flaked with dandruff and scraps of hair. Turner wished to dust the jacket off. He looked away.

"*Englisch?*" the old German asked.

Turner shook his head. The man was so close that his dark cuff was brushing the melting pat of butter on Turner's bread dish.

"American."

"Indeed." Light glinted off the old man's spectacles, obscuring his eyes. "Und are you enchoying Berlin?"

"I'm here to rest really. To get away."

"Ah? From what, *cher ami?*"

Turners fingers trembled as he lit a cigarette. He no longer wished to speak, but could in his anxiety see no way out. "I've not been well, my nerves, you see. My wife. . . Berlin, it seems so clear and pure."

The German stared at him.

Turner thought of Eileen, the parties, the drink, thought of the children, so young still. He thought of the Star War figures they had requested when he asked what he should bring back for them. He had stood in the toy shop at the airport, studying them. Some of the monsters, he knew, were symbols of good, but he didn't know which and couldn't determine it by their appearance. So he bought them all; then, outside the shop, he came face to face with the realization of what he was contemplating, that he might never see their young faces again, and he dropped the bag of toy figures into a refuse can and fled from it.

The old German was still watching him. His spectacles had slipped down on the bridge of his nose, revealing a red growth on his trembling eyelid. Turner stared. The man was smiling. Abruptly, the Turk's photograph reappeared in Turner's mind.

"This is a *filthy* city," he snapped and rose, flinging his soiled napkin to the table.

The old German raised his brow.

"Forgive me," Turner said quickly. "I'm not well." His heels reported sharply across the marble floor.

He smoked a cigarette in the garden. Stood in the agreeable September chill watching the night green trees and misted sky, trying to see his place in the truest order of things. The hotel at his back was a nest of turn-of-the-century copies of the antiquities commissioned by a steel merchant. It was all fake—fake Rembrandts in ornate frames, fake Roman murals, fake Sistine ceilings, a fake castle. He recalled again watching Eileen with two men while the children slept upstairs. He breathed, thought, exhaled, saw his dead breath catch light from the moon.

In his room, he sat in an armchair and glanced idly through a folder of literature the management had provided on the desktop. The brochure announced a downtown "MacDonald's Cup" bicycle race, sponsored by the local MacDonald Hamburger emporium. Another, which purported to be a map of the city, was fringed round with ads featuring photos or sketches of half-naked women: *Intim, pikant, exotisch, erotischste, Lady Lydia Domina aus Passion, phantasievoll, Club Petite Surprise, Lady Bizarr. . .* Turner flung the map into the waste pail and paced the room, muttering curses.

He ended at the bathroom mirror, watching himself place pills on his filmed tongue, drink water, stare into his wasted face until his eyes began to droop.

He woke smiling to the sound of chill air fingering the brittle leaves outside his window. He rose briskly, did push-ups on the carpet before the open window, breakfasted on cold meats and cheese, brushed his teeth, voided, showered, shaved, patted his jowls with stinging fluids. He tied a paisley scarf beneath the collar of his blue serge shirt and set off on foot for the wall, strong again, determined.

On one shoulder he carried a pair of binoculars in a black leather case. In his breast pocket was his passport and all of his money and credit cards, which he intended to dispose of at the earliest possible moment, a small spiral pad and his silver Cross pen. He had left the photographs of Eileen and the children on the desk in his room. Leaving them there had taken resolution, a moment of decision torn from his heart, a victory over love. The sensation had been not unlike the experience of deciding to remove a bandage crusted upon a healing wound: You look at it, know it will hurt, bleed; you fear, decide, tear. And then it's over.

The morning sun lit gold on the wings and robe of the Victoria Angel on its pedestal above the city's scummy streets. Turner could not determine from his map whether the angel were on this side or the other. He headed toward its gleaming wings, but in the looping of a side-street lost it, found himself again at the wall, climbed up the metal steps to the observation platform. He put his binoculars to his eyes, saw the young East German soldier watching him from the tower opposite.

Turner trained his binoculars to right and left of the tower. He could not see behind the seventy-five meter zone of desolation. Midway across, a Doberman paused, one paw raised in mid-motion, glared. Turner's field of vision encompassed barbed wire, wilted grass, deserted pathways, parklamps, strobes, the wall here, the wall there, the tower, the young German watching him.

He returned his glasses to their leather case and climbed down again. At the base of the wall, three young men in metal-studded leather slacks stood drinking bottles of brown water sugared with caramel. Their teeth were edged in brown, and they were sharing a cellophane bag of crisped fat clumps. Their fingers and lips and cheeks glistened with the grease. Stenciled on the wall behind them was a multi-colored series of the Statue of Liberty in black, white, pink, lavendar, green. The three young men watched Turner. One raised the middle finger of his left hand and flicked it upward, dark eyes smoldering beneath dark brows, begging Turner for an excuse.

Emotion staked Turner's heart; hatred, desire, fear, disgust. Rage simmered in him. He wanted to fight them. Let them kill me, *filth!* He slung the binocular case off his shoulder, stopped, glared at them. He wanted to fling the case at them. Smash one of their brazen faces. Their feet shifted. They looked away. Turner felt power, tested it by remaining another moment. They would not meet his gaze. He felt the light of fierceness filling his eyes as he headed away from them back into the city, the light of righteousness, wrath.

At the mouth of U-Bahn, the Turk waited, grinning. His teeth were scored with a yellow stripe of childhood rickets. Turner focused the light of his eyes upon him. *Please,* he thought. *Try something. Anything.* But the Turk only grinned as Turner passed, descended the stair to the subway.

On the platform, two men argued over a bottle of gin. Their shirts stretched at the buttons over their guts, and their knuckles were scabbed and cut. A tall slender young man with pink hair was kissing a woman with patches of acne at the pit of each cheek. A child with dull black eyes chewed a bar of chocolate. Posters on the walls advertised cigarettes, whiskey, candy, condoms. A fat woman with dirty hands sat on a bench and read a book whose cover depicted a doctor and nurse kissing.

The train rolled into the station. Turner opened the door and boarded, sat beside a middle-aged woman clutching a cardboard suitcase. A woman seated across from him made him think of Eileen—her eyes perhaps, so pale, her slender fingers. He steeled himself to tear off another bandage. *Goodbye*, he thought. *Goodbye.* A word so strange, demanding, frightful; a word that drew boundaries upon his will: you can do this; she will be left; they will be away from you; you will join the other.

He leaned his head back on the window glass behind him and thought: *Commie. Jew. Russian. Kraut. Cunt.*

The Friederichstrasse station made his stomach move. Not a single poster or notice marred the uniform green drabness of the walls. His breath was shallow. To stand in a roomful of people in a public station devoid of advertisements had an eerie feel to it. There is no business here. No business. He was afraid. He saw again Eileen with the two men and the babies asleep upstairs and his business office, the receptions, drinks, sugar-rotted teeth of that world of yesterday, please god . . . But god, he knew, had died to make way for greater themes.

A muscular young man with sensuous lips and blond moustache, a diamond in his earlobe and shirt open to the sternum, stared at Turner. An East German policeman emerged from a booth, shook his head, handed papers back to the young man, escorted him back to the subway. Another policeman came out, steering a girl away, motioning impatiently for her to button her blouse up to her throat. The girl's hair was electric blue, and she wore a pin through the center of her nose.

Turner prayed. *Please, god, let me come over.* As his line dwindled toward the invisible screening place, he watched people disappear through to the other side: a middle-aged man wearing a fat tie and carrying cardboard boxes with twine handles; a woman in an autumn coat and fur collars; a mother and a child; a black man; a couple.

When Turner entered the inspection tunnel, he saw chill blue eyes inspecting him, his passport, him, his passport.

"*Funf mark,*" a mouth said.

Turner paid, was motioned through, paid again, received a crisp piece of east currency, climbed stairs through walls up to the street.

On this side, the sun shone. A parade was in progress. Smiling workers with good strong teeth carried red banners that flowed in an even-currented wind. Men and women, clean people in modest, clean clothing, of equal height, all walking in pace.

Turner backed against a wall, dazzled, questioning what he saw, challenging it to be certain it were real before he would accept it.

The parade was swift. Glockenspiels, drums, brass, smiles of strong good teeth. A blushing woman glanced at him from the ranks. Their eyes met. She looked so glad, right into his eyes, and Turner looked back at her as at a sister, fellow human, all of them, fellows of this world, brothers, sisters. The rattling chimes of the glockenspiels rolled past, trailing away with the tail end of the parade.

Turner strolled: along the bank of the River Spree, past the Pergamon. He strolled the length of Unter Den Linten, beneath the small yellow leaves of September, to the Brandenburg Gate, staring west now across the zone of desolation to the dirty city of the west.

He turned his back on it, gazed down the broad quiet boulevard of Lindens, free of the stinking belch of traffic. He recalled pictures from the forties of Hitler on the balcony as military parades rolled past his crooked salute, and the nostalgic grandeur of the image consisted in the fact of the annihilation of its source — cleared away for a new history to begin a new course. He strolled back toward the center with an easy sense of conquered destiny as the afternoon shadows began to lengthen, followed to Alexanderplatz, a peaceful vast expanse of open square surrounded at comfortable spacings by buildings, some new, some old. The ancient Marienkirche stood with its red brown steeple before the looming modern Teletower and the pastel skyscrapers with reflector windows. The church's grandeur was humble beside its tall, young neighbors.

Turner gazed up at the Teletower. *L'heure bleu* was approaching. He entered the tower and joined the queue waiting to ride an elevator to the top of the city.

He sat at a table 207 meters up in a cafe that slowly revolved within the tower's globe. He drank *Berlinder kidl* and *doppelkorn schnapps*, iced to a mist, and watched the city turn below him. He could see the island of the west nestled in the shell of its wall, connected by a fenced-off highway through East Germany to the other end of Europe. Alongside the winding River Spree below, a white-topped train snaked through the East. Inside the tower, the light was low, darkening gradually with the blueness of the city. The *doppelkorn* chilled his lips to an agreeable numbness.

At the table across from him, a young German family sat eating ice cream. The mother glanced at Turner with large brown eyes. Her child's blond head lay in her lap; she and her husband's hands were touching on the tablecloth, but her eyes held Turner's. Her lips were full, chiselled, and her dark hair fell in curls across her forehead. Turner drew his gaze free, stared out the window again and saw the last fading of the light. Pale copper streetlamps flanked the roads. Here and there the headlights of automobiles cast wandering beams. And a sadness that showed itself only in the dark seeped toward him.

The brown eyes still watched him. Turner looked at her hair, the graceful line of her shoulders. Her breasts were full; the nipples pressed against her blouse. She turned away. Light glistened on the surface of an open sore at the corner of her mouth. And from behind Turner, a voice whispered,"*Deutscher*, hey. You fick mit Trallala. Big meat. What you like, *nicht?*"

Turner froze. His mouth opened. Then he was rising. "*Enough*," he hissed. Louder: "*Enough*." Bellowing, "*Enough!*" — as he rose, turned, saw the hated face, swung his fist at the sagging eyelid, missed, swung again, felt knuckle bone bite soft lip. The Turk fell backward off his chair, blood smeared around his mouth. He scrabbled away on hands and knees, but Turner's fingers clutched into the oily hair and jerked. The Turk cried out. Turner was upon him, thumbs searching the stringy neck to find the windpipe. The Turk gagged. Spit flecked the corner of his mouth. Turner's thumbs pressed, squeezed. He glared into the eyes, the sagging eyelid, and his thumbs dug deeper into soft throat, felt the passion of destruction. He did not realize that he was grinning until he saw the pained glee in the eyes of the dying Turk.

Turner jerked his hands away. The Turk coughed, gulped in air, eyes all the while lit with pleasure as they stared into Turner's.

Then hands were seizing Turner from behind, dragging him away. The Turk watched, sitting up on the floor, his sagging eyelid, his lip curled in amusement.

The duty officer was the man Turner had watched through his binoculars: young, blond, clean-faced. On his right hand he wore a wedding band. His eyes, gazing upon Turner, were chill, his mouth without sympathy.

"Vi haf your name, Mister Turner," he said. "Vi haf your name on paper. Vi do not wish you to return here no more. You are not velcome. Now you must go out of zis land unt return to the vest, Mister Turner. Forefer."

Turner said, "I watched you. From the other side. I loved you, your life. Do you have a family? Children?"

The German officer glanced at the sergeant who waited by the door. "This vill be all," he said. The sergeant stepped forward. The young officer spoke in German to him; then, without looking at Turner, he left the room.

Turner said, "I came in good faith. I came with love in my heart for this land."

"*Ja, ja*," said the sergeant calmly and took hold of Turner's bicep as though it were the handle of a suitcase. He smelt of sen-sen and chilly grey wool.

"You are all in danger, sergeant," Turner said. "Corruption and decay are just around the corner."

"*Ja, ja*," said the sergeant, lifting Turner to his feet. "You go bye-bye now."

Slowly, Turner climbed up out of the U-Bahn onto the Ku'damm, to the rev and beep and stench of traffic, the quick jerky movement along the boulevard. From a shop front, electric boogie rhythms bumped ceaselessly. A magazine rack at the mouth of the station displayed a long row of naked body parts: lips, breasts, buttocks, thighs rising into the shadows of intimate clothing.

Turner's eyes swept along the rack semiconsciously, came to the end. The Turk slouched there against the wall, grinning, his shirt collar pulled open to reveal the bruises, his full red lip distended, dried blood between his teeth. Turner's eyes continued in their sweep past him, though not without having seen the shiny red growth that weighed down the sagging right eyelid.

"Hey, *deutscher*," the Turk whispered, and nothing more. His swollen lips smiled, his eyes presumed intimacy. "*You deutscher*," he whispered, as to a lover.

Turner said nothing. He kept walking, pretending that he had seen nothing, heard nothing, felt nothing, desired nothing.

THE FORGIVENESS OF SINS

We can give some gods the benefit
of our doubt, the granite cringe of millstone,
our life's grain sacked in burlap. But as for
the boy whose name we have forgotten, whose
father's farm on Seven Mile in Northville
hedged the mental hospital and held such
falterings, such deviltry, we can't be so sure,
so forgiving.

A long medieval glance through the pounce
of sideshows, the turn of decades, and we see
in the mottled sunspots of the barn the two-headed
calf, the aberration positioned by artistry.
And through the strawdust of that particular day
in our childhood, we can retaste the incredible
silence rising slant-light from the gapped
barnboards in the hayloft.

"Yes," he had answered, "it was born alive."

But alive it wouldn't have lived as long, this
practical joke we hoped it was, unable — or unwilling —
to lay our hands upon its glass case, to screech
the barndoor open further and verify it: two
pairs of spindle legs locked in top-heavy upthrust;
two pairs of cow eyes pleading for the lost
teats of the mother that we knew — though he never
said it — had died in the birthing;

two glass-eyed planets positioned to look
past us, one to the white meadowpond where the child
who becomes our mate ice skates to the vision
of her heart, having as yet to take the fall
that blinds her — and the other one beyond the child,
to her infidelity, the misery of mistressing.
We can't convince ourselves to this day that it was
real, as real as we now know real to be.

§

So maybe I have seen my god as a two-headed calf
and continue to shuttle our children to Sunday school,
faithfully, disbelieving in the principle, not
the practice. And while I cannot see through
the motley accumulation of our marriage either head
more clearly, more duplicate—the one of compassion,
the one of grief—and while I cannot believe
to this day the boy whose name I meant to forget

waiting in the hot faint at the bottomstep
of the farmhouse for my mother's trustworthy car,
I can believe in the deliberate bread you
have worked and served to me, the imperfect
flesh we have borne, the doubt we have benefited
from.

VARIATIONS ON A THEME BY RILKE

i

Two crows circle
the old logging trail
and I find the body
of the raccoon they want
alive with maggots.
Walking off I watch them
closing in their circles
spiraling down
twining their two helixes.

ii

And trees have their knots
convolutions of grain
like wheat whipped by wind,
as when a nail is driven in
to tack up a sign against trespassers;
the wood whorling around the rust
taking in even
this thorn.

iii

And when I climb the intricate ironwork spiral
to the dead quartz lamp of the lighthouse
I see a freighter
that for the earth's curve
could not be seen from shore,
as if risen from sinking,
fire stoked and smoking from its stacks
and the whole Lazarus-crew
frightened again by life.

THE DANGER OF POETRY

This poem takes place in another country
and if that country is Canada
it takes place in Quebec, though one might

prefer Mexico of those countries bordering us
on aesthetic grounds and it may as well
take place somewhere else. It is a poem

about my father, who came from Canada
though that was when he was just a boy.
Since the poem is from my memory

I will be in another country
though I haven't traveled out of the U.S.
since a trip to Jamaica five years ago

which, by the way, would make a perfect setting
for this poem, unless it is already taking place
in Mexico or Quebec.

I am remembering my father coming home
from the plant, metal shavings sticking
from his torn hands. In reality he was a purchasing

agent for a chain of movie theaters, but in that case
his hands would not stick metal shavings.
Anyway, he gets home and we dance

in the kitchen, my stocking feet on top
of his workboots, though he really wore wingtips,
my ear scraping against the belt buckle.

There must be a bottle of whiskey somewhere
in this poem—yes, there it is over there
on the cutting board, a fifth of Jack Daniels

Black Label which is filled only to the ⎺ on the No. 7.
The remainder of the whiskey I will place
on his breath, though in truth my father was a strict

scotch man. After dancing awhile he scoots me
off to bed, and on the way upstairs I tell him
how stubborn he is and how much I hate him.

For twenty years after that I travel around
waiting for that time when we will meet and make
our peace, which is why this poem is taking place

in Jamaica or Mexico or Quebec in Canada where I
very likely have been studying something esoteric
my father has no use for. But, of course, this too

is not true. None of this is true.
This is the danger of poetry:
what it will get you to do for more.

RESTORATION

I love to recover the quality
of things in decline.
To scour bricks, scale paint from stone,
to compel, with wire brush,
the flourish wrought by iron.
To refinish wood, solving for
forgotten grain.
To give, by weeding, our stone wall
back its dignity.
To left and right the borders of our lot,
to square the corners of our keep.

I have even dreamed: pushing a pushcart
I stop anywhere and start
doing what needs to be done.
The first building takes time:
replacing windows, curing the roof.
I know compromises must be made
and make none, a floor at a time.

I work along an interstate
a century after Johnny Appleseed.
A modest people makes me chief.
(They, too, enjoy the hazy shine
of finished work by last light.)
Storm drains relieved, brick walks relaid,
a heritage of dust and wrappers
is renounced. The square square,
trim trim, the town for once
is like an artist's conception of the town.

YESTERDAY, WHY I DIDN'T CALL

I sat all day at the base of a burned tree,
watched ants set up their sad architecture of rules,

and wondered if one among them watches for their futures
sailing off, multiplying along the shore like loaves.

Somewhere under a bridge, mateless washed-up shoes slopped
in the cattails. I remembered one lonely soldier

in the murdered boy's uniform who walked on water
across the Aegean, and then, requiring religion,

formed a great city under the teats of a wolf.
Grandmothers slowly lose all interest in small talk.

I remembered Jefferson's library
making its slow journey to Paris and back

in a pegged chestnut paddleboat, his magnolias,
like a carnival strip show all spring wagging their sex at him

through the puritan windows, and one bloom floated on its back
in a crystal bowl, turned slowly in the still room. What we call progress

lands on its feet each time practicing its catechism. Today
there are undiscovered women packing nothing but peaches,

scalded and skinned, halved, stuffed
like bare asses down the mouths of sterile hungry jars;

and in 1912 the sore and sick at heart inventor
of another perpetual motion machine was murdered by his cows.

The brain, a self-congratulatory mechanism, riding its dark column
of rope like a dumbwaiter, is thrown to the floor with a splat

not unlike the sound you'd expect a squashed brain to make.
I'm clapping today for myself from somewhere in the backrow,

hat in my lap, hoping Jefferson might return,
take me by the hand and whisper so only I can hear,

that not only is everything going to work out in the end, but
there are words that may not be uttered.

HOW WOMEN WRITE POEMS

A woman told me
that poems walk into her kitchen
while she is loading the dishwasher
or rolling dough for a quiche.
She pencils them on her white formica
table, and later sponges them off,
squeezing melted words into the sink.

I know another woman
whose poems arrive on horseback,
gallop up behind her, grab her
by the throat and demand to live,
and one who holds lines all day
under her tongue, like unmelted
mints, until her babies are in bed
and the last dish is washed.
Then words roll out
neat as a package of Lifesavers.

A woman poet told me she has days
when, as she writes a line,
another tumbles after it
and then another, like a row
of irrepressible clowns
falling over sideways one by one.

But mine are another story.
All day I sit in my house
with the doors and windows wide,
waiting for the wind to blow something in.
Nothing has come this summer but flies,
and my tables are heavy with dust.

DETONATING THE POEM

is a last resort. But this poem is bitter,
and sorely frightened by all those children

whose waving arms would spill so casually the milk
of the world. These thin lines, too, are a weapon.

Imagine the explosion. At the weakest edge of this poem,
all symbol will cease. Flags will droop in the breeze,

silly patterns of material. Heroes will have no meaning,
crosses, awards, the names of countries.

Borders will just be fences and men with guns.
One step closer to the heart of the poem,

and the only metaphor left will be this one.
The sea, its thrashing surf, will be alien, chemical.

No longer will bright tipped birds wing away,
troubles attached like strings to a kite.

Closer yet, and simile will end. Nothing will be like
a horse's velvet nose, or like a summer's day,

or like the soft pulp of an orange as its juices
sting your tongue. Like nothing, nothing to like.

And finally here, in the vacuum heart of the poem,
all that will be left is the thing itself, the particular

in its lonely quest for a mate, a brother, for a way
to see itself as other, as more. What will a man

say when he is only biology, when the words he has left
are only about himself, spoken to a mirror?

This poem is made of readily available parts, and copies
have been placed in every major city, mining each

important port. I tell you, I am frightened.
Unless this madness is stopped, I will aim

one at the moon. I will place your children,
your lovers, within the teeth of this desperate poem.

THE TROUBLE WITH POEMS

Say that you are reading this poem
and something you don't want to happen
does. You remember your father
chasing you down the street with his belt.
What was it that you did?
Can you remember, or were there
too many times to remember?
That's the trouble with poems.
You never really know just
where they're going to take you—
like this late afternoon light
and outside the window
fir trees laden with cones
bowing like dancers in the wind.
That's better, isn't it?
Then what about that wind,
the storm coming, the trees
disappearing into waves of snow
and you stuck somewhere miles from home
in a snowdrift, with no more than
a few minutes of gas left in the tank
that you should have filled yesterday,
but you forgot, so now you might die
alone way out here because you're stupid,
because you don't know how you'll
ever explain this to your father
who is out searching for you.
Poems are like that, you say,
and he just looks at you and shakes
his head. If I had my belt with me,
he says, I'd teach you about poems.
And you know that he already has.

DOOR HANGING

Upstairs I have paced all day
hammering on intangibilities.
Downstairs in the kitchen
the old Finn kneels in shavings
finding a special grace
in the cough of plane on wood.
His tools circle him like toys.
Ancient hands dance
in the sweet music of grains.
This old man knows
the value of a snug fit.
The door and jamb will meet
as tightly as his beveled days.
When he leaves he says with a smile:
"Today I have made a door.
What have you made?"

Old man, perhaps for you
the setting sun latches into place
but do not be fooled
by the confidence of tools.
Days, private worlds
cannot be engineered like cabinets.
Hard jobs cry for
(but cannot find)
the proper hinge.
We shim ourselves
not through well-made doors
but the empty spaces they fill.
The warps and cracks
that leave our frames out of square,
our lives mercifully ajar.

LISTEN

The man on the forklift
with the star tattoo keeps
paper beside him,
writes when no one is looking.

At four, a woman arises,
white specter through the house,
to gather words left
like gifts at the door of sleep.

The teacher takes a notebook
from her locked desk,
closes the classroom door,
makes poems as neighborhoods rush
by the bus window.

Everywhere at odd hours
someone is writing.
And these words are their words,
the same conjunctions.
Words are all we have:

Talk at the corner station,
legends on subway cars, the clatter
of dishes on a convent kitchen
remembered twenty years, machinery grinding
away at itself, dry leaves clapping.

Something pulls us into words.
Loneliness caught
in the throat,
clumsy invitation
to pull up a chair and listen.
Listen!

INDEX

Elinor Benedict, who grew up in Tennessee, keeps moving farther north. She now lives in the Upper Peninsula of Michigan, where she and several other writer-teachers developed *Passages North* during its first decade, 1979–1989. She won an Editor's Grant from the Coordinating Council of Literary Magazines in 1987. Her own poetry and fiction have appeared in a number of journals and anthologies. With the publication of this anthology, she passes the editorship of *Passages North* literary magazine to Ben Mitchell of Kalamazoo, Michigan.

Charles Baxter, fiction writer, poet, critic, and professor at the University of Michigan, has published two short story collections, *Harmony Of The World* and *Through The Safety Net*, and a novel, *First Light*, as well as two collections of poetry and many articles.